My
JOURNEY
To
EPHPHATHA

Discovering Ways God Guides
Us to Our Purpose

BONNIE JEANE-MARIE

COPYRIGHT

DEDICATION

I'm dedicating this book to my first Sunday school teacher and elementary school bus driver, Josephine (Jo) Thompson, who continued to keep in contact with me throughout my life to remind me that God loves me and so does she. Her unconditional love was from God and everyone she met knew that and loved her, too.

Jo called me frequently until a few months before she died at the age of 94. If I wasn't home, she left a voice message to remind me that she loved me and so did God. Although she has been gone for over five years, I can still hear her voice.

Good Morning!
Has anyone told you today that they love you? Well, I do!
"And do you know what?
God Loves You, Too!"

Jo working on her quilts
"A bushel and a peck and a hug around the neck!"
Thank you, Jo!
I know God has a special place in heaven for you. You will never be forgotten.

Acknowledgments

First of all, I would not be who I am today if it were not for my parents who changed their lives and ours by becoming Christians and making sure our family attended church regularly. Because my grandmother truly believed and reminded me often that God had a purpose for me, I went through life wondering what God had in mind. And, of course, I was truly blessed to have Jo as my Sunday school teacher. She, too, repeatedly reminded me of God's love and her love for more than sixty years until her death.

I am thankful for two of my closest Christian friends, Jan Brock and Bobbi Bach. Bobbi has been encouraging me for the past fifteen years to write about Martha, the deaf girl who appeared at my door and the impact she had on my life for years to come. Jan supported and encouraged me throughout the process of writing my story. Both Bobbi and Jan were excited and more than willing to read my first version of "My Journey to Ephphatha" and give me feedback on what I had written.

I am grateful for Mary Tyler, my creative writing teacher, for encouraging me to stay in her class when I thought writing stories or poetry was beyond my ability.

Although at the time, I didn't appreciate it, I am now thankful to Pat Tober, who insisted on introducing me to Tricia McDonald, who eventually became my writing coach and led me through writing each chapter of this book. Tricia helped me to recognize and stop listening to my internal gremlins which only created anxiety and filled my head with negative thoughts about writing this book.

I was more than blessed to have had the support and encouragement from Pastor Neisch, Pastor Karl Stumpf, and Pastor Fremer throughout my journey with the Deaf and throughout the Deaf ministry.

I am very thankful to have met Father Coughlin, the first Deaf Catholic priest, who without knowing it, helped me to recognize my weakness of doubting and to acknowledge my need to trust God, fully.

I would also like to thank Rich Lohman for leading masterminding classes which helped me to learn not only what is needed to become successful in any walk of life, but to grow spiritually as well.

Although she has requested to remain anonymous, I am very appreciative to the pastor who has given me permission to use her examples from her children's sermon which focused on the message that everything and everyone has a purpose in life.

I am thankful for a loving, interactive God who is available to each of us daily and overlooks our mistakes, apathy, and when we forget that He is always with us.

And, finally, but not least, I am so grateful to my husband, Don, who has always been there beside me to support me and allow me to step out of my comfort zone to become what God had planned for me. He has always been helpful and patient with me, especially when I found computer technology challenging and I was ready to throw my computer out and quit writing.

Introduction

I believe throughout my life, even when I wasn't paying attention to Him, God was always there providing me with opportunities to learn and grow. He taught me to unconditionally love others, especially those who were difficult for me to love. He provided me with spiritual experiences that extended beyond what I knew or understood at the time. He gave me the gift of intuition and sense of internal knowing, which I could not and never have been able to explain. Yet, I know it comes from my heart and not just from my head. I have learned to listen and meditate on what bothers me until I know the direction or the path I need to take.

I have always felt close to the Lord. I believe that is the reason I seemed to be led to doors for me to either choose to walk through or not. Jesus says, "Abide in me and I will abide in you. As the branch cannot bear fruit by itself, unless it abides in the vine." [1]

I chose the title, "My Journey to Ephphatha" for my book because it seems to apply to the way I have led my life. It comes from the story of Jesus touching the ears and lips of the deaf man. After doing this He spoke and said "Ephphatha", which means to be open. This phrase has became a motto for my life. It has taught me to become aware, brought me to a closer relationship with God, and a better understanding of what it is to be a Christian. I hope my journey, although far from being perfect, is an inspiration to others to become open to where God is leading you. We never know where our path my lead us. Be open and enjoy your journey through life.

As St. Jerome wrote, "Let us learn upon earth those things that can prepare us for heaven."

Author's Note to Readers

You may question why I used the capital "D" for Deaf and other times I used the lower case "d" for deaf when writing this book. The reason for capitalizing the D as in Deaf is because that signifies I am talking about the cultural Deaf population or a person who usually uses ASL, with body movements, facial expressions, etc. and subscribes to the norms of their society.

When using the lower case "d" for writing the word deaf, it signifies anyone who has a severe hearing loss and is not part of the cultural Deaf nor adheres to the norms and culture of the Deaf population.

CONTENTS

The Foundation
Chapter 1

Sometimes in life, a sudden event occurs that changes everything. One moment everything is fine, and the next your whole world is turned upside down. This is what happened to me. One moment I was outside playing. The next moment I was fighting to breathe. The following story is a true story of what happened to me as a young child. It isn't directly part of "My Journey to Ephphatha"; however, this event did have an impact on the lives of my parents, resulting in changes they made in their lives that laid the foundation for who I am today.

It was an early morning in June and since it was Monday, it was a routine laundry day at my house. I stood next to my mother watching as she wheeled her wringer washer out from the bathroom into the kitchen, hooked up the hose from the sink to the tub, and began filling the tub with water.

I loved to smell the fresh clean aroma of the detergent she used. The scent reminded me of our huge lavender plant which grew next to our front porch. I watched as she put the clothes into the basin. After the clothes had finished agitating, she picked them out of the washer and put them through the wringer before dropping them into the huge galvanized tub for rinsing. Then she put them back again through the wringer at the top of the washing machine.

Our neighbor, who lived across the street from us, had just walked in to have coffee and chat with my mother while she washed clothes.

"Where's Tony?" I asked, looking around and hoping he had come over with his mom.

"He was just behind me. I think he found some stones that caught his eye outside before coming over."

I ran to see what he was doing and asked him to come to play with me.

Tony was the youngest of six children in his family. It seemed there was always a swarm of people coming and going at his house. The night before was one of those occasions when his family had a big party and lots of people came and stayed late.

Before coming over to our house this morning, Tony had been helping his mom pick up empty glasses and beer bottles left outside in their yard from the night before.

Tony was six years old and had just finished kindergarten. I was an only child and just getting ready to start school in the fall. I loved to be around Tony and would listen to him describe what school was like. He knew so much more than I did about everything and often spent time teaching me things he had learned at school. I felt very special around Tony and often thought of him as my big brother.

Tony and I often played with cars and trucks or marbles in the sand. But today was different. I wanted to use my new set of cups and saucers to have a tea party with him. Tony said he didn't mind. We sat down on the cool sand which was still damp from the night before. The sun had created a shadow of my house across the driveway where my dad's 1949 Chevy was parked. We began making cookies out of the damp sand, and then I put one sand cookie on each of my toy saucers. We got up and walked around to the other side of my house where we put dry, warm, loose sand in my toy tea cups. We walked back to the shaded side of the house and put the cups down on the running board of my dad's car before pretending to drink out of them. Tony talked about the party at his house the night before. He showed me how the guests filled their glasses with beer and then clicked them together and said, "Cheers!" Tony suddenly looked up and noticed a big barrel next to our back door.

"Wait right here," he said. "'I've got to go home to get something. I'll be right back." He ran across the street and returned with two empty beer bottles and proceeded to fill them from the spigot at the end of the barrel. After he filled them, he gave one to me. Then we clicked our bottles together and said, "Cheers!" just like he said the guests had done at his house.

I took the first gulp expecting it to taste like Kool Aid, not knowing it was fuel oil. Suddenly, I couldn't breathe! I tried to gasp for air and began choking. Terrified, Tony ran to the kitchen door screaming for help.

Both of our mothers ran outside to help. Thinking I had something caught in my throat, my mother picked me up, and while holding me upside down, she began shaking me. Tony's mom ran back home to phone the police for help.

Soon there were two police cars, a fire truck, and lots of men rushing toward me. The fire chief talked to Tony about what I drank as the police rushed me into the backseat of their car. They laid me across the laps of my mom and Tony's mom. The fire chief climbed in the back seat with us as the police rushed us off to the hospital.

I could hear the siren and knew we were traveling fast because I could see the treetops as we passed them. My mom started crying as we passed a red brick building with a big green awning stretching out toward the street. (When I was older, I learned this was the entrance to a funeral home.) She was sobbing as I heard her say, "She's dying! We'll be going there soon to plan her funeral!"

It was then I felt something strong inside me say, "No! I'm not going there! I'm not going to die!" I don't know how I knew that or why that voice had said that. I had never been to a funeral home and at that age I'm sure I had no idea what a funeral home even was.

When I arrived at the hospital, the nurses met us at the door and rushed me down long, narrow, yellow colored corridors into a brightly lit room where they laid me face down on a table, my head hanging over a big stainless steel bowl. They inserted a tube down my throat and started to pump my stomach. I don't know what happened after that. My parents said they labored over me for quite a while before one of the doctors came out to speak to them.

"We believe we got all of the fuel oil out of her stomach, but she does have chemical pneumonia. The next 48 hours will be touch-and-go. But, with careful observation from our staff and lots of prayers, there's a good chance she will live. She will need to be kept in an oxygen tent to help her with her breathing. We will keep her here until we're sure she's ready to return home, which could be quite a long time."

Being in a Catholic hospital, and my parents not having any religious affiliation or minister of their own, a priest came to support my parents through this ordeal and to pray for me. My protestant, paternal grandmother didn't like having a priest with us. She called her minister and told him what had happened and requested him to come to the hospital. My parents said he often came to pray for me. As I watched from the small, opaque plastic window of my canvas oxygen tent, it seemed everyone who came was either worrying or praying for me.

When I was much older, my parents told me they had been called to the hospital several times during the middle of the night in the weeks that followed because the hospital staff didn't think I was going to make it. They also called my grandmother's minister who would rush over to be with them during times of crisis. He often stayed with me after my parents left to go back home so my mother could get some rest and my dad could get up to go to work the next morning.

I don't remember the minister or the priest, but I do remember the nuns. I especially liked the nun who wore all white and sat behind me at the head of my bed. She was there every night all night long after my parents left. I recall her as an older nun with white hair. She wore wire-rimmed glasses and smiled all the time. I felt so comforted and loved by her, but never knew her name.

During the weeks I was hospitalized my parents had become very close to my grandmother's minister. After I was discharged, my parents started taking me to church and decided to join the protestant church where we were all baptized at the same time.

About twenty years later, while talking to my mother about the experience of being in an oxygen tent, I asked her about the nun who came to sit with me every night. I wanted to know if she knew the nun's name because if she was still alive, I wanted to let this nun know how much it meant to me to have her there comforting me.

"There wasn't any nun there and those nuns didn't wear white, either," she said. "The nuns at the hospital all wore black. We were there almost every night with you and never saw any nun like you're describing."

"I know she was there!" I said. "I saw her face and her warm loving smile. I felt her warmth, but she never talked to me. She just sat there as if waiting and watching over me with her hands folded in her lap and smiling as if she were content and pleased."

"How could you possibly have seen her?" my mother asked. "It would have been impossible if she sat behind you at the head of your bed. You could barely see what was in front of you with that oxygen tent completely covering your head, except for that small window for you see out."

I sat back in the rocking chair feeling stunned by the realization of what my mother. I had never thought about that! It would have been impossible for me to see someone sitting behind me. I wondered if this person was real or if I had imagined her. I also wondered if, perhaps, she was my guardian angel and just maybe it was her voice I had heard in the police car telling me I was not going to die.

I'm sure this near-death experience, with my vision of the nun sitting behind me and my maternal grandmother continually affirming God had a plan for me, affected how I began to view my world and the presence of God. My grandmother had planted a seed about the possibility of God having a purpose for my life. This seed continued to grow and was supported by the church in which I was raised and by my Sunday school teacher, Jo, who was the most loving and caring Sunday school teacher anyone could ever ask to have. Every time she had an opportunity she reminded me (and everyone else, too), "God loves you and so do I." I would giggle as she always continued to add, "Remember, a bushel and a peck and a hug around the neck!"

I looked forward to going to church every Sunday, loving how our Sunday school always started out with singing lots of joyful songs. Our parents and the older generations also joined us during the opening session of Sunday school. We had competitions between the kids and the adults to see which group could sing the loudest and we always sang "Happy Birthday" to everyone who had a birthday during the week, no matter what his or her age. We could win medals for memorizing scripture each week and also for regular attendance. I looked forward to getting mine every week. We had "Family Night" potlucks once a month with a hymn sing afterward. Sometimes we had guest artists come and draw characters from the Bible while sharing

Biblical stories. Other times someone would tell a Bible story with flannel graph pictures. Our time together was like being in a huge family full of love and fun activities.

My family didn't have much when I was growing up and we never went anywhere for a summer vacation, but I enjoyed my summers by going with my friends to every Daily Vacation Bible School available. I loved to hear the stories of Jesus, sing songs, and make crafts. Second to visiting and spending time with my grandmother, this was my favorite thing to do every summer. When missionaries came to visit our church or showed up at other church's Bible school events, I loved meeting them, hearing their stories of faraway lands, and seeing the pictures they shared about their works.

I dreamed of someday becoming a missionary like them, but surmised God called them because they were special in some way. As I continued to grow spiritually, I often wondered if becoming a missionary was what my grandmother meant when she said God has a purpose for me. I often asked her how and when I would know what His plan was for my life. She would just tell me to listen and someday he'd let me know.

And so my foundation in the Lord was laid. It's a foundation that prepared me for many events to come and how I would handle each of them. As you read my story, you too will notice that God led me to several doors and opportunities to serve Him. With my spiritual foundation being strong, I only had to open the door to see what laid ahead for me and my journey.

"Train up a child in the way he should go and when he is old, he will not depart from it."[2]

The Stranger
Chapter 2

It was an ordinary summer afternoon in the mid 1950's. Well, not exactly ordinary. I was nine years old, but wasn't allowed to play outside in the hot summer sun after lunch. Polio epidemics had been reported across the United States and thousands of children were dying or left paralyzed from polio. There were no vaccines to prevent these devastating effects and no known reason for the cause. Everyone, including my parents, seemed to believe they could prevent this dreaded disease from affecting their children by keeping them inside during the mid-afternoons of summer and making sure they got plenty of rest by napping.

On these summer afternoons I sat next to my mother on the sofa while she knitted and watched her favorite afternoon television stories.

On this particular day I heard something out on our back porch that sounded like it fell or was knocked over. I suspected it might be a dog, cat, or even a squirrel that found its way onto our unfinished porch my dad was in the process of building.

I got up from the sofa and walked to the back door to see what was making such a noise. I was shocked as I looked up and saw a tall thin girl with long dark hair pulled back into a pony tail standing at the door. She seemed to be about my age and was nicely dressed in a pink summer outfit, but she didn't smile or say anything as I approached her. She just stood there on the other side of the screened door as if she were a statue staring at me.

"Hi," I said with a smile. She didn't reply. "Did you want something?"

She continued to stand there staring at me. I felt goosebumps rise on my arms, and my breathing became shallow as I suddenly felt afraid of her. "Do you want to talk to my mother?" I asked, as I started slowly backing away. Still, there was no response from her.

I stepped back toward the living room and looked around the doorway to where my mother was still sitting on the sofa.

"Mom," I whispered, afraid this stranger might hear me. "There's a strange girl at the door and she isn't saying anything. I asked if she wanted to talk to you, but she just stood there staring at me."

"Have you ever seen her before?" My mom asked as she put down her knitting to get up and follow me into the kitchen.

"No. I've never ever seen her!"

My mom moved toward the door. "Hello, did you need something?" she asked curiously.

Still, there was no response from this stranger.

The silence was as deadening as if a thick brick wall separated us. Being somewhat afraid of her, yet curious at the same time, I wondered what she wanted and why she was at my door. Where did she come from? Part of me wished she would go away and not bother us.

"I think she is deaf and dumb," my mother said as she opened the door to let the girl inside. "It's hot outside. Why don't you give her a glass of cold water? She might be thirsty from all this heat, or maybe she is lost." My mother continued, "You know how much you love to spend time during the summers with your grandmother. Maybe she is visiting her grandmother or has some family around here and wandered off and then couldn't find her way back home. Or, perhaps she saw you outside and wanted someone to play with her. Invite her in."

My heart sank. Reluctantly, I did as my mother had asked. I handed her a glass of water and motioned for her to come inside. I really didn't want to entertain someone who couldn't talk and was dumb. I had never heard the term "deaf and dumb" until that time, and I didn't understand that dumb meant she couldn't hear or speak.

She slowly walked in like a cat searching and investigating the surroundings while looking at everything on the walls of the kitchen and living room. Then she wandered down the hall to my bedroom where she stood in the doorway looking around at my bed, my dresser, and things I had left lying around. After checking everything out, she walked back to the kitchen door and left as quietly as she came in. She didn't say "Goodbye" or even wave.

"Whew! That was creepy!" I said to my mom as we walked back into the living room. I was glad she had left. *I hope she doesn't come back*, I thought as I returned to the sofa with my mother.

A few weeks later, while washing dishes, I felt as if someone was watching me. Out of the corner of my eye, I saw something move and looked up toward the screen door. This same mysterious girl was standing there watching me as she had done before.

I felt a lump in my throat as I wiped my hands and said, "Hi." Once again, I opened the door to let her in. *Why did she come back? What does she want?*

She headed straight to my bedroom and looked around exactly as she had done before. I walked around her toward the closet and took some of my dolls off the top shelf to show her. She seemed to enjoy holding and studying the face of my Indian princess doll who had long black hair like hers, only braided instead of in a ponytail.

My mom heard me moving around in my room and peeked in to see what I was doing.

"Oh, your visitor has returned!" she exclaimed. "She seems fascinated by your doll. Maybe you could also show her your new music box with the ballerina that twirls. I bet she would like to see that."

I lifted the music box from my dresser and opened it as the ballerina began dancing. The girl reached toward the ballerina. I pulled my music box back feeling afraid she would break it; but, instead, she put her fingers on the box under the doll's foot and began smiling.

"What is she doing?" I asked my mom. "She has her fingers too close to the ballerina. She's going to break it!"

"She isn't going to break it," my mom responded. "I think she can feel the vibration of the music through her fingers."

For the first time since I met this stranger, she smiled while she held my Indian doll and watched the ballerina dance. Then, as quickly as she came, she handed my doll and music box back to me and got up to leave.

As I followed her to the back door and watched her walk down the driveway toward the street, I felt very bewildered.

Maybe mom is right. Maybe she is just looking for a friend, I thought. *But, how could we be friends if I didn't know her name or anything about her? How could I be friends with someone who can't hear or talk?* I didn't know what to do and felt so helpless around her.

I wondered what life was like for her. *How did she learn? How did she and her family communicate? How did she tell others what she needed or wanted or let them know what she likes or doesn't like?* From the joy she seemed to show while touching my toys, I wondered if she had any dolls or what kind of toys she had.

She came one more time before the end of summer and we colored together for a while, then she quickly left again. By the time school started in the fall, I hadn't thought much more about her. I was going into fourth grade and was excited about lots

11

of new experiences I was having at school. I was busy with an after-school class at church, learning to sew at 4H, music lessons, and helping my mother with folding clothes, washing dishes, and other chores when at home.

One day after returning to school following Christmas vacation, our teacher walked our class down the hall and into the library. "We are going to work on writing book reports this year." she explained. "I want you each to find a book that interests you because you will use that book to write your first book report. If you have any questions or can't find a book you would like to read and write about, let me know."

I circled the library several times pulling books off the shelves and looking at the covers, but I couldn't find anything that interested me. I also didn't want a book with too many pages to read for fear I wouldn't have enough time to read it and continue with all my after-school activities.

At the end of the hour, our teacher noticed I had not picked out a book. She walked over to me with hands on her hips asked, "Why haven't you chosen a book? Can't you find at least one book that you would be interested in reading?"

"I don't know what interests me," I said, my face turning red as I looked down at the floor.

My teacher turned around to the bookshelf behind her. "Do you like to read about people, or animals, or fiction?"

"I guess people," I said, feeling ashamed because I was the only person who hadn't found a book.

"If you can't choose one, I will!" she said as she grabbed a book titled, "Anne Sullivan Macy, The Story Behind Helen Keller", and put it in my hands.

I found this book to be a very interesting story about a woman named Anne Sullivan and her struggle as a private teacher for an incorrigible blind and deaf girl named Helen Keller. Anne Sullivan was able to help Helen overcome her disabilities and her outrageous behaviors to eventually become an author and an advocate for others with similar disabilities. Later in her life, Helen Keller was acknowledged as one of the most literate and admired women in American history.

Yet, as I read the book, I didn't make any connection with the blind-deaf girl in the book and the "deaf and dumb" girl who had come to my home the previous summer. Perhaps the reason was because I perceived Helen Keller to be predominately blind and ignored the deafness; or, because the strange girl who had come to my door didn't exhibit any of the negative and unmanageable behaviors like Helen Keller did when Anne Sullivan started working with her.

By the time the school year ended, I had forgotten all about the deaf girl who had showed up at my door the previous summer. I certainly didn't expect to ever see her again.

Then one day, a few weeks after summer vacation began, the mysteriously silent girl showed up at my door in the same way as she had the summer before. Only this time I was not stunned by seeing her standing silently at my door. Once again, I let her in and she walked back to my bedroom as she had done before. She found the coloring book we had been coloring the previous summer, took it off my bookshelf, and scribbled, MARTHA.

She tried to say something, but I couldn't understand her speech. She pointed to what she had written and then pointed to herself. She looked up at me and smiled. Then she put the crayon in my hand and pointed to the coloring book where she had written her name.

I wrote my name, BONNIE and pointed to myself.

She smiled and started to color the pages. About fifteen minutes later she got up and left as she had done before. After that, each time she came to visit she either held the Indian princess doll and rocked back and forth or colored in my coloring book. She seemed happy and content to just be with me in my home.

"Mom, can I walk with Martha to the end of our street?" I asked one day as she was leaving. "I promise to not go any farther than the corner. I want to see if I can figure out where she lives."

With my mother's permission, I walked with her to the end of our street. I would have preferred to walk with her all the way to her house, but my mother was adamant about me not going any farther than that corner. When we reached the corner, I stopped and waved goodbye as she turned to leave. For the first time, she smiled and waved back to me. I stood there watching her as she walked two blocks then turned the corner and walked a few more steps until she was barely in sight. I had learned her first name but still had no idea exactly where she came from or anything about her family.

Martha came twice more that summer and each time was just like the others. I wished I could communicate with her, to learn something more about her, and her reason for choosing to come to my house. Each time she left, I walked her to the corner and watched as she walked away and turned down another street until she was out of sight.

When school started again in the fall, our bus stopped at the corner near where I thought she might live. I had hoped this would be her bus stop, but, she was never there. I started asking others on the bus if they knew someone named Martha who couldn't hear or talk. No one knew or heard of her and laughed at me for trying to find someone who couldn't hear or talk. During recess and before school, I would walk around the playground searching for her, but she was never there. *What happens to her during the school year? She must be somewhere!* I thought as I continued to look for her.

The following summer, I waited and watched for Martha to return. I began to look forward to seeing her, but she never came back.

After several weeks, I asked my mother if I could walk past the corner on our street and a few blocks further to look for Martha. With her permission I walked to the end of my street, turned the corner and walked a few more blocks up to a yellow house on the corner where I thought Martha might live. I thought if this was not her house, perhaps someone there might know where she lived.

I walked up the steps and knocked on the door feeling afraid it might be the wrong house and concerned I might be bothering someone who lived there.

The door quickly opened and a tall, heavy-set grumpy man looked down at me. "What do you want?"

"I was wondering if a deaf girl named Martha lives around here," I said.

"Not anymore! We put her in an institution to be with others like her. She will never be coming back here! Now go along and don't bother us."

An institution and never coming back, I thought. *How awful to be put someplace away from your family. What about her birthday and Christmas?* I pondered those thoughts as I walked back home feeling empty and sad. I was genuinely sad for what had happened to her, and sad that I had lost a playmate with the hope of someday being able to communicate with her.

So, People who can't hear or talk go to an institution. I kept replaying this in my mind as I walked home. I figured that an institution must be like a hospital as I recalled my great grandpa living in a nursing home that was like a hospital. We used to go visit him, but there was only a bed and a chair in his room.

"Mom, what's an institution?" I asked as I walked into our kitchen where my mother was cooking dinner.

"Why do you want to know that?" she asked.

After I told her what the man had said, she explained it was a place where people lived who can't go to school or live with others in the community or don't fit in. *Just because a person can't hear or talk, they get rid of people like her?* I wondered. I went into the living room, sat down, and turned on the television. I guessed that was why I had never seen anyone like her before.

I was surprised about how much I missed Martha unexpectedly showing up during the rest of that summer. I felt sad knowing I would never again see this silent friend who seemed to enjoy visiting me. Even if we couldn't talk, there was something intriguing about not knowing anything about her or what she thought or felt. I continued to wonder what her reason was that she chose to come to my house. I wished I could have had the opportunity to learn more about her. Little did I know that this experience was eventually going to have a significant impact on my life.

"Do not forget to entertain strangers, for by doing some people have entertained angels without knowing it."[3]

Lessons Learned from Those Least Expected
Chapter 3

I was five years old when my brother, David, was born. My parents were delighted to have a son who would carry on the family name. He was special and he knew it! By the time he was three years old, he had taken my place as the number one child by going everywhere with our father. While he got to go places, I stayed home to help my mom with household duties.

As his older sister, watching David became part of my responsibility. When he was playing outside, I had to make sure he didn't run off into the creek or go out into the road to play. I didn't mind playing with him in the dirt with his cars and dump trucks or showing him how to make a hole with his feet and shoot marbles into it. In the winter I took him sledding with my friends and their siblings. We built snowmen and snow forts for snowball fights. However, resentment set in when taking care of him interfered with my opportunities to go to my friends' homes to play board games. He was too young to play because he couldn't understand the rules.

By the time David was four years old, he had learned to play practical jokes on people. He loved scaring me by jumping out of the closet wearing his furry Davy Crockett hat and pointing his toy rifle at my face. I would scream and he would laugh. Our parents got mad at me for screaming because we had a new baby sister who was often asleep in that same room when he played these stunts.

My brother was well liked at church and Sunday school. My parents were proud of him. But that all seemed to change once he entered school. Shortly after he started kindergarten, the teacher called my parents for a special meeting. When they got home, my mother was in tears. The teacher had told them my brother was "retarded". (In 1956, this was the term used for children who could not learn in a regular classroom setting. The current term is cognitived challenging. However, David was also behaviorally challenged.)

Later that night, when my mom called my grandmother, I overheard her repeating what Dean's teacher had told them. "He doesn't pay attention." she said. "He refuses to do anything asked of him in the classroom and causes disruption with other children." Then she paused before continuing. "I just can't believe he would kick his teacher when she bent over! He's never done anything like that before."

I couldn't help but snicker after hearing that. *He must have seen that when watching The Three Stooges on TV,* I thought to myself. I certainly didn't think there was anything wrong with him. Instead, I thought he was just plain spoiled.

My parents took his diagnosis very hard. They became very concerned and overly protective of him because he was "different" than other kids. It often became my responsibility to continue to stay near him when he played with other kids in the neighborhood and make sure they didn't bully him. I had never perceived him to have any learning problems or to be different from the others, and I never believed there was anything wrong with my brother that couldn't be managed by a spanking. *After all, I had my share of spankings, why shouldn't he?*

After my parents met with his teacher, they made an appointment with a psychologist to have David evaluated for placement in special education classes. My parents were told he had a lower ability to learn and Minimal Brain Disorder, which would later be known as Attention-deficit/hyperactivity disorder (ADHD is a very common diagnosis today). My mother blamed herself for taking some medications while she was pregnant for him and believed God was punishing her. She cried almost every day and didn't want to do housework or attend church functions. She was becoming deeply depressed until my dad took her to a psychologist who helped her understand it was not her fault and that God was not punishing her. My parents eventually found a Sunday school class for kids who had special needs like my brother and told me I would be going along with David to watch out for him.

Although I loved going to church and Sunday school, I didn't like the idea of attending with these kids. Plus, this was way across town in a church I had never been in and I didn't know anyone who went there. But, my parents wanted him to learn about Jesus with others who were like him. From what I experienced, I thought he was doing fine at our church. He memorized Bible verses, remembered the Bible stories we heard each week, and participated in the Christmas pageant just like I did. No one ever said he did not fit in, but my parents were adamant and I had no choice.

Every week they dropped us off at this church after Sunday dinner. After we entered the red-bricked building and walked up the tall flight of dark wooden steps while holding onto the wide polished wooden banister, we entered into a huge room where the afternoon sun colored the room with bright rays of light from the beautifully designed colored stained glass windows.

The first time we arrived there, I was shocked to see a lot of weird looking kids. Some were sitting in wheelchairs with their arms waving in the air. I saw some kids with their heads leaning on their shoulders. Some sat with their mouths open, tongues hanging out, and drooling. A few of them were missing an arm or a leg. The friendly ones, who came right up to us and tried to hug us, had short necks, small rounded heads with slanted eyes, and their hands were short and stubby.

I tried to back away from these kids. I didn't want them to touch me or to sit anywhere near them. I had never seen kids look so strange or were unable to move about without help. I just wanted to go back to my safe, comfortable home.

One Sunday as I sat looking around the room at all these strange kids, I thought about the girl who was "deaf and dumb" and had come to my door. I wondered if she might show up here at this Sunday school, but she never did. I also wondered if these kids, who were so different from anyone I knew, were also living like Martha in an institution.

We continued to attend this special afternoon Sunday school for the next two years and I never met anyone who was like Martha. There were kids who talked funny and were unable to pronounce words and some who couldn't talk in complete sentences which made sense. Yet, no one seemed to be "deaf and dumb" like Martha.

During those two years, I began to appreciate these very kids who had seemed so strange when I first met them. They had hearts full of love which they easily and willingly expressed and were so happy to share with everyone without any inhibitions. They were completely open and honestly shared what they thought and felt. They were filled with joy as they sang "Jesus Loves Me". After Sunday school was over, these kids would rush right up to me and look me in the face and say "Jesus Loves You!" Then, with a huge smile, they would each give me a big bear hug. As I grew more comfortable with them, I stopped trying to find a place to sit as far away from them as possible. I began to enjoy sitting next to them, singing songs along with these special people. Each week I was amazed at their outward expression of God's Love. When it was time to leave their Sunday school class, I left feeling deeply loved. They were "different", but in a good way. Although my Sunday school teacher, Jo, had always reminded everyone in our class of God's love, those in our class, including me, never seemed to share that love with one another as these kids did and they did it with so much ease.

This experience, during which I had started out feeling awkward around these kids with major disabilities, also proved to have a tremendous impact on me for years to come, even into my early career. I have never forgotten how stunned I was by their tremendous love for Jesus and their ability to be so open by sharing that with their world. Unlike most of my friends, these kids exhibited an awesome and close relationship with God. They knew that God loved them no matter what. They shared their joy in their outward expressions of His love among each other and with everyone else. They had something special I had never seen in any of my friends or at any of the other churches I had attended. They knew God and they knew He knew them.

"And he said, 'I tell you the truth, unless you change and become like little children, you will never enter the kingdom of heaven. Therefore, whoever humbles himself like this child is the greatest in the kingdom of heaven."[4]

Becoming Aware of Choices
Chapter 4

My life had changed from being an only child prior to the age of five, to the oldest of four by the time I was ten years old. I continued to help out at home with more chores and care-taking, especially after the birth of my two youngest sisters. I was active in the grade school band, took saxophone lessons, attended after-school 4-H sewing classes, and continued to attend all church events.

During my early teenage years, I helped out at Bible School and was given permission from my pastor to join a Moody Bible Study with the adult Sunday school class. I got lots of support from the older people in our church for being so young, yet having a very deep interest in the Bible lessons. I think much of this was due to listening to the Moody Bible Institute Hour with my maternal grandmother during the summers when I visited her.

When I was sixteen, I toured Chicago and Skid Row with our youth group. We walked along the streets with our chaperones and saw night life through the windows from outside the taverns. We saw drunken men staggering as they walked down the streets. Some of them slept on the sidewalk outside the tavern or sat on curbs along the road holding their beer bottles or paper bags with beer or alcohol bottles inside. For the first time in my life I also became aware of prostitution.

To enhance our stay, our youth group was provided an opportunity to sleep one night in a slum house or flop house as some called it. These places were unlike the motels we had. There were mattresses on the floor, or on a plain metal bed with no sheets or blankets. This experience helped us to get a better understanding of the lifestyle of those who lived there and those who had become addicted to drugs and/or alcohol. Some had lost hope as well as good paying jobs, family, and everything meaningful they possessed. We saw many people from a variety of different cultures. We had an opportunity to tour Moody Bible Institute and radio station. The staff talked to us about why it was important for Christians to reach out to these people and give them hope for a different way of life.

The summer before I graduated from high school I was able to attend a Christian camp. The camp counselors were from a University in the Chicago area and were studying to go into the ministry. Our counselors stayed in the dorms with us and took time to meet with us individually to get to know us better.

When it was my turn to meet with my counselor, she led me down to the shores of Lake Michigan where we walked along the shoreline until the campground was out of sight. We sat down on the warm sandy beach, watching the late afternoon sun go down on the horizon while listening to the waves beating against the shore. It was such a beautiful and peaceful scene.

"I hope you're enjoying your camp experience," she said while smiling and looking into my eyes.

"Oh, yes. I love being here. I have never been to a camp before."

"It is a beautiful place for a camp and a great opportunity to be with other Christians or just spending some individual private time with the Lord."

"It's been a lot of fun," I replied. "I have enjoyed being so close to nature. It feels so peaceful, almost sacred."

"Yes," she said while seemingly pondering her thoughts. "Well, you are probably wondering why each one of us take time to meet with the campers. Am I right?"

"Yes. The others have mentioned they enjoyed spending some time with their counselors and the opportunity to share their thoughts and feelings about what they are learning here."

"Yes, Bonnie, that is all part of this camp experience. But, we also want to take the time to explore what goals each of you are thinking about for your future and the rest of your life. Have you given any thought of what will happen beyond your high school graduation? And, how does God fit into your plan?"

"I haven't thought about how God will fit into my life because He is already in my life! As far as what I will do upon graduation, I don't really know. I do know I love to hear the missionaries who come to visit our church and tell about their work in other countries. Sometimes I think I'd like to be a missionary, but don't know if that is something I could do, or what I would do if I ever got to be one. I don't see myself as a doctor or nurse, like some of the missionaries." I paused and looked out at the lake. "At other times I think I would like to be a teacher. Sometimes, when I watch you interact with the others and lead us in Bible discussions or activities, I think that is something I would like to do, too; but, I don't know how."

"Don't worry about the how. Just ask God for guidance and it will come," she said. "Tell me more about your choice to be a teacher. Have you picked out a college or applied to any?"

"No, I don't think that is going to ever be a reality. When I told my parents that I was thinking about going to college to become a teacher, they were upset because it cost a lot of money. They said they weren't rich and didn't have any way to help me." I blinked as tears formed in my eyes. "My mom and dad said no matter what, even if they could help me financially, it would be a waste of my time and their money because I would just end up getting married and having kids."

"But do you want to go to college to become a teacher?"

"Yes!" I replied emphatically.

"Then listen to your heart. What does your heart tell you?"

"It tells me I would be a good teacher. I love to learn and like sharing what I learn with others. I do very well at school and have a lot of experience with kids. I have three younger siblings I help take care of and have babysat neighbor kids since I was ten years old. Their parents say I am very responsible and love to have me take care of their kids."

"Then follow your heart and don't worry. Ask God for help and if this is His plan, He will guide you."

As we managed our way back to the campground, tears started to flow down my cheek as my counselor reminded me of a Bible verse, "...If God is for us, who can be against us?"[5]

Is my dream a real possibility? I wondered finally feeling relieved that someone had listened to my desire and was so supportive and believed in me.

As we walked up the wooden steps to our cabin, she made one last comment that stuck with me for a long time. "From what I have learned about you so far, I don't think you would be happy unless you follow your dream and find out if that is God's plan for you. I will keep you in my prayers as you make your decision to go to college or not."

I continued to be actively involved with church and youth group throughout my teenage years. When I started dating, my parents started showing more concern about where I went and with whom. I had several male friends, but no serious boyfriends. Although they were nice guys and I liked going to the school and lake dances with them or ride with them to McDonald's after-school, they were not someone I would think of marrying. Although I enjoyed their company, most of them didn't seem to have any specific goals.

Once again, during the last half of my second semester of my senior year of high school, I began thinking seriously about my desire to go to college. I had worked part-time jobs since I was fourteen and saved enough money to pay for two or three college classes; but, I was uncertain as to how well I would do academically in college and I didn't want to waste money. I decided to enroll in a six week English class starting the first week after high school graduation. If I did well in this class, and if I could save enough money during the summer or get a loan, I would continue with more classes in the fall.

I wrote a lot of essays that summer and was surprised by how well I did in that English 101 class. I became even more excited about taking more classes in the fall. Considering the cost, I knew I would have to begin searching for a scholarship or loan to augment my income so I could become a full time college student.

My experience working at the theater as a cashier during high school opened the door for a full time job as a cashier at a local dime store. I worked nights and weekends and I went to school during the days. However, this was not going to be enough money to pay for all my needs and to continue my schooling for the winter semester.

During the Christmas holidays, one of my regular customers, a teacher, suggested I apply for a teacher aide position in the Head Start Program. I applied and in January I was hired to work with underprivileged kids in a poverty-stricken area. I fell in love with these kids and learned a lot about minorities, their culture, and issues of poverty.

The pay as a teacher aide was good and I could afford to go to college full time in afternoons and evenings while still working at the school during the day. For the first time in my life, I felt I was on the right track and I would be able to reach my dream of becoming a teacher. I also met with the financial aid adviser at the college who helped me search and apply for some small scholarships and a loan.

"Delight yourselves in the Lord and He will give you the desires of your heart."[6]

Early College Years
Chapter 5

I was thrilled to be able to attend college and loved learning, even if it meant a lot of reading, writing, and scrambling to find time to fit in working, attending church, and helping at home. Two of my closest friends, Sheila and Lynn, were also attending our community college. Lynn often talked about two students who were brothers in her chemistry class and said each had hinted about taking her out on a date.

"Oh, Bonnie," she said. "They are so nice and helpful. They are both really smart. I just can't choose which one I'd accept to date if I actually could go out with one of them. I'm afraid I might hurt one or the other's feelings and I don't want to do that to either of them. I just can't make up my mind what to do. So far, I've had to turn them down each time one of them made a suggestion we go somewhere after class because I already had other plans."

"Two guys want to date you and I don't have any," I said. "Actually, I'm glad I don't have that kind of problem. I'm too busy just going to class, working and studying. I'm overwhelmed just trying to get through each day."

"Bonnie, if you could meet them, you would understand my predicament," Lynn responded.

A few days after this conversation Lynn and I were sitting in the corner of the student lounge talking when a guy came up to her. He seemed really nice and very polite. We had a good conversation and I found him quite interesting. After he walked away, Lynn turned to me. "Well, what to do you think of him?" she asked. "He is one of the two brothers."

"He seems very nice," I replied. "Just like you said, he's intelligent and seems knowledgeable about a lot of things. I don't know what I would do if I were in your shoes."

A week later I walked into the student lounge and noticed this guy who looked like the young man Lynn and I had met recently in the lounge. He was now standing across the room talking to another student. I walked over to him, smiled and said, "Hi!" hoping to join in their conversation.

"Do I know you?" he asked. "Have we met before, or are you in any of my classes?"

"No, I'm not in any of your class, but we did meet last week. Remember? We sat over there," I said, pointing to the corner. "You came over to talk to my friend, Lynn, who is in your chemistry class and she introduced you to me." He still looked as if he was clueless about meeting me. "Don't you recall?"

"Sorry," he said. "I've never met you before. You must be talking about my twin brother." He turned to continue talking to the guy standing next to him who was chuckling after hearing our conversation.

I felt embarrassed by his rude rejection, especially in front of someone else. I could feel my face turning red as I turned to walk away. "Oh, of course everyone has a twin brother!" I said as I stormed out of the lounge.

A few weeks later, I arrived at school early and was waiting outside my English classroom for another class to be dismissed. When the door opened, I noticed the first guy walking out of the classroom was the same one who had so rudely denied we had met. I felt my face turning red again and wished I could crawl under the carpet.

Then Sheila walked through the door behind him and over to me.

"You will never guess what our next assignment for this class is!" she said as she continued, "Are you ready for Shakespeare? Because our class has to go to the theater to watch Hamlet when it comes to town next month and then we have to write an essay comparing that movie with the story as it was originally written. I've got to get going to my next class now, but let me know if your class gets the same assignment. Maybe we can go see Hamlet together."

"That sounds good. I'll call you later tonight or tomorrow and let you know."

A few days later, I didn't have any transportation to class and called Lynn for a ride. I shared with her my experience about seeing her friend in the lounge and how he had denied ever meeting me.

"Oh, that's so hilarious!" she said laughing. "You must have met his twin brother!"

"What? Is this a joke? Those are the exactly the words he said to me!"

"It's true! They are identical twins. That is why I'm having such a difficult time choosing which one to go out with first, if at all. I keep having conflicts in my schedule and finding excuses to not go out with either of them!"

"Well, why didn't you tell me they were identical twins instead of being just brothers? Now I feel really embarrassed about my response to him!" I said as I described my snotty remark and how I stormed out of the lounge.

"By the way, do you know which one is taking the Wednesday night English Class with Mrs. Churchill? One of them is in that class just before mine."

"I'm not sure, but I suspect it is Don," Lynn replied. "Why not ask Sheila? She's in that class and maybe she knows his name."

"It's probably Don because he doesn't stop to talk with me or others after class. It just seems like Ron is more friendly and outgoing."

"I think if it is Don, he probably has other things on his mind or it might be his last class after a long day. If it is Don, you could tell him you just found out he has an identical twin brother and apologize for your behavior."

"I'm just not sure how to approach him with that. When he walked out of class, he didn't even seem to notice me standing there."

It was common for me to often wait outside the door for Sheila's class to let out so we could chat a little before my class started. On one occasion, Doug, a guy I had met in another class, walked along with me to this class.

"I have a friend in that class who gets out just before yours starts and I need to check to see if I can hitch a ride with him next week," Doug informed me as we walked down the hall together.

When the door opened and students came rushing out, Doug nodded to the guy, whom I now suspected was Don.

"Hi Doug, what's up?" he said as he walked toward us with a broad smile.

"I need a ride next week while my car is in the shop getting fixed. I'm hoping you can give me a lift." Then he turned toward me. "Oh, by the way, Don, have you met Bonnie? She's in my history class."

"Well, we sort of met. She thought I was my twin brother and stomped off when I didn't seem to recall meeting her!"

"Oh, are you two playing that game again?" Doug replied and looked over at me smiling before turning back to Don. "You two get into so much trouble by looking so much alike. Remember how the nuns always got you two mixed up in class? That was a blast watching them get so confused over which one of you was Don or Ron."

"We were not trying to play any games! It is just something that happens to us all the time."

Week after week, I started to meet with Don after class and often ran into him in other places on campus. Each time I saw him he became friendlier. I loved the way his face lit up with a warm deep smile as he looked at me and I felt like I was melting into a pool of butter. And, the more I looked forward to talking to Don after class, the more my heart felt like a drum roll while I waited for him.

"I can't help but think I could easily fall in love with Don," I told Lynn. "I love his smile and soft confident voice. He is so intelligent it amazes me. I haven't seen Ron much at all since I met him that day with you. Although Ron is pleasant and friendly, there is just something special about Don that makes my heart beat faster and I feel so excited when he is near me."

Lynn agreed they were both special and was glad I had met them. "Wouldn't it be something if you eventually married Don and I married Ron? We would be sisters-in-law!" Still, she couldn't decide which one to agree to date if she ever had the opportunity. As a result, she never took either one up on their subtle offers.

Hamlet was scheduled to be at the movie theater soon. So, Sheila, Doug and I had met after class to make plans for when we could go to see Hamlet at the same time. She needed a ride because her parents wouldn't let her take their car. Doug had already asked me if he could take me to see Hamlet. Sheila was hoping to go along, but she didn't want to feel like a third party tagging along with us. Later, Sheila confessed she was jealous of me because she liked Doug, but he never seemed to notice her.

As we were standing outside the classroom looking over the movie schedule, Don walked over to us.

"I couldn't help overhear all of you talking about going to see Hamlet. Have you decided what day and time you're going?"

"Yeah, we are thinking Thursday night would work for all of us. Would you like to come along?" Doug asked.

Sheila spoke up. "We could all go out afterward for something to eat and talk about writing our papers."

"I guess we could do that," Don responded. "Shall I drive?"

"I've already asked Bonnie to go with me and it would mean a lot of driving around town before the movie if one of us drove to pick everyone else up," Doug responded. "Maybe we can just meet at the theater."

"That will work," Don replied.

"That won't work for me!" Sheila chipped in. "I don't have any transportation unless one of you guys would be willing to pick me up."

"Where do you live?" Don asked.

"Not far from here, near the cemetery," Sheila said. "I would really appreciate it if you would come to get me. I won't be able to go or do this assignment without a ride. I can be ready on Thursday night by 6:30 pm. Will that work for you?"

"That should be fine. Give me your phone number and I'll call you for directions to your house. I'll see the two of you at the movie," Don replied as he walked away with Doug.

After the intermission during Hamlet, Sheila and I returned from our bathroom break. She scooted into our row and sat down next to Doug leaving me to sit next to Don. I didn't mind her doing this. In fact, I really enjoyed getting this close to Don; but, it did seem rude of me since I had come with Doug. Yet the guys didn't seem to notice that we were sitting in different seats. They were seriously watching the movie while Sheila and I were bored with it. When the movie was over, it was much later than we had expected. We all decided to head for home and call it a night.

Not too long after that event, while driving another girl home from school, I noticed the car in front of me looked familiar.

"Hmm," I said. "I think that's Don's car in front of us. I wonder where he's going."

"Why not follow him and find out?" Francine asked.

"That sounds like I would be stalking him!" I said.

"Not much anyone can say about you just driving down the street behind a car that happens to look like Don's," she said.

"Well, okay. This is sort of the direction of your home. Maybe he's on his way to work," I said as I continued to follow him.

Suddenly, Don waved out his window for us to move over to the side of the street. I followed and stopped behind him. He got out of the car.

"Oh, oh! I think he recognized me," I said as I tried to smile looking at Francine while opening the window.

"What are you doing? Are you following me?" Don asked seemingly upset.

"Actually, I was just driving down the street and didn't realize your car was in front of mine until just a few minutes ago," I said, feeling guilty but still trying to smile.

"So how far are you planning to drive down this street?" he asked.

"To the end of this street or as far as it goes. I haven't been on this street before," I said naively.

"Well, you can't do that! I live at the end of this street."

"Oh. You mean I can't drive down this street because you live on it?"

"No, I mean, you can't follow me home. This street ends in my driveway and my parents would not appreciate two girls following me home. So please, don't follow me any further."

"Hmm, 'tis a predicament," I said wondering what to say and feeling guilty for being so brazen as to follow him. *I should have turned off this road long before and taken Francine directly home,* I thought to myself.

"Look, promise me you won't drive into my driveway and I'll take you out for lunch tomorrow. Is that a deal?"

Stunned about finally getting a date with him, I could hardly hold back my excitement. "That's a deal! But I work until 3pm. If you promise to take me out after I'm done with work tomorrow, I won't drive into your yard."

"It's a deal!" he said. "Thank you! At least I don't have to explain this to my mom. I'll meet you tomorrow at 3:30 pm in the lounge if that works for you."

So that's how our relationship began. We often brought our lunches or snacks to school and sat together outside, in the lounge, or in his car eating and studying between classes. Whenever he held my hand, my whole body felt the warmth generating from him. He started calling me every night including weekends.

"If we confess our sins, He is faithful and just and will forgive our sins and purify us from all unrighteousness." [2]

*Note: Because this kind of behavior was so far out of my character, I felt embarrassed and was ashamed for pursuing Don as I did.

Religion and Relationships
Chapter 6

My parents were becoming keenly aware and very concerned I was possibly getting serious about someone from college. They wanted to know more about my new boyfriend and when they would meet him.

I told them how nice he was and how he opened doors for me and that he spoke gently, was very religious, and intelligent. "He graduated in the top 10 of his class with a full scholarship to Michigan State University in the engineering program!" I said hoping to impress them with all of his good qualities.

"Did he go to high school with you?" my mom asked.

"No, I met him at college," I replied.

"Did he go to any of the high schools around here?" My mom continued to ask.

Knowing they would be upset with me for being interested in someone who was a Catholic, I hesitated. Even though this was the era of Civil Rights and Woman's Equality movements, they considered dating a Catholic as bad as a white person dating an African American. I knew they would not be very accepting of Don and would frown on him because of his religious difference. They believed all Catholics were hypocrites who went to confession on Saturday and afterward went out drinking and carousing. But I knew I couldn't lie to my parents and responded, "He went to Catholic Central."

My parents looked at each other and then looked at me with disgust. "Why are you dating a Catholic when there are plenty of Christian boys you could date?"

"Because he is one of the nicest boys I know and we have a lot of the same interests."

"You don't have the same religious interests!" my mom said scornfully. "You realize we will have to meet him before the two of you go out together."

I felt as if a ton of books just fell on my shoulders and my eyes dropped to the floor.

"You <u>do</u> know that, don't you?" my mom asked.

"Yes, I'll tell him he has to come inside to meet you first before I can leave with him," I said as I turned to walk to my room. *What are they going to say to him?* I wondered. For the first time in my life I felt very sick to my stomach bringing a new boyfriend into my house to meet my parents. I decided to prepare Don for this encounter before he came over. Although I suspected it, I was hoping they wouldn't say anything about him being Catholic when they met him.

When I told Don I couldn't go out with him until he came in to meet with my parents, he said he was fine with this. He had planned to come early to meet them anyway. "It's not unusual for me to meet the parents of the girls I date. I don't know why you seem so worried."

"Well, normally I wouldn't worry, but you don't know my parents. They don't regard Catholics very highly," I said, feeling ashamed of them. "They might say something offensive to you about your religion.

That evening when Don arrived my mom and dad were not at all very friendly toward him. My dad sat down and asked Don to have a seat. He opened his Bible and started reading the passage about not be unequally yoked with a non-believer (II Corinthians 6:14 NIV). He talked about how important being

37

"equally yoked" was for those who married and planned to bring up children in their family.

I felt horrified! Don and I were not even discussing marriage! This was just our first real date.

I couldn't believe my dad was accusing Don of being an unbeliever. I sat there feeling as if my stomach was doing somersaults. I wondered if after this encounter Don would ever want to take me out again.

I was shocked to hear Don's response. "You're right," he said. "Both a husband and wife need to believe in God and share that belief with their kids. I see you are both Christians who care a lot for Bonnie. She has also shared with me her deep belief in God and the importance of her church and religion. You must be proud of her." He paused. "But, you are wrong about one thing. We Catholics don't all go out carousing and then think it can all be wiped away by going to confession on Saturday. We worship the same God you do."

Then my dad started finding fault with Catholics for praying through Mary and the Saints instead of through Jesus.

"We do pray through the Saints and Mary is a Saint," Don replied. "But, we also pray through Jesus and in Jesus' name."

I can't believe how well he is handling this interrogation, I thought to myself.

I interrupted my dad who was starting to argue about how wrong it was to pray through anyone except Jesus. "Dad, we are just going to dinner and then the movie. We need to get going now or we will be late."

"Okay, for tonight," my dad said with a stern tone and looking at me as if he was very irritated. "But we need to talk more about this!"

Once Don and I got in the car, I was still feeling pretty shook up. I looked over toward Don. "I'm so embarrassed about how my dad spoke to you and I am so sorry for how you must feel."

"Don't be," Don replied seeming to understand. He didn't appear to be as shocked as I was by what had just happened. "Your dad has his beliefs and must care a lot for you to be so concerned that he scrutinizes your dates."

"He has never done this to any of my dates before," I replied. "But you are the first Catholic I have dated."

After that, every time I went out with Don my parents became more and more angry with me and read Bible verses to me about relationships with non-believers as well as reminding me of the fifth Commandment to honor your parents.[8] One day, while getting ready to leave to go to work my mom asked, "Why do you continue dating him? He's a Catholic and not right for you!"

Although Don and I had never talked about marriage, I blurted out without thinking, "I'm going to marry him!"

"No, you are NOT!" she said as I opened the door to leave.

My dad rushed to the door and attempted to block me from walking outside as my mom grabbed my hair and tried to pull me back inside. I managed to get out the door and as I ran to my car I could hear my mom yelling, "We're going to call the minister and have you put into a Psychiatric Hospital! There is something very wrong with you to continue as you are! You know better than to disobey the Lord by continuing this relationship with a Catholic!"

Although I was in tears, I didn't perceive Don as a Catholic per se, but instead a very devout Christian who worshiped the same God as I did. I felt we were soul mates in our spiritual life, but maybe not in the same theological process of worshipping.

With the stress from living at home increasing from my parents' yelling and condemning me while I tried to study and keep my sanity, I soon realized I needed to move out of my family home to gain some peace and give myself some space to rethink my relationship with Don. I consulted with Glenda, who had been my Sunday school teacher during my high school years. I explained all that was going on at home and how I felt about Don. Her opinion meant a great deal to me. She was also a friend. Before Don and I had started dating, I often went to Christian movies or concerts with her. She had helped me purchase a car so I could drive back and forth to college and work because the family car was not always available.

"I'd like to meet him," Glenda said. "He sounds like a gem and I don't doubt your relationship with God. If you ask Him, he will guide you. I can't give you answers, but I will pray that God will lead you."

I had developed a deep appreciation and love for Don that I had never felt with any previous boyfriends. He was really wonderful with all that was going on in my home life. He was patient, kind, and understanding which was the reason I was shocked one day when he said, "If you feel you want to break off our relationship so it would make life better for you, I will understand."

"I don't want to break up with you," I said. "Do you want to break up with me?"

"No, I really want to keep our relationship, but I know this is hard for you."

When I got home late one night after-school, my dad met me at the door. He said my mother had been taken to emergency earlier in the evening and was admitted to the hospital. "She may have had a heart attack or stroke," he said. "She has been so upset and stressed out since you started dating that Catholic."

I started crying. I felt responsible and sad if I had caused this to happen by following my heart and dating someone they were totally against. In the morning, I went to the hospital to visit my mother. On the way up to her floor, her doctor happened to step into the elevator with me. I told him how concerned I was and how guilty I felt because I had caused this to happen to her.

The doctor looked at me and said, "My dear child, you did not cause this to happen to her. Your mother cannot blame you for what is happening. Some of this is due to her genetic inheritance. But your mother is responsible for how well she has or has not taken care of herself and that is what has brought on her heart problems. It has nothing to do with your dating someone she does not approve of."

I began crying. There was part of me that had thought what happened to my mother was not my fault. The doctor validated my thinking. I was so thankful the doctor had taken time to listen to me and relieved me of my guilt feelings. I knew I had no choice but to move out of my parents' home as soon as I could and before this blaming continued to escalate.

I spoke with a friend of mine whose mother had died while we were in high school. Her father had recently remarried and had left her with their family home. She offered to let me stay with her if I would help pay for utilities and food. Although this was not the ideal way to handle this situation, one day while my family was away I moved my things out. I knew if I had tried to move out when my family was home, they would have preached, yelled, and condemned me to the "everlasting fire". I did not want to have to go through all of that and have that kind of scene in front of my younger siblings.

At the end of summer that year, Don and I said goodbye as he returned to Michigan State University and I headed to Central Michigan University. I worked 20-25 hours a week while in Mt. Pleasant to support my education. Don and I wrote each other weekly and talked once a week or more on the phone. I was growing madly in love with him and wanted to be with him all the time. My friend, Lynn, also attended MSU and lived in the dorm next to Don's. Lynn offered me her dorm room key and meal pass if I wanted to visit Don when she went home on the weekends. I also had friends at CMU who often drove to Lansing on a Saturday for the football game, spent the night, and would return back to CMU on Sunday. I went along with them two or three times that fall to spend some time visiting Don. Although we spent a great deal of time doing our homework together in the library, I really enjoyed our walks across the campus holding his hand and listening to the sound of the Clarion bells ringing.

When it came time to pay for my second semester at CMU, I didn't have quite enough money to live on campus, which was required during those years; nor could I afford to pay for all my classes and books. I had no choice but to return home to my parents and siblings. Since it was almost Christmas when the semester ended, it was easier to be at home; but my parents continued to preach to me about my relationship with Don.

After Christmas, I got a full-time job as a bank teller and moved into a rooming house near town where it was a short walk to the bank. Don and I were now starting to talk about marriage. Both of us were concerned about our different theologies and decided before we got married we would have to resolve whether he turned Protestant or I turned Catholic. We met with different ministers and priests to discuss how their theological doctrines were or were not like the others and compared our beliefs. We began to narrow it down to the Episcopal or Catholic Church. Don said the sacraments meant a lot to him and since the Catholic Church included two more sacraments than the Episcopal Church, he asked if I would be willing to take some classes on Catholicism while he was away at school. We could discuss what I was learning over the phone. I agreed.

One weekend, when Don came home from college, he bought me an engagement ring and showed it to his mother before giving it to me. Up until this point, his parents had not said much about our dating or that I was a Protestant.

"After all the religious training we provided for you, you are not going to marry a Protestant! What is wrong with any of those girls you dated in high school?" his mother asked angrily. "If you give her that ring, you will not be welcome to come back home!"

With the conflicts from both sides of our families trying to prevent us from marrying, I prayed daily that we were doing the right thing and asked God to either create some divergence to stop our relationship or to bless us. In my heart, I felt strong about our relationship but very uncomfortable about the turmoil it was creating in our families.

Don gave me the ring just before Valentine's Day. When classes were out for the summer term, he returned to Muskegon to work as draftsman and found a rooming house not far from where I was staying. During the summer, we attended pre-marital classes together offered by the priest at the Catholic Information Center. In the fall, he returned to MSU and I stayed behind working as a bank teller and taking one college class in the evening.

One Sunday afternoon in the fall, just after his term started, Don came home from MSU to visit me. I asked if he had any thoughts of when he wanted to get married.

"How about getting married the next time I have a break from school?" he said with a smile.

"What? That's only two months away," I said feeling both excited about the possibility of becoming his wife so soon and overwhelmed with the thought of how much it would cost and the time needed to prepare for our wedding. "That will be Thanksgiving! I don't think we will have enough time to get ready for it by then. What about in the spring after-school is out?"

"I think Thanksgiving is a perfect time," Don said.

Long before we before we had started dating, I knew when I got married I would want a husband who had a strong relationship with God and would be involved with bringing our children up in the church. Don had all those qualities I felt were important. By this time, I had decided I would support him by becoming Catholic so our family could worship together and grow strong in the faith.

Although my parents said they would not step into a Catholic church for a wedding and his parents said they would not come to a Protestant wedding, we found a semi-neutral chapel at the Catholic Information Center. The priest, with whom I took religious training, said he would be happy to perform our wedding there. "It will be the first wedding ever to be held here!" he said with excitement.

Sheila and Lynn agreed to be my attendants. Don's brother agreed to be his best man and Doug agreed to be Don's attendant. Now we had to tell our parents about our plans.

Don came home from MSU a few weeks later on a Sunday afternoon to tell my parents we were planning to get married at Thanksgiving. My parents were upset, but not noticeably angry about it. They knew it was coming. They said they weren't sure they would attend a Catholic wedding and had to think about it. We told them they were invited and we would love to have them be part of it, but if they decided not to come, that would be their choice.

On November 25, 1967, Don and I were married and our parents, along with both sides of our families, attended. Both of our families held bridal showers for us and Don's aunt made my wedding gown. My mother bought my veil. My maternal grandmother adored Don and his grandmother and aunts showed me lots of love and acceptance. I felt I as if I was part of their family from the beginning. The ladies at my church were happy to make and serve the dinner for our reception.

Right after our wedding reception, we left for our new apartment in East Lansing. I had been blessed with a job waiting for me at a local bank and started working on Monday morning following our wedding.

Every morning, Don and I could hear the Clarion bells chime from campus as we walked a short mile into the city of East Lansing where we parted. He headed to classes while I went to work at the bank across the street from campus. We developed friendships through church, my work, and his classmates. We attended a Catholic Church where they held Friday night movies and entertainment with popcorn, dances, or other events for a small fee to students.

It was easy becoming a Catholic those first few years while living near campus. The priests and nuns seemed very friendly and full of joy and excitement. They also became more personally involved with those in their parish and kept up with what was going on in their parish members' lives. This church reminded me so much of the church where I grew up. When we had our first two children in Lansing, one of the nuns came to the hospital to visit me. Once I returned home, she stopped by our apartment to check on how we were doing and offered to help fold diapers or just hold our baby. She invited me to join the Mom's Club in our apartment complex and introduced me to other young mothers. This nun always had a smile and I appreciated having her come around because I felt so alone being far away from home in my new role as a wife and young mother. But still, something was missing in my spiritual life. While I enjoyed the worship services with guitar folk songs, I missed attending Sunday school and singing the old familiar hymns from my childhood.

After Don graduated, we moved back home near my parents. Although by this time we had been married for almost six years, Don had never really been accepted by my parents until my sister, who was only sixteen at the time, became pregnant. My parents had made it very difficult for her to live at home. They called her disgraceful names and shamed her to the point she left home and moved in with us. Don was upset about how they were treating her and finally decided to do something about this situation. He made an appointment with my parents to talk to them alone without any other family members present. Taking his Bible with Him, he went to their house and listened to how hurt they were. I don't know what he said, but the next day they called my sister to move back home. After that encounter with Don, my parents showed tremendous respect and love toward him for the rest of their lives. That dark cloud had finally been lifted between Don and my parents.

"And we know that in all things God works for the good of those who love Him." [2]

Growing Awareness
Chapter 7

My husband was informed the semester before graduation that there would be no job openings in the field of mechanical engineering when he finished his degree. After meeting with his adviser to discuss options, he decided to spend his last semester at college as a student teacher in an Industrial Arts Education Program. As a teacher in this program, he would be able to utilize all the skills he had learned in the engineering program. He decided it would be fun and rewarding to inspire young students to trouble shoot, build, fix and repair things. Just prior to graduation from Michigan State University in March of 1970, Don applied for a teaching position in our home town. He was accepted immediately as a full time substitute to fill an open position teaching wood shop, electronics and auto repair. That fall he was offered a full time position at the school as a teacher in the Industrial Arts Program.

At the beginning of the school year, the intermediate school district hosted a "kick-off" party for all the teachers, staff, and their spouses. We met many teachers, but I was intrigued by one particular teacher who caught my eye. Every time she spoke, her fingers moved as fast as her mouth. I had never seen anything like this before. But, being shy and not wanting to appear stupid, I didn't ask her what she was doing.

Although I became aware of a classroom for the students who were deaf or hard of hearing across the hall from Don's classroom, I never met any of the students or the teacher when I came early to pick Don up after-school.

One evening after a home football game we were invited to join some teachers at a get-together for a party at one of their homes. This same teacher, who had caught my eye before, happened to be there. Once again, her hands were moving as fast as her mouth.

Finally, I got enough courage to ask her, "What is that you are doing with your hands? Every time I see you, you are moving them whenever you speak."

"Oh, I'm just talking with them!" she said with a giggle.

Everyone laughed and someone said, "She is really good at that!"

Is she joking with me? I wondered, feeling confused because I still didn't understand what she was doing with her hands. However, I did enjoy watching her.

A few years later, during the last week of school, I gave birth to our third daughter, Tracy. My husband had taken a day off from school to pick me and our newborn daughter up from the hospital to bring us home. I couldn't wait to get home to meet her older sisters: Kady, who was 4½ and Dawn, who was 3½. I had everything packed and ready to go way before breakfast and sat rocking Tracy for what seemed like forever before Don finally appeared.

"Hi Honey," he said as he walked in and picked up our newborn baby. "Ready?"

"Yes. I can't wait to get home!" I replied. He took our baby from me as I got up to call for a nurse to discharge Tracy and me.

As we drove out of the parking lot and started down the street, Don appeared anxious as he looked over and smiled at me. "How do you feel about stopping by the high school? I would love to show off our new baby to my students before class is dismissed and stop by some of the other classrooms to show her to the teachers. How do you feel about that?"

"Sure, we can do that," I replied beaming with a smile and happy he was proud to be a father again.

"You don't have to go in if you don't feel like it. You can wait in the car if you prefer."

"What? Are you kidding! I want to go in with you to show her off, too! Besides, I want to hear what they have to say."

Class was almost out for the day and the end of the school year. The students were just waiting for the bell to ring to start their summer vacation.

As he opened the classroom door, the students looked up. Some got out of their seats and rushed over to the door to greet us. "How old is she? Is this why you weren't here today, Mr. V? What's her name?" Everyone wanted to touch her tiny fingers and hands while they gathered around us.

As we made our way further into his shop, I noticed a young woman with two teenage girls standing near the door to the inside hall. Seeing girls in his classroom surprised me since I thought only males were allowed to take shop classes. "Are those girls in your class, too?" I asked.

"Yes, they are two of my best students," Don said as he waved at them.

"Who is that woman with them?"

"She's a para professional teacher aid. The girls are mainstreamed from special education into regular classes. She attends all classes with them to help them understand."

As we walked up to them, the girls started moving their hands just like the teacher I had seen make similar hand movements at the parties we had attended. Then the young woman standing next to them began moving her hands, too. We walked over to them and Don started to introduce me to the lady and the girls. The woman started moving her fingers as Don spoke.

My husband leaned over and whispered to me, "These girls are deaf. This is Barb. She's their interpreter". Then he introduced me to her.

It seemed very confusing for me to listen to the woman speaking on one side of me while the girls who stood on the other side of me were looking at me with inquisitive looks and moving their hands as they tried to voice something. I wasn't sure whether to listen to the girls or the woman, but it seemed it was the girls who were trying to communicate with me. So, I looked at them as I spoke.

"Is this your baby?" the young woman asked while the girls stared at me.

"Yes," I replied. "She is two days old."

Then one of the girls tapped my lower arm and moved her fingers up to her chin while the interpreter said, "She is so cute!"

The girls moved their hands again. "What's her name?" the interpreter asked.

This seemed so awkward and confusing to me. Two people used hand signals and moving their lips, while another person stood next to me voicing everything they tried to say to me. I focused on the girls' faces as I tried to respond directly to the girls while listening to Barb verbalizing the girls' questions.

The girls smiled and touched Tracy's little hand and her forehead just as the bell rang and everyone ran out the door.

I asked the interpreter how she learned to communicate with deaf people. She said her parents were deaf and this was her first language. "Family members who were not deaf taught my sister and I to speak English. When we were older, my sister and I had to go with our mother or father to appointments and interpret for them. Sometimes it was hard to understand what the doctors were talking about, but other times interpreting was quite interesting. For example, deciding what to share with our parents when interpreting at a parent teacher conference and deciding what to tell our parents the teacher said about us."

Just then, Mrs. Thomas, the teacher for deaf and hard of hearing students hurried over from across the hall. When Tracy began to move her fingers, Mrs. Thomas proudly announced, "I have just taught your new baby to talk with her hands!" I couldn't help but laugh, not knowing at that time, babies can learn sign language very quickly and have a better concept of language if taught at a very early age.

Don noticed I was getting tired and our baby was getting restless. We said our goodbyes to everyone and headed for home.

"Are those two girls the only students who are deaf at the high school?" I asked my husband while he drove home.

"No. There are others throughout the entire school system."

"You know, I only met one deaf person in my whole life before today. I never even knew there was such a thing as sign language or interpreters," I said as I told him about Martha, the deaf girl who came to my door when I was a child.

"Really?" Don said. "That's interesting. My dad works with a deaf man who signs and has for a long time. I never met him, but I remember my dad talking about him since I was a kid."

We pulled up to the curb in front of our house just as my mom, Kady and Dawn came running out to greet us. I was thrilled to be home with my three beautiful daughters and husband.

"Children are a gift from God; they are His reward."[10]

Family Matters and
Spiritual Growth
Chapter 8

After lunch, while the girls were down for their nap, my mother said she needed to discuss some problems which occurred with Dawn while I was in the hospital.

"I hate to tell you this on your first day home, but you or Don will have to wash Dawn's clothing and a load of diapers right away, or else go buy new ones because all of her clothes are wet. I put Kady's pants and clothing on her for now, but they are really too big. She kept wetting her pants even though I put her on the toilet frequently. I think she might have a urinary infection."

We had been trying to potty train Dawn since last summer just before I became pregnant for our third baby, but she continued wetting her pants. I had thought the frequent wetting was psychological because I was often exhausted and unable to give her the time and attention she might have needed. But, this had continued to be a significant problem, especially when we were trying to get ready to go somewhere.

Don started the wash and left to get new underwear for Dawn while I called our doctor. He wanted to see her that same afternoon. When Don returned home, he helped me dress Dawn and then took her to the doctor's office.

A urine sample showed she had a severe urinary tract infection, and they were sent to the hospital for a catheterized specimen and culture. An appointment was made for her to see a urologist. After a number of tests, it was determined Dawn had three kidneys with three separate ureters to the bladder. Each time she had an infection, there were mixed results from the urinalysis because the fluid came down a separate ureter from a different kidney. Two of her kidneys were working well, but one was not. That meant we had to take her to the urologist regularly every two weeks or more to monitor the amount of bacteria and protein she was spilling into her urine which could also mean there was something more serious going on with her kidneys. Because of these repeated infections, Dawn was given antibiotics frequently. They seemed to be helping but she still needed to be carefully monitored by her doctor.

Our oldest daughter, Kady, was never sick and always very easy going. She played well with Dawn and often helped me by running to get diapers for Tracy, making her own bed, setting and clearing the dinner table and folding towels. But, she would be starting kindergarten in the fall and I would soon miss her helpfulness.

When Tracy was about six months old, we started her on some table food and milk. She began having frequent ear infections, frequent bronchial infections, and projectile vomiting when she ate anything with milk or wheat, indicating she was intolerant to both milk and wheat. I began researching information on food allergies and also the causes and treatments for urinary problems. I talked with other mothers whose children had food allergies and also with some workers at the health food store who seemed to be more knowledgeable in these areas. My life seemed be become a series of medical appointments, dispensing medications, taking temperatures, or walking the floor at all hours of night when Tracy couldn't sleep. I read everything I could find that might become helpful for my children to overcome their health problems. I began to feel like a nurse and dietitian as I made many changes to their diets.

It was not unusual for us to take longer getting ready to leave for family gatherings or church because we had to stop to change Dawn's clothing, nurse Tracy, or clean Tracy up after something didn't settle with her digestive system. This seemed especially true on Sunday mornings when we rushed to get ready for Mass.

One Sunday after our regular rituals of getting ready for church with several interruptions and then waiting for the next scheduled Mass, we finally got to church just in time to hear an announcement that really hit me hard.

"We have several Masses available on Saturdays and Sundays. If it is difficult for those of you with young children to be on time, please consider planning ahead. Also, once seated, please do not walk to the back of the church or walk out early as this is disturbing to other worshipers."

Although to some extent I could understand how this was interrupting to others, I felt embarrassed, shocked, tired, and angry. *If he only knew how hard it was to get here, I don't think he would say what he just said.* I wondered what kind of church expects young children will not interrupt during the Mass.

A few days later while sitting outside watching my kids play with our kittens, my neighbor walked over to ask how I was doing. I offered her some ice tea as we sat and talked. I shared how hard it was to get ready and to be on time for church on Sunday mornings and how I felt about what had been said at Mass the previous Sunday.

"It seems every time we get ready to go out the door, something happens and we have to start all over, again. There are so many interruptions in the mornings. I have to give medications to Dawn and Tracy, but sometimes I get caught up in getting everyone ready to go, I forget and we leave without giving them their medications on time. I am getting so exhausted just trying to get everything done. I feel like I'm just a failure. Now that Don has to go Grand Rapids in the evenings after-school to attend classes to get his permanent teaching certificate, I feel even more alone and overwhelmed."

"Bonnie, God knows what is on your plate. I know it is important to go to church and the Catholic Church frowns on lack of attendance. But, God gave you a very important task and that is being the best mother you can be. Those kids are His gift to you. It is your job to take the best care of them and right now, taking care of them is your highest responsibility. He wouldn't have given them to you with their special needs if he didn't think you could handle it. Jesus' mother and father couldn't get to the temple very often either. They lived too far away. Jesus learned about His Father through His parents. Do what you know is right in your heart."

Not too long after that, my best friend Lynn stopped by our house. I also shared with her what the priest had said and my internal struggle of trying to be a good Catholic; yet, really yearning for a church like I had attended as a child.

"You might be interested in visiting my church. It is a Lutheran Church and very much like the Catholic Church in worship. If you and Don go there, you may not even notice it is not Catholic except for the actual Mass or Eucharist part of it. We have a Sunday school and kids are more than welcome."

"I'll think about it. You know we did talk to many ministers and different denominations before we were married. I don't know why but we never considered a Lutheran Church."

The next Sunday, I woke up very early before it was time to get up to go to Mass. I heard someone say, "Stop, don't go there." I looked around. Don wasn't next to me. I got up, put my bathrobe on, and walked out into the kitchen where he sat reading the newspaper.

"Did you say something" I asked.

"No, did you hear someone who sounded like me?" He replied.

"I'm not sure who it sounded like but I heard someone say 'Don't go there'."

Don said he hadn't said or heard anything. So I went back to bed and fell asleep. I dreamed God was mad at me and did not want me to go back to the church where that announcement had been made about disrupting the service when taking children out or for those who came late. Knowing my parents were still upset with me for switching to Catholicism, I considered the voice and dream might be just my own subconscious speaking to me. But, if that were true, then I knew I did not belong in the Catholic Church. My own wisdom was trying to tell me I needed go elsewhere and take my kids with me, even if Don wouldn't go, too.

I worried about how I could share this with Don. *What would he say if I told him I didn't want to go to that church anymore?* I felt like I'd be really letting him down and he would feel betrayed. *Am I really betraying him or am I betraying myself if I believe God is telling me to go elsewhere?*

I finally got up the nerve to share with Don how I had been affected by what had been said in church a week ago and how much I had been struggling trying to be a Catholic.

"Don, I need to talk about something with you and I'm concerned you won't understand. I have not been happy with the Catholic Church since we moved back here. I miss attending Sunday school and want my kids to have the same kind of experience I had growing up in a church. It was so important to me then and now." I continued to share with him what Lynn had said about her church when she stopped by. "I'm thinking of visiting Lynn's church. I'm sorry. I hate to do this because worshipping together as a family is also very important to me; but, I just have to make some changes for me and our kids so we can grow closer to God."

Don listened carefully to what I said and then gently spoke. "I have also experienced some of the same thoughts and feelings as you since last Sunday. I'm concerned especially after hearing what was said about interrupting others when taking the kids out. There is no other place in church to take the kids when they are acting up but outside the sanctuary. I don't know anything about the Lutheran Church, but I guess we could check it out, if that's what you want to do."

We visited my friend's church and found the parishioners friendly and welcoming. It was very much like Lynn had described as being very similar to the Catholic Church. There was a Sunday School Program for young kids which Kady and Dawn visited. I felt so happy when they said they liked it. The church also had a parochial school and we were invited to consider sending Kady there for Kindergarten. I loved the idea of having my children in a parochial school, but I also loved the public school system in which I had grown up.

There was a young vicar at the church who seemed to take a liking to Don and Don liked talking with him, too. It wasn't long before we were taking Adult Information and Confirmation classes. We joined the Lutheran Church and looked forward to Kady starting school there.

The minister of this church and the young vicar stopped by often to see how we were doing and how the kids were. It felt so good to have a close relationship with our spiritual leaders who soon learned what was going on with our daughter, Dawn, and prayed with us for her.

Dawn continued to have problems with her kidneys. By the time she was almost six years old she had become immune to penicillin. She often had fevers, but sometimes we didn't know she was ill except when we noticed a change I her attitude and moods. She would become more irritable or her face would be flushed which we learned was often due to her medications. She was also photosensitive, which meant she could not be outside in the sun. I discovered certain foods irritated her bladder more than others, especially red dye in Kool Aid, candy, and pop. I started to buy more natural foods and food with less sugar and no dye. We changed to non-fat milk and cut down some dairy products. It was working and Dawn was getting better.

I also changed Tracy's diet and began to make rye bread and other types of bread and cookies from oat flour. I bought rice cakes and healthier items from the health food store. I continued to learn a lot more about nutrition, additives, and dyes put into foods and causing health problems. What I was doing was helping both Dawn and Tracy.

To help me make sure I gave her medications on time, we bought Dawn a watch with an alarm on it to notify her to come see me for her medication, especially while she was outside playing with other kids. It had been difficult to keep on top of everything with making special diets, household chores, doctor appointments, events at school and now having four children under seven, with another baby on the way. My life was definitely centered on our home and care-taking. Sometimes, I felt as if I was surviving each day by helping my kids survive.

The next year, Dawn got really sick just before her sixth birthday which was only a few days before Christmas. She had become immune to not only the penicillin, but also Septra and Bactrim. She ran a fever of 106 degrees and we could not get it to come down. Her urologist admitted her to the hospital because her urine was full of bacteria and nothing was helping to control the infection. The second day she was in the hospital, I couldn't help but notice the extremely worried look on her doctor's face as I stood outside the nurses' station watching him review her chart. His facial expression looked as if he was struggling with what he was reading. I became alarmed and feared Dawn could die because she had built up immunity to everything and nothing was helping her.

Overwhelmed with fear and anticipatory grief, I walked into the nurses' station and looked directly into her doctor's eyes. I could barely get the words out of my mouth before I started crying as I asked him if she was going to die.

He looked very concerned as he turned to me and replied, "I hope not, but I am only a doctor, a tool in God's hands. I can't honestly answer your question. But, I will do everything I can in my power to prevent that from happening."

I left the nurses station choked up with my tears flowing down my cheeks. I walked down the hall praying for God to heal her, but I also prayed if that was not His intention, would He please give me the strength to cope with whatever was to happen.

The next day Dawn showed some improvement. The doctor said he thought he finally got a handle on the infection. Dawn quickly took a turn for the better. Although she was weak for quite a while, this was the last time she was seriously ill or ever hospitalized again with any kidney problems. God had answered our prayers and the prayers of others who had been praying for her.

As I thought over what had happened and how close to death she had been, I realized God was in control. Not me. Perhaps he was trying to show me I needed Him more than I had realized. It seemed as if I felt I had carried the entire burden and 100% of the responsibility for the outcome of keeping her healthy. I had watched her diet so very closely and made many changes which had helped her tremendously. However, even though I was doing all of this, I had forgotten to pray and give my concerns to God until I was finally, literally, on knees begging for His help.

This incident not only humbled me, but brought me closer to God. My eyes and heart was opening up to the realization that God does care. He knew what was in my heart and answered my prayers. It seemed I had become so busy I had forgotten about Him and what I had learned earlier in life, as a child, a teenager and young adult, to ask and then believe He will answer that prayer.

I've been forever grateful for the answer He gave me. I have never forgotten the impact of this experience on my life and my need to continually be in a relationship with God.

"Do not let your hearts be troubled. Trust in God; Trust also in me."[11]

Changes at School and Home
Chapter 9

As the summer was coming to an end, Don went to check everything out in his classroom and to make sure his supplies had arrived before school would start. When he returned home he went inside to grab a glass of tea before walking outside to talk with me.

"We're losing Mrs. Thomas," he said, as he sat down next to me in the shade and gentle breeze of the big oak tree in the middle of our back yard.

"Oh, no, what happened?" I asked.

"Her husband was transferred out of state and she found a teaching job close to their new home."

"What's going to happen with the deaf kids at the school?" I asked being interested about this unique classroom for deaf and hard of hearing in our own community.

"I don't know. They're searching for a teacher who can work with them, but from what I hear, they haven't found anyone, yet, and school will start in two weeks."

"You know, I'm really disappointed she is leaving. Ever since I met her, I had hoped to learn sign language and thought someday, when our girls were older, I might be able to spend some time as a volunteer in her classroom."

By the time school started, Kristy, who was young and single, had been hired as the new teacher for the deaf and hard of hearing. She had just completed her degree as a teacher for deaf at a college which only taught oralism (lip reading). I was surprised she was hired because she was not at all familiar with using sign language; but, the school system also had hired interpreters, who would work as teacher aids and could help her in the classroom.

Kristy's family lived approximately three to four hours away in the Detroit area. She was all alone in our community without friends or any family nearby. She often walked across the hall at school to talk to Don between classes and loved to greet our children when I came to pick him up after-school. Occasionally, we would go shopping together or we would invite her to join our family for dinner.

One evening after-school, Kristy called to ask me how to get to another high school in our area. I tried to give her directions, but she didn't know the streets well enough to understand how to get there.

"What's going on there?" I asked out of curiosity.

"They're offering a six week community education class in beginning sign language. Since I'm teaching deaf students without that skill, I'd like to take advantage of this free class and learn to sign."

"Oh! That sounds so interesting! I've been thinking about learning sign language, too. If you don't mind, I'd like to go along with you. Then you won't have to worry about getting lost." We discussed the time and dates of the classes. Don was going to be available to watch the girls on those nights and supported me taking this class with Kristy.

By the time Kristy and I arrived for the first class, the room was already filled with parents, children, teachers, and others who were interested in communicating with deaf people. The class was fun, easy, and I learned quickly. I attended three more of these six week sessions offered through community education, but they all taught the same beginning level of sign language. I was thirsty to learn more.

I asked one of the sign language teachers how I could learn more signs and if there were any advanced classes available to increase my skills. She suggested I write to Gallaudet University, a college for the Deaf in Silver Springs, Maryland, and ask for a list of sign language books from their bookstore. I followed her advice and ordered several books which showed how to make the signs in the Signing Exact English (SEE). I showed the sign language teacher my books and she offered to help if I had questions about hand or finger movements. She suggested whenever I had a question, to ask any of the interpreters when I picked Don up from school. She also suggested I come early to the community education classes and ask any of the teachers there for more help. As I became more fluent using sign language, I started reading stories and singing songs to my children using the SEE language.

What I didn't know at the time was the SEE language was not the language of those who were in the Deaf Cultural. It was what hearing people thought would help the deaf understand the English language by speaking English and signing the words in English word order. This sounded fine with me, but later, as I became more involved with the Deaf community, I learned there were several other sign languages including American sign language (ASL), Signed English and Pigeon, at which I became more fluent as I continued to learn more about sign language.

I continued to attend every sign language class available through community education, even if the lessons were repetitive. As my skills progressed, the teachers, who were interpreters and children of the cultural Deaf adults, invited me to help in classes with those having difficulty learning the signs. But, I still wanted to learn more of the language and once again, shared this deep desire with one of the teachers.

"If you want to learn the language of the Deaf," she said, "You have to go where the Deaf are."

"I don't know any Deaf people and have never seen Deaf people in public," I replied.

"The culturally Deaf like to bowl and spend almost every night of the week at one of the local bowling alleys. Just go anytime to any one of the bowling alleys until you find them. You will see them signing to each other," she said. "You know enough of the language to introduce yourself and let them know you are learning sign language. They will be more than happy to communicate with you and invite you into their group."

I started searching bowling alleys and like she said, I found them. At first I felt awkward walking up to introduce myself to those standing around in a group signing; but it was just like the interpreter said, they welcomed me. Although I hadn't expected their signing to be so fast, they did slow down so I could understand what they were saying. Whenever I had an evening available to get away from home for a little while, I would spend some time with the Deaf community. I made many Deaf friends and they were happy to having me join them. As my skills continued to increase, I became more fluent in signing and was asked to substitute teach for the beginning level classes in the community education program. Eventually I was offered a job to teach classes of my own.

Sign language was becoming very popular as a second language and more advanced classes were starting to spring up all over town. Part of the reason was due to Section 504 of the Rehabilitation Act of 1973 and the Americans with Disability Act. These two important Acts obligated public schools and all public places to provide equal access to communication for those who were deaf or hard of hearing. The other reason for the increase of sign language classes was due to the increased cost to school districts to send deaf students to the Michigan School for the Deaf in Flint, a residential school where students stayed all week and returned home on weekends.

Whatever the reason was to offer more sign language classes, I found myself becoming enthusiastically and totally involved in learning more. I was learning about the issues of the Deaf and recognized how much they were missing out on things I enjoyed such as movies, television, plays, concerts, educational presentations, church services, politics, community meetings and more. I also became acutely aware of how much they were ostracized by the hearing population that didn't seem to want to include them, or didn't know what to do when a deaf person was present. I thought about Martha and how I, too, had been like that when I first met her.

As I continued to expand my vocabulary and became more fluent, I began teaching our daughters sign language. They caught on quickly to some of the signs like popcorn, cookies or other treats my husband I would sign to ask the other if we should give them that treat. Even five-year-old Tracy learned a lot of signs from the songs and stories I practiced signing while reading to her.

When we attended Tracy's first kindergarten parent-teacher conference, her teacher had a pressing question for us. "Tracy is a bright student, but I do have one question. I often ask my students to get up in front of the class to say their ABCs individually and every time I ask Tracy to recite her ABCs, she does something with her hands. Do you have any idea what she is doing?"

Don and I couldn't help but look at each other and start laughing out loud. "I taught her to say her ABCs in sign language! In fact, I'm not sure I ever showed her a picture of what the alphabet actually looks like!" I said feeling guilty I had omitted something that important in her education.

"Well, that explains it! And, she does know the names of the letters and what they look like."

As we drove home that night, I turned to Don. "I wish Mrs. Thomas was here now. I think she would have enjoyed hearing this story about Tracy."

"If you remember, she said she taught Tracy sign language the first time she saw her!" Don said with a smile as he glanced over at me.

"I will instruct you and teach you in the way you should go; I will counsel you and watch over you." [12]

Not Me!
Chapter 10

One evening during dinner I noticed our daughter, Tracy, who was about three years old, seemed to be studying the dining room clock with an inquisitive look on her face.

"Tracy, what are you looking at?" I asked.

"That clock. Why does that clock make so much noise?"

"That clock doesn't make any noise," I said as my family stopped eating and stared at me.

"You can't hear that?" Don asked as he put his fork down.

"Hear what?" I asked. Why are you all looking at me like that?"

"That clock makes a very loud tick sound," Dawn said.

Kady spoke up. "I've been wondering why you bought a clock that makes such a loud noise and you never seemed to mind it."

"Stand up and get closer to that clock. Let's see just how close you have to be to hear that thing tick," my husband said.

I stood and backed up against the wall until my ear was flat against it. "Oh, now I can hear it ticking."

"That does it! When are you going to make that appointment with an audiologist or do I have to do it for you?"

"I guess I'll do that, but I think you and the girls have superior hearing. It's not like I can't hear."

From very early in our marriage, Don had been encouraging me to get my hearing checked. Several times he had noticed I couldn't hear simple sounds that he heard such as the water boiling on the stove while sitting in the next room or water dripping from the bathroom faucet. He also noticed I had trouble hearing what others were saying to me in a crowded room or when there was background noise interfering with communication. Although we really enjoyed attending the Civic Opera and school plays, Don was now getting less interested in going.

"It seems I have to interpret what the actors are saying every time we go and then I miss out," he complained.

"That's because they don't speak loud enough or project their voices," I'd respond.

Sometimes he would get frustrated with me and accuse me of not listening. I'd accuse him of talking too low or defend myself by responding, "Maybe I just have a lot on my mind."

"Well, I would appreciate it if you would at least get your hearing checked," he often urged.

"There is nothing wrong with my hearing!" I would respond. "You just have very sensitive ears. You should have YOUR hearing checked to find out why YOU hear so many sounds and everything is too loud for you."

Reluctantly, I agreed to make an appointment, although I still believed Don and our girls had very keen hearing. During the time between making that appointment and actually seeing the doctor, I became more attentive to my hearing. I wondered if I was actually not hearing or if I might not be fully paying attention. I was beginning to notice things such as delaying before I responded and misinterpreting what was being said. I really thought other people were just not speaking clearly. I kept searching for reasons I was missing parts of conversations and not hearing all the sounds of the spoken words. I decided I just needed to be more focused on what was being said.

When I met with the doctor, he asked if I had noticed anything wrong with my hearing. "Not really, but everyone else in the family seems to think I have a hearing loss," I replied.

"Sometimes it takes others to notice when we can't hear because it can be such a gradual loss. Over time it doesn't seem like we are having hearing problems. We become used to it."

His answer was not what I wanted to hear and not very consoling.

"Actually," I continued, "recently I have noticed something, but I really think something is wrong with my brain, not my ears. I didn't want to mention this to my medical doctor because I'm afraid I might have had a stroke that has caused me to not comprehend what is being said."

"Go on, tell me more about why you think that," the doctor said.

"Well, it seems as if I pause after someone finishes talking and before I respond. It's as if a train is passing and I wait for it to be out of sight before I move. I wait for what seems like several minutes after they finish talking before I respond. I feel really dumb when I do this. Sometimes I do make mistakes when I try to answer them. When I repeat what I think was said, sometimes it causes others to laugh. They ask me what I'm talking about. I also say "huh?" or "what?" a lot. I thought I was probably distracted and not following the conversation close enough. Most the time I thought the other person was just muttering. Sometimes I wondered if I just wasn't interested or if I was getting tired or bored of the conversation."

"What you are describing is similar to what many people describe when they first find out they have a hearing loss," the doctor said as he continued. "It takes a lot of effort to strain to hear and follow the communication and of course you would be getting tired. That would not be unusual."

Oh, no! Not him, too. He's convinced I have a hearing loss. I thought.

"Your brain is putting together the soft sounds you are missing and creating the words for you," he explained. Sometimes when your brain fills in the gaps it is right and sometimes it isn't. There are many consonants that sound alike. Let's have my audiologist check your hearing to find out what your hearing level actually is. We'll go from there."

When the testing was completed, I met with the doctor again. "Well, it's as I suspected. You have a sensory-neural hearing loss. That is very common with older or even some of the younger adults, especially those who listen to loud music."

"Maybe that's why my husband gets upset when he turns the car radio on and I keep turning it up. Then he complains it's too loud because it hurts his ears. Yet, I think it sounds normal."

"Yes, this is typical of the hearing loss you have."

"What caused this?" I asked. "I haven't had a head injury and never listened to really loud music."

"Well," the doctor continued as he sat patiently with me. "Sometimes it is just genetics. But, it can also be due to repeated ear infections or certain antibiotics, especially those ending with myosin which can deaden the little hairs in the ears that transfer sounds to the brain. Diseases like meningitis or having high fevers can also be the culprit. We probably won't ever know for sure why you have a hearing loss, but we will need to keep checking it annually until you need hearing aids."

"Do you know how long it will be before I need them?"

The doctor explained that they never know how long it will take. "It's hard to say. Everyone is different; but, eventually you will lose more and more of your hearing. At some point, you might become deaf. It will help a lot if you ask people to look directly at you when they speak."

I was really shaken up by this news and recalled Martha, the deaf girl, who was put into an institution because she was deaf. I thought about the girls at school who needed an interpreter who talked for them and to inform them what others said. I thought about the Deaf adults at the bowling alleys and how much they were left out of community events because of their hearing loss. I thought about my husband and my four little girls at home, who now had a mother who was going deaf and someday would not be able to hear them or attend their school events. I felt very alone, discouraged, and afraid. I struggled to hold back the tears that were flooding my eyes.

"There's nothing to be upset about. You are just like millions of others who have a hearing problem," he said as he patted me on the shoulder when I got up to leave. "If you have any other questions, feel free to call. Otherwise, we'll see you next year for an annual check-up."

I drove home, took a deep breath and wiped my tears as I drove into the driveway. Don was not the least bit shaken when I told him the results of my appointment.

"That's what I expected," he said. "There is a lot that can be done to help people with a hearing loss. Now that I know what is wrong, I will try to speak more clearly and make sure you hear what I say."

"He will have no fear of bad news: his heart is steadfast, trusting in the Lord."[13]

A New Branch and Connection
Chapter 11

My mother had always wanted to do something significant with her life after raising the four of us. Once we all left home, she began selling Christian books at home parties, schools, churches or wherever she could set up a booth. She loved reading these books, too, and made many new friends as well as re-connecting with many of her friends from her past.

At one of her in-home book parties, she met Leah, a young mother who was new to the area. Her husband, Harley, had recently been hired by the local school district to coordinate programs for the hearing impaired classrooms. It was also his job to interview and hire interpreters and teachers for this program. While talking to Leah, my mother discovered Leah and her husband attended the same church as Don and me.

My mother called me right after she arrived home from this party. "Bonnie Jeane, I met someone I think you might know from your church, but she didn't recognize your name. They've just moved to this area. Her husband coordinates the hearing impaired program at the school where Don works. I thought you might know who I am talking about."

"Mom," I answered, "There are so many people at my church, I haven't noticed anyone new," I said. "Just getting our girls dressed and ready for church and Sunday school takes a lot of energy and when I get there, I sort of sit back, relax, and listen. I guess I really don't pay much attention to who is new, unless someone comes up to me or introduces me to them."

"Well, I told Leah about you learning sign language and she said both she and her husband would like to get to know you. She gave me her phone number and told me to ask you call her."

I called Leah the next day and we made a plan to meet after church and before Sunday school at a corner of the church near the entrance.

"I hear you are learning sign language," her husband said when we met. "Where are you taking classes?"

"From Community Education Programs and books I ordered from Gallaudet bookstore."

"Do you ever use sign language to talk to any Deaf people?"

"Yes, but I am not as fast at signing as they are. I visit them at the bowling alley and have made a few friends. I am trying to learn more from them, but they have to slow way down for me and sometimes finger-spell until I understand the signs. They are very patient with me! I also practice using sign language while reading bedtime stories to my kids or singing songs while listening to the radio.

"That's great. I wish there were more people like you who wanted to learn. We have a hard time even getting parents to learn to sign to communicate with their children. But, here you are a hearing person teaching your children sign language! You don't know how valuable that is going to be for them. Are you aware that our current educational program is based on total communication?"

"I've never heard that term. What is it?" I asked.

"It's exactly what you are doing with your kids at home. Using voice and sign together in English word order."

"I wasn't aware it was called that; but, I sign using my voice so my kids can see the signs and hear the words. I thought they could learn the words that way."

"Exactly," he said. "Well, I'm glad to meet you. Keep up the good work," he said as he and his wife turned to leave.

By November of 1978 I had talked with Leah and Harley almost every Sunday after church. Then, one Sunday, Harold rushed up to me alone.

"I have been thinking about you and our Deaf students," he said. "Most of them never go to church because there is no reason. They can't hear and people don't communicate with them. Some have no idea why Christmas is an important religious holiday. They do know Christmas songs about Santa Claus and Rudolph, but they don't understand what Christmas is really about."

My heart sank when I heard this. Church had been my whole life. Celebrating the birth of Christ meant a lot to me. I believed God had always been present with me and my husband. Without Him, we couldn't have gotten through what we did with our daughter, Dawn, a few years ago when she was so ill and I thought she was going to die. To not have experienced God and His love, hit me like a steel ball.

"I thought maybe you might be interested in helping me out with our youth group. I would like to have a little Christmas party and invite some of the deaf students to visit our youth group. I thought about you and wondered if you would be willing to help teach our youth some signs and finger spelling to help break that communication barrier. You could just teach some simple signs so they could introduce themselves and wish the deaf kids a Merry Christmas. What do you think? Would you be willing to help? We could have some punch and Christmas cookies, but nothing very elaborate. I thought maybe the deaf students would be willing to sign some Christmas songs they know. I think our youth group would enjoy seeing these songs in sign language. It would be a great exposure to both the kids from school and our youth. It wouldn't be have to be very long; maybe just an hour on a Sunday night during the regular youth group meeting time. What do you think? Would you be willing to help me put this event together?"

"Yes! Definitely," I replied eager to be part of this.

"You don't know how happy this makes me feel that you are willing to help," Harley said. "You have no idea what this could mean to the Deaf students. They are mainstreamed in the school, but no one talks to them or pays attention to them. Most of the students will talk to the interpreters, but ignore the Deaf students. They seldom have an opportunity to mingle with hearing people their own age. I really appreciate your willingness to help. Thank you so much!"

"I'm really excited about being part of this and I would also love to see the students sign those Christmas songs."

I left church feeling thrilled with the idea of using sign language and teaching it to our youth in church. I was even more excited about bringing the deaf and hearing students together and exposing the hearing to deaf while giving the deaf an opportunity to come to church and meet kids who would be open to interacting with them.

The night finally came for our little party. I was so happy to see our youth group excited about this event, although they were somewhat reluctant about interacting with the others who could not speak. Both groups gathered with their own friends, just like you would see at a middle school dance with girls on one side of the room and the boys on the other, wanting to move toward each other, but being too shy and feeling too uneasy to do that. Harley and I stepped in to help with the introductions and mingled among both groups helping them to communicate.

We were so thankful the evening had gone very well as both groups began to interact. Everyone seemed to enjoy the party, and for me and Harley, it was a step closer to increasing awareness of the deaf in our community and providing them an opportunity to feel included, especially in a church atmosphere. For many, it was the first time they really felt welcomed in a church.

"Let the word of Christ dwell in you richly as you teach and admonish one another with all wisdom, and as you sing psalms, hymns and spiritual songs with gratitude in your hearts to God. And whatever you do whether in word or in deed, do it in the name of the Lord Jesus, giving thanks to God the Father through Him." [14]

A New Adventure
Chapter 12

The Christmas holidays were over and with the start of the New Year, our three older daughters were back in school. I sat rocking our 22-month-old daughter, Lisa, while her older sister Wendy was playing with Legos on the floor next to me when the phone rang. I got up to answer it.

"Hello, Bonnie! This is Harley from church. I hope I'm not interrupting you, but I have an urgent request of you. Our interpreter at the high school fell and tore a ligament in her leg. It's really urgent I get an interpreter to come help our deaf students immediately. Can you come and interpret for them?"

It took a minute for me to grasp what he had just asked of me and to catch my breath. "Wow, Harley, I'm really impressed you thought of me. I would love to help you out, but I'm not an interpreter. I'm just learning and only know some sign language. I don't think I would be very good as an interpreter. Besides, I still have two small children at home."

"You're probably better than you realize. But here's the scope of the problem. I would have to first get approval from personnel to create another interpreter position before I could put an advertisement in the newspaper. There is a lot of red tape with that and if I got the approval, it would take about four to six weeks to go through resumes, interviews and the entire hiring process. Plus, I doubt if anyone would even take the time to apply for such a temporary position without benefits. By the time I finished that entire process, our interpreter would be back to work. I think I can get personnel to allow me to hire you temporarily because of your prior experience in our school system with Head Start." He paused. "I need someone now and don't know anyone else to call who has any skills in signing. Even if you just come to take notes during their mainstream classes that would help significantly. After the classes are over, when the students go back to their classroom for the hearing impaired (H.I.), the teacher or one of the other interpreters could help them from your notes. Please consider this. I will do what I can to help you from this end to make it easier for you. You would be so much better than getting someone right off the street to just take notes but not be able to communicate at all with our students."

"Harley, I have two small children under four at home and a five-year-old to get at lunch time after kindergarten gets out. I don't know anyone who could take care of them."

"Well, I will keep asking around school if anyone knows someone who can interpret, but please see what you can do about getting a sitter. Maybe someone at church would like to make a little extra money. You could call our church office and ask the secretary if she knows anyone or to ask her to ask others at church or school who might be willing to do that. Please get back to me as soon as possible. The pay is good and it is only for about four to six weeks. Maybe I can work something out with the other interpreter for a half day for you. Let me know what you can do. I'll be praying all works out for both of us. Just tell me you will try to find someone."

"Okay, Harley, I'll try," I said. Still not believing he really asked me to interpret. Going to work part-time for a few weeks after being a stay at home mom for the past twelve years sounded very interesting, and I liked the idea of having some spending money of my own.

I wondered if God was answering the prayer I had been praying secretly for years, asking Him to guide me into a career that He wanted for me when the time was right. *Is this the direction I should go at this time?* I couldn't help but wonder about this while having mixed feelings of excitement and apprehension.

Before we were married, Don and I had talked about whether or not I would work when we had children. We both believed raising our children was the most important job for me and I made a choice to stay at home until they were all in school. But having a large family often meant pinching pennies or going without to make it from one payday to the next. *It would be nice to have the extra money to take the girls places to see and experience things we haven't been able to afford.* I felt torn between wanting to take the job, or continuing to stay home another four or five years. But this job was for only four to six weeks. I promised I'd try to help Harley out. Now, I had mixed feelings. I prayed for God's guidance.

While ruminating over my beliefs and this offer, I decided to search for a sitter for just a few weeks. I believed if this was not the direction I should be going, I wouldn't be able to find anyone to take care of our kids.

After I had called friends, neighbors and the school without any luck, I walked out to the mailbox and picked up our neighborhood newspaper. I noticed an advertisement for babysitting in a home not far from us. I didn't know the woman by name, but I knew some people in the neighborhood where she lived. Although I hesitated, I decided to give her a call. She sounded like a bubbly, happy person and after I explained my situation, she invited me to come over with my girls to see if our children would get along.

I liked her as soon as we met and the girls got along fine. The interview went very well and I felt positive about this working out except for one other problem that needed to be solved. The principal at the parochial school where our daughters attended said he could not allow the bus driver to transport our five-year-old to the new babysitter's house after-school because it was too far from the planned route. I didn't know anyone else who could get her at noon hour and thought that was God's answer saying "not yet".

When Don came home from school, I told him about the call from Harley and his request. I told him how things almost worked out except I couldn't find anyone to take care of Tracy when she got out of school. He was excited about my job offer and said he thought I should take the short term position if we could resolve this one issue.

"Hey, doesn't the school bus go near my aunts' church?" He said during dinner. "That is really close to their house and they are home almost all the time. They might like having Tracy come there until you can pick her up after you're done. It would be right on your way home, too." Don's aunts had never married and lived with his grandmother their entire lives. They were very special people who were always helpful and loved to stop over to our house to visit.

"I'm not so sure," I said. "They never had any kids of their own. They probably have other things they would prefer to do."

"Call them. They loved it when I used to stop over to visit after-school. When we were kids, they often took care of us on weekends to give my mom and dad a break."

Once again, I checked with the principal to find out if it would be possible for Tracy to ride a different bus route near Don's aunts' home at lunch hour for the next four to six weeks until I would be done with this part time job. He was very agreeable and said they could accommodate this change.

Everything was moving along smoothly. Now, I just had to call Don's aunts.

They all said they would be thrilled to meet Tracy at the bus stop, feed her lunch and take care of her until I picked her up in the afternoons.

I called Harley right away.

"Thank you so much!" he said. "Come to the H.I. classroom as soon as you can tomorrow morning. The closer to 7:45 am the better, but we will start as soon as you can get here. You don't know how much this means to me and how much the students will appreciate having you."

Although it was a cold, blustery day when I arrived at the high school, I was too excited to notice the cold gusting wind and snow hitting my face.

Harley greeted me at the classroom door. "Your first hour class is Family Living in room 126," he said. "It's already in process. Do you want me to take you down there or can you find it yourself?"

"I know where the room is, but it might be helpful for you to go with me so the teacher knows why I'm there. I might know her, but she won't know why I would be walking into her classroom, especially since class has already begun."

"I'd be glad to do that for you, but you will be on your own the rest of the day," he said as he showed me the schedule with room numbers. "I'm sure the students will help out if you get lost! Right after this class, you will go to the math class upstairs, followed by a science class and then return to the H.I. classroom. After lunch, you will go to an English class and then you can leave. Tomorrow you will have auto shop and wood shop in place of English and math. Call me later today at my office, or at home tonight to let me know how it goes for you today. I'll look forward to hearing from you."

I joined the Deaf students who sat near a corner in the back of the room. They waved and smiled when I came to sit down with them. At first, it was hard for me to keep up with the speed of the teacher's voice during lectures. When I was not familiar with a sign for a word, I would start to use finger-spelling. The Deaf students would interrupt me and show me the sign for those words. I often combined sign language, finger-spelling, and note taking to make sure the students got all the information from their classes. It took a lot of concentration on my part and patience from them to put up with me at times; but they never complained. After classes were over, I reported back to the H.I. classroom teacher and informed her of what was covered in each class, the assignments given and gave my notes for her and the interpreter to go over with the students. Even though at times I signed slowly, I was surprised at how fast I could sign and how well this was going.

I continued to work on learning more signs and if I knew I was going to be substituting in an auto shop class, electronics, or wood shop, or any class in which I might need more knowledge of that subject's specific terms, I would pull out my dictionary for sign language and study all the words which I thought I might need to use in those classrooms.

Those six weeks passed quickly. Tracy loved going to the aunts' home and spending time with them and her great grandmother. Lisa and Wendy had fun playing with Sandy's girls and were ready to come home for a nap when I picked them up. I enjoyed the opportunity to work in the school system, particularly with the Deaf students, and Don liked to have his wife bring in some extra spending money. When the regular interpreter returned, I was asked by Harley if he could keep me on a substitute list in case the need would arise again. I agreed and was called often, sometimes for just a few hours while an interpreter needed some personal time off.

Having a part-time "on-call" substituting job meant that if I wasn't available to go into work because my children were home from school for some other reason that particular day, I didn't have to go in to work. However, I seldom missed a day I was asked to interpret and continued this position for the next five years.

"For I know the plans I have for you, declares the Lord, plans to prosper you and not to harm you, plans to give you hope and a future."[15]

Ministering and Growing in Christ
Chapter 13

Spring was in the air and my second year as a substitute interpreter was almost over when I received a call from one of the interpreters who worked at the elementary school.

"Hi, Bonnie, this is Wanda. I thought of you today when I interpreted for a young couple who are planning to get married this summer. After their pre-marital session with the minister, he asked me to stay a few minutes to talk about how the church could be of spiritual support for this Deaf couple after they are married. Although he didn't have the time today, he asked if I could set up a time to meet with him next week to discuss a ministry for the Deaf. He asked if I knew anyone else who might be interested to join us. I know you're involved in your church and since you have worked with this Deaf couple at the high school, I thought of you."

"Yes, they often mentioned they were planning to get married, but when I questioned if they had picked a date, they signed summer. Sounds like it will be soon."

"Yes, in June," she replied.

"When are you thinking about meeting with the pastor to talk about this ministry?"

"He said he could be available after-school on Tuesday or Thursday, but could change that if that doesn't work out for everyone interested."

"Oh, Tuesday will be fine," I said. "Now that my children are older, I don't have to rush home after-school. Thank you for thinking of me, Wanda. This is something I would be thrilled to become part of."

After-school on the following Tuesday, I arrived at the church just as the pastor was walking the young couple outside. It was a beautiful bright warm sunny May afternoon. The sun bounced off the beautiful red, yellow and green stained glass windows as if to say "welcome".

The Deaf couple was just leaving and waved at me as I walked up to the entrance of the church.

"Hi, you go to church here?" The young man questioned in sign language.

"No, I go to another Lutheran Church. I'm here for a meeting with the pastor", I signed.

"We are getting married here," Greg signed with a big grin while squeezing Melissa's hand as she smiled and blushed. "We finished meeting with the pastor. Happy see you!" he signed in deaf syntax.

"Happy see you, too," I signed back to them. "See you at school tomorrow. Be sure to study for your English exam tonight," I signed as I followed the pastor and Wanda into the church office.

"I'm very happy you both came," said Pastor Karl Stumpf as he grabbed a cup of coffee and poured some for us. "I've been thinking about this ever since Greg and Melissa first came to me requesting to get married here. I don't know anything about the Deaf or how they worship."

"Most of them don't," Wanda said. "There has never been a reason for them to go to church around here. No one communicates with them. They can't hear the music or understand the sermon without an interpreter. When they try to speak or start signing, people look at them as if they are weird. There has never been any positive reason for them to visit or attend any church."

"That is why I wanted to have this meeting," Pastor Karl continued. "I've been thinking about them. They have parents, friends, and others who are deaf and might want to come with them someday. They will eventually have children and will want to have them baptized. I'm sure there will be other life events such as illnesses or deaths, good times and bad when they will need support of their church family. We need to be here to support them just like others in our church, but we can't do that if we can't communicate."

"Are you thinking of hiring a church interpreter?" I asked.

"No. An interpreter might be available sometimes, but not always. I'm actually thinking of starting an entire program for the deaf. If we start a deaf ministry, we will need a lot of help getting that started and keeping it going. Yesterday, I called a friend of mine who is a pastor for the Deaf in the Flint area and is fluent in sign language. He said he might be able to give us some ideas. However, he already has a full schedule working as a pastor at the church there and with the Deaf students at the school. I'd like members in our congregation to learn to communicate with the Deaf members in sign language. I want the Deaf to feel welcomed as they come into the sanctuary, just like we welcome the hearing people in our congregation. I want them to feel this is their home and family, too."

"So, you're thinking of having sign language classes for those in the congregation who want to be part of the Deaf ministry?" I asked.

Wanda interrupted. "I agree it would help to have people in the church who can Sign. Have you thought about how to get the Deaf to come here to worship? We can't just say that we are now going to have church services for those who are deaf, because the Deaf do not trust the hearing people for many reasons."

"Like what?" Pastor Karl asked. "I think we need to know about their experiences so we don't make similar mistakes."

"Well, the hearing population has a history of forbidding Deaf to use their hands to communicate in sign language. Instead, they have tried to make the Deaf use their voice and read lips, which is difficult for even hearing people. Even the best lip readers make mistakes because so many of the sounds look alike on the mouth. Only one third of the words are actually made on our lips. Many of their own family members do not use sign language or will make up home signs that don't make sense outside of the family environment. When decisions are to be made, the Deaf are often left out and their opinion or feelings are not considered. The hearing population has often shown a punitive attitude toward people who are deaf or hard of hearing. Most of the Deaf community doesn't feel welcomed by them. Even at school where Deaf students attend regular education classes with hearing students, those who can hear very seldom interact or try to communicate with the deaf students. The list goes on. If you want to start a Deaf ministry, you have to start with the Deaf and find out what they want."

"So, are you saying we need to let them lead us?" Pastor Karl asked. "That seems like it might be quite a challenge for them if they never have been involved in a church. Do you have any ideas how to bring this about?"

"I think teaching sign language is the first step and also for the church to obtain a TTY as soon as possible so those who are deaf can get a response when or if they call here needing something," I said.

"What's a TTY?" Pastor Karl asked.

"It's a teletype for deaf people to make phone calls," I said. "You type a message and it comes across the LED screen on their phone."

"But, how do they know the phone is ringing?" He asked.

"Because it is also connected to a light which goes on and off when the phone rings," I replied.

Pastor Karl was amazed that such a device was available and something very easy to obtain. "I can understand how important that would be for our office. I'll put a request in for that right away."

"You know," Wanda said, "the Deaf love to get together with other Deaf people. In the past, they got together every weekend for picnics and potlucks wherever they could find a place to meet and where they could communicate face-to-face. Perhaps we could start with a group of people from your church who are interested in learning sign language. After they learn some basic signs we could have a potluck and invite the Deaf to our class. How does that sound, Bonnie? What do you think?"

"I'm on the same page as you," I said, feeling thrilled that everything was coming together as if God was guiding this entire conversation.

"I think we have a plan," Pastor Karl said. "We can offer sign language classes in the fall. Then we could follow up a little later with a potluck and invite the Deaf community to join us. I have a council meeting coming up soon and would like to present this idea. Would either of you want to teach the sign language class?"

We both agreed that we would be committed to starting Deaf ministry and teaching sign language at the church in the fall. I walked out of the church exhilarated and thought about what had just happened all the way home. Three of us, who had never been involved with each other before, had just come together for the first time today. Now, we were working together as a team to provide an opportunity for those who were deaf to be included in church with other Christians. It was like becoming a missionary; but, not leaving home to go off to some faraway place.

Once again, the words from my grandmother kept popping into my head. "Bonnie Jeane, I know God has a purpose for you and someday you will know what that it is."

Although, I had grown up knowing God was always with me, and I could pray to Him when I was troubled, I never had a real conviction that He actually involves Himself in our daily lives until our daughter was in the hospital and I thought we were going to lose her! Perhaps He really does have a certain plans for each of us. The things that had been occurring in my life during the past two years were things I never dreamed would happen or become part of my life experience.

While starting dinner that night, I shared with my husband what the pastor, Wanda and I had talked about at the church.

"Sounds to me this is right up your alley!" Don replied with a smile.

"Don, it means I will be away from home two nights a week. Is that going to be okay with you? You would have to be in charge of making sure the girls do their homework and get to bed on time those nights," I said, trying to get a feel as to whether or not he would really want me to be gone that much.

"You don't think I can do that?" he asked.

"Oh, I think you can, but you do have homework to check every night, lesson plans to prepare, and at times you do get distracted with what's happening on TV or something around the house that needs to be fixed. I'm just concerned you might forget to watch the time."

"You worry too much. I know this is something you would like. Just do it! You can do other things, too, besides staying at home. I think it would be good for you to get out and do this. I know you would enjoy the time away and you won't really be gone that much. We will be fine. Besides, this will give me some time to be more involved with our kids."

I was so glad he was supportive, even if I felt guilty leaving our kids for two or three hours two nights a week. That night I prayed, "Dear God, please direct me in the way you want me to go. You know my heart and love for my children. You also know my desire to help others and how blessed I feel about this opportunity to serve you. You also know how much I want to be a good mother and wife. Please guide me to make the right decision."

"Trust in the LORD with all your heart, and lean not on your own understanding; in all your ways acknowledge him, and he will make your paths straight."[16]

A Deaf Wedding
Chapter 14

Greg and Melissa's wedding day had finally arrived. As we drove over to the church, my husband seemed a little nervous. "I've never been to a Deaf wedding before. I don't know if I know how to act or what to do."

"Act normal," I said. "After all, you know Greg. He was in your class. You'll be fine."

"But I don't know many other people who are deaf or how I can communicate with them. Besides, Greg always had an interpreter with him in my class. I doubt if I will know anyone at the wedding. I already do feel very awkward."

As we walked into the church, Don was surprised to see we were greeted by so many of the teachers, students, and interpreters from high school.

"See, you do know many of the guests," I said as I nudged him.

The wedding was beautiful. We watched as the interpreter signed while the minister spoke. We could hear soft music in the background, but no one was singing. This simple ceremony was followed by a reception in the school gymnasium where we were surrounded by people moving their fingers and hands, just like Mrs. Thomas had done at many of the events we had attended while she was still at the high school.

As we joined others in the food line, I noticed a man, whom I recognized from my high school study hall years ago. He looked up smiling and waved for me to come over and sit with him.

"Who is that?" my husband asked.

"A guy who often came into my study hall during my senior year and always sat in front or behind me. He couldn't talk, but he wrote notes to me. He was always smiling, just like he is now."

"You aren't supposed to talk in study hall, so how do you know he couldn't talk?" my husband asked.

"Well, he did try to talk, but the words never sounded right. I had a hard time understanding him. I think he had a speech impediment," I said. "He never brought homework with him and just sat there the entire hour. The only thing I knew about him was his name, Ray. He wrote that down on paper and showed me while pointing to himself."

"Maybe he's deaf," my husband said.

"I never thought about that!" I replied, stunned that this had never even occurred to me before.

When we finished going through the food line, once again, this man, Ray, motioned for us to join him at his table. As we sat down, He began signing, "My wife, name Marcia".

"Hello!" I voiced and signed to her. "My name (is) Bonnie. My husband name Don."

"Happy meet you. You know my husband, how?" Marcia signed back to me using Deaf syntax.

"He was in my high school study hall a long time ago."

Ray smiled and signed, "Same class, sat close (to her)."

Just then, another Deaf man, whom I had met at the bowling alley, came over to talk (sign) with us.

"Oh, Don, this is Billy. I met him at the bowling alley," I voiced and signed so Billy knew I was introducing him. "Billy, this is my husband, Don."

"Billy?" Don asked while I signed for him. "My dad used to work with a deaf man named Billy when I was growing up. Did you ever work in a machine shop?"

"Yes", Billy shook his wrist and smiled while nodding his head. "Your dad, name, what?" he questioned as I continued to voice his signs for my husband.

After I signed Don's dad's name, Billy smiled and signed "Yes, I know him."

Suddenly we heard clapping from behind us. As we turned around, we saw a band setting up along with a disc jockey.

"What's this? A band and disc jockey at a Deaf wedding?" my husband asked as if surprised.

"Maybe the families of the bride and groom were being considerate of all the guests and hired the band for the enjoyment of those of us who are able to hear," I said.

Billy signed, "Dance" and pointed to the dance floor shaking his head with a smile, "Yes". Many of the Deaf guests started dancing and if I had not known differently, I would have thought they could actually hear the music. They kept excellent time to the beat. They were dancing just the same as other non-deaf young people their age.

"They're dancing! I didn't know deaf people could do that!" I said out loud as an interpreter came up to join our little group.

"Oh yes! The Deaf are great dancers!" Barbara signed as she spoke.

"How do they do that? They can't hear the music," I asked.

"They can feel the beat from the floor," She said with a laugh. "Deaf can do anything hearing people can do except hear!"

Both my husband and I tried to feel the beat from the floor, but neither of us could feel it.

That night as we drove back home, Don and I couldn't help but talk about how interesting it was he had just met the deaf man he had heard his father speak about when he was growing up. We talked about so many wrong assumptions we had made about the Deaf such as thinking they would not enjoy music, couldn't dance or that only those who were deaf would come to the wedding. The barriers and differences between hearing and the Deaf were similar to other assumptions many of us often make about other people and cultures which stemmed from our own limited knowledge, but that doesn't make them true.

"Do not judge, or you too will be judged."[17]

A New Ministry
Chapter 15

It was late August when Pastor Karl called to update me on the plans for the Deaf ministry.

"Since we last met, our church council not only gave us permission to start a ministry for the deaf, but was very supportive of our plan to start sign language classes and encourage our parishioners to enroll in the classes for free. The council set aside a special fund to pay for a sign language teacher and to purchase a TTY. I just spoke with Wanda and hired her to do the teaching. She will be able to start the classes the second week of September. We already have a good number from our congregations, who have voiced an interested in this class."

"That's great," I said feeling a little downhearted since I had wanted to be involved teaching the class and felt I was being left out.

Pastor Karl continued. "I recall you expressed an interest in Deaf ministry and thought you might like to join us. We will be meeting twice a week on Tuesday and Thursday evenings, and twice a month on Sunday evenings at about 5:30 pm for a potluck, followed by worship. Pastor Neisch has agreed to come from Flint to lead us in worship and singing."

"I'd be glad to attend and help out as much as I can. Although I'm not sure I can make it to every Sunday evening worship service. We have huge family on both sides and usually spend Sunday afternoons visiting our families, but I will be there on

Sunday evenings as much as I can and I will come to help out during the week.

"I understand. If you can work it out to be here once or twice a month for our Sunday services, that would be so beneficial to the members of the sign language class and the Deaf who will be joining us."

"I'll be glad to do what I can." I said feeling very happy I was included in this mission.

I hung up the phone and filled my husband in on our discussion. "I thought it was only going to be two nights per week, but now we will be having a late Sunday afternoon potluck followed by a church service twice a month. I'm afraid adding on a Sunday evening may be too much."

"It will probably work out fine. He's only asking for two Sunday nights a month. I believe you think too much and worry when it's not necessary. Our kids usually finish their homework on Sunday nights, anyway. You should do it." Don said with his blessing and put me at ease.

Although we didn't have addresses for those in the Deaf community, we passed out fliers to those with whom we had contact, inviting everyone to a potluck for the last Sunday in September. Pastor Neisch from Flint would be offering a worship service in sign language after the potluck for those who wished to join us. All were welcomed.

We didn't know if any Deaf would come. However, we were thrilled when the day came and more than what we had imagined joined us. Some of the Deaf said they already knew Pastor Neisch from the Michigan School for Deaf where they had attended years before. It was like a class reunion for many of them. Although it had been over 40 years since he had last seen several of them, Pastor Neisch still remembered all of them.

During our potluck, we talked to the Deaf about having a ministry for the Deaf at this church. We asked those who were deaf how the church could be available to them for their needs and assist them in their spiritual growth. They all agreed they would like to have a minister who could sign to be available to them. They were delighted to have Pastor Neisch join us and wanted him to come regularly. Pastor Neisch agreed to come as often as he could, especially at first while this ministry was developing.

One of the first things the Deaf requested was to have a Halloween party and potluck in October and to invite all ages of deaf people from surrounding counties. Potlucks and socials were a big part of their culture. They said their children no longer got to participate in the Deaf socials that were so much part of their culture. Before the advent of the TTY and Relay making contact and communication easier and quicker, they had to travel to one another's homes or parks to see and talk to each other. Now, many of them were getting older and it was becoming harder for them to get around or to attend outside events.

The Halloween party had been a huge success! I brought my husband and our kids. Other members of our sign language class brought their families, too. Everyone wore costumes and as might be expected, all of us who could sign had to interpret for those who could not. It was a good experience for all of us. The Deaf mingled with the hearing members and were very supportive and patient with those trying to communicate with limited sign language ability. They made up fun games unfamiliar to most hearing people and everyone participated.

When the party was over, we all agreed it had been a very successful evening and a fun event for all. The Deaf enjoyed interacting with us so much they brought many more people with them to church the following week. During our interactions with them, we learned that most deaf parents did not have deaf kids because deafness normally skips a generation or two. As a result, most of these deaf adults did not have the support of their children interacting with them and their community anymore.

The younger children in a Deaf family usually left the care taking of their parents and the interpreting to the oldest child (usually able to hear) in the family.

One of the Deaf couples who came to our potlucks and church services for the Deaf were in their 90's and had emigrated from Sweden. I really enjoyed watching them sign and using facial expressions to communicate. They had arthritis in their hands so severe their signs and finger spelling were difficult for the rest of us to understand, but to watch them was certainly something else! They seemed to interpret the thoughts of each other through facial expressions, not any language as I knew it. They could understand what the other person was going to sign before the other one finished signing.

One of the elderly Deaf women often teased me, "You sign baby signs." When I told one of my interpreter friends what she said about me, the interpreter said she meant "you are new to signing." Yet they were all very accepting and helped me by showing me their preferred signs that were a little different from some of the ones I had learned at school from the deaf kids or from the sign language books.

Our ministry was growing. Just before or after a service and before he headed back to Flint, Pastor Neisch would teach me a little more about church signs or differences in signed words or phrases which, in some cases, were sort of like a short hand, so to speak. Another new experience for me happened when he asked me to lead in scripture reading. I didn't want to get up in front of church. I guess I was still influenced by the era before the Woman's Equal Rights Movement. I still believed that this was a male's position, especially in a church. Traditionally, women were not part of a formal church service anywhere that I attended and I felt awkward stepping into that role. However, I quickly overcame my hesitancy to stand up and read the Holy Scripture.

Being able to sign seemed to make it okay because someone was needed to do that regardless of gender.

In November, we learned to sign a few Christmas songs. Our sign language students were learning fast and having so much fun, too. Many more Deaf started to join our classes to help out. Then, just before Christmas we all decided to go Christmas caroling to those shut-ins at home and in nursing homes. The Deaf community had never gone Christmas caroling before. The hearing group sang and signed along with the Deaf who followed us in sign. It was such a heartwarming experience to watch the faces of those who were not deaf and had never seen songs in sign language as well as the Deaf shut-ins who had never had anyone come to sign Christmas carols to them.

After Christmas, the interpreter who had been teaching was unable to continue and I was asked to teach the sign language class. By now, almost everyone knew how to communicate at some level with the Deaf using this language. Some still needed help and finger-spelling was often employed when they didn't know the word they needed to sign. As usual, the Deaf would show the sign to help the finger speller out just like the high school students had helped me when I first started working with them.

In my classes, I taught mainly religious signs which were used in church for singing songs or for worship. I felt this was the direction God wanted me to go and felt the Holy Spirit was giving me the energy and knowledge I needed to do this. I believed God put people in my path like Pastor Karl and Pastor Neisch, and even Wanda, to open the door and then to use me to open the doors for others to learn about Him.

I couldn't help but realize God's plan for my life was unfolding when that job had first opened up for me at school after the interpreter had fallen. I had grown so much since then by following His direction to where He was leading me. God created a path for me to follow and at every turn, there as a new door. I was thrilled to open those doors and become part of all He had planned for me.

"I know your deeds. See. I have placed before you an open door that no one can shut..."[18]

An Invitation!
Chapter 16

One day in early April, I received a packet in the mail from a community college in Kansas. Since I didn't know anyone in Kansas, I thought it was junk mail and almost threw it away. Yet, out of curiosity, I opened it and was surprised to read an introductory letter from the sign language Program coordinator, Daniel Marshal. Mr. Marshal indicated my name had been submitted as a candidate for a pilot program called Project Brother's Keeper, which was to be held for an entire month during the coming summer at Concordia College in Seward, Nebraska. This program was designed as a training for those who worked with Deaf and hard of hearing in churches. The program would focus on understanding and interpreting parts of the Bible in addition to creating a better understanding of addressing this population's spiritual needs. In his letter, he was personally inviting me to be one of the ten participants from across the United States to join this program.

My heart leaped for joy as I jumped up and ran into the house. *How did he get my name and address?* Suspecting it was Pastor Karl I immediately picked up the phone and dialed the church office.

"Is Pastor Karl still there?" I asked his secretary as I felt my heart beating like a hammer against my chest while I waited for him to come to the phone.

"Hello Bonnie. How's everything going with you?" Pastor Karl asked.

"All is fine! I just got an invitation to attend Project Brother's Keeper out in Nebraska this summer. Did you submit my name?" I blurted out.

"No, I didn't but Pastor Neisch might have. I read a little about that program in the newsletter from Synod a few months ago. Just after that, Pastor Neisch asked me what I thought about sending you to that program. We talked a little about it and we both agreed it was something that would benefit both you and our church. It would really be a boost for our Deaf ministry as well as an excellent opportunity for you. I never heard any more about it after that discussion. So you received some information, huh?"

"Yes! I just got the invitation and application in the mail and can't believe it! I was considered to be one of ten people invited to participate! Do you have Pastor Neisch's phone number? I want to call and let him know how much I would love to go. But, I am also concerned about what my family would do if I went away for a whole month this summer."

"Your husband's a teacher. Isn't he off work during the summer?"

"Yes and no," I said. "He has to work during the summers to help pay for our girls' parochial schooling."

"Maybe a family member could help out for those few weeks?" Pastor Karl asked.

"I don't know. I can't ask my mother. She's had a lot of health problems. My mother-in-law works full time during the day. She's not available either."

"Well, I will pray that everything will work out for you and your family so you can go."

I hung up the phone and called Pastor Neisch right away.

"I'm glad they contacted you. I sent them your name and address and wrote a letter about your involvement with the Deaf ministry you helped to get started. I thought you would be an excellent candidate for this program. I know you will learn so much in those four weeks. I'm sure it will have a huge impact on our participants who attend Deaf ministry. From the excitement in your voice, it sounds like this is something you would be willing to do."

"I'm willing and I'd love to go, but I can't leave my five kids at home for four weeks without someone to take care of them. Our older two girls are only twelve and thirteen and it would be too much for them to take care of the three younger ones. My husband works full time every summer to make extra money to pay for our children's school tuition. My kids have to come first. I'd go in a heartbeat if I could find someone to take care of them while he works," I said. "Yet, I really would prefer to take my family with me. I would feel much less stressed if I could see them and know what is going on with them every day."

"Well, I can understand your predicament. However, it may not be possible to take anyone with you. How long before you have to respond to the invitation?"

"Registration is due back in six weeks along with a $500 deposit."

"Okay. For now, don't worry about the deposit. Just pray things work out for you to go. Discuss this with your husband and family. See what comes up. Meanwhile, I will find out more about the program and if there might be some way to help you bring your family along. I'll get back to you in a few days," Pastor Neisch promised before he hung up.

The next day, he called back. "I spoke with Mr. Marshal, who is in charge of this program. He said they could not change the living arrangements for those attending this training. He reserved just enough rooms in the dorms for those individuals who would be attending. The women will be staying in one dorm and the men in another. There were no plans made for those with families. I did some further research and called Pastor Jay who is the pastor of a church near the campus. We graduated from seminary together. He said there is a campground just outside the city limits and not far from Concordia College Campus. Do you have a camper?"

"No, we've never camped."

"Is there anyone who might let you borrow a camper and some things you would need for camping for just one month?"

"I don't know off hand, but I can ask around."

"While you are at it, you might want to show that letter from Daniel Marshal to your pastor and see if your church might be willing to help offset some of the cost. Sometimes a benefit dinner, bake sale or even a special offering is taken to help those in the ministry. It won't hurt to ask."

I really hated asking, but I did as Pastor Neisch suggested. My pastor didn't think there was enough time to raise much money, but said he would get back to me.

The following week, while helping to serve hot lunch at our children's' school, I showed the school cook the invitation I had just received to go to Seward, Nebraska and asked if she knew anyone with a camper. The school principal, who was eating his lunch near the kitchen, overheard our conversation. He got up, walked in and asked, "Does it have to be a camper, or could you use a huge tent?"

I had never slept outside nor camped in a tent. I felt nervous about the idea of mosquitoes, snakes, coyotes and who knew what else might be roaming around outside, especially at night out West. However, I took a deep breath knowing I might have to overcome these anxieties. Then I responded, "No, it doesn't have to be a camper, but I don't know how we could all stay together in the same tent for a whole month. It would have to be huge."

"It IS huge," he replied. "I'll go up in the school attic and get it down this weekend and lay it out on the ground to air out. You can take it home and try it out to see if it'll work for you."

That Saturday we drove over to the school parking lot to look at the tent. It was dusty and dirty, but it had four different compartments where the kids could sleep and there was a separate area for us. There was also an area to store our coolers, suitcases and whatever else.

Although this would work, I really didn't care for the idea of staying in a tent for a month. However, I decided that if that was what God was asking us to do, then I would learn to accept that. After all, it was only for a month and it could be a lot of fun and quite an adventure for all of us. I felt very appreciative and thankful this was going to work out for my family to go with me. God listened and was answering my prayer. What more could I ask? We thanked the school principal for getting the tent down and allowing us to use it.

A few weeks later, a good will offering was taken and a potluck was held for us at church. Several individual donations were also received. Pastor Neisch said he received some money to help finance our travel expenses and handed me a check for $500! The registration fee was paid and everything was ready for us to go. Don's summer employer agreed to let Don take the month off and start working as soon as he returned from Nebraska. To make up for the four weeks of loss work and pay, when we returned, Don was allowed to stay and work after hours for his summer employer.

While everything was working out, I continued to feel somewhat uneasy about the thought of living in a tent with a lake nearby on the campground. My fears of "what if" kept growing. *What if my kids, who love the water, went out wading or swimming and drowned all because I wanted them to be near me.* Then I would rethink my negative thoughts and change my self talk. *Don is a good swimmer and he will be with them all day. It will all work. God is in charge and everything else is working out for us.*

A few days before we planned to leave, as I was packing things for camping, the phone rang. It was Pastor Neisch.

"I know you are all set for camping, but Pastor Jay just called me. He found a place for you and your family to stay about three blocks from the college and close to his church. It's a small apartment with only two bedrooms and a laundry room, but no dryer. He said he hopes you won't mind sharing the backyard clothesline with a missionary couple from Libya who are on leave for three months. However, they will be staying in an adjacent apartment for only ten of the days while you and your family are there. After they leave, the whole yard will be yours. The owner won't charge you anything. Do you think this will work for you?"

"I can't believe it," I said, as tears started flowing down my cheeks. "You don't know how much I prayed something else would come up for us. I am so thankful and relieved we won't be living outside in a tent."

"I should mention there is no air conditioner in the house and it gets quite hot in that area during the summer. If you can, you might want to bring along a fan."

"I don't care. I love the warm weather and this is so much better than staying in a tent for a month. I'm so grateful to you and Pastor Jay. Thank you both so much!"

"I also have another message from Pastor Jay. He said when you arrive on Sunday, even if it isn't in time for church, his church is planning a picnic that afternoon. You and your family will be guests of honor. The whole church is looking forward to doing this for you and your family. Just let me know the approximate time of your arrival so I can inform him. He will take care of the rest.

I was amazed at how things were falling into place and felt overwhelmed with being so blessed, I couldn't stop crying. *Thank you, Lord. You knew my fears and answered my prayers even more than I had expected.*

We arrived in Seward, Nebraska late Saturday afternoon and stopped by a little grocery store in this small town. Our car was filled with pots, pans, dishes, luggage, and plastic containers full of flour, sugar, a few boxes of cereal and many other things I would need to set up home while there.

We got out of our car and locked our doors before we went into the store to buy some meat, eggs, bacon, milk and bread for dinner that night and breakfast in the morning. Everyone was extremely friendly in the store. One man smiled and said, "You must be new in town. No one else around here ever locks their car doors. We don't even lock the doors to our homes."

Don answered the gentleman, "We're from Michigan and plan to be here for a month. My wife will be attending some training at Concordia College."

"Well, almost everyone here has something to do with Concordia. I'm sure you will have an enjoyable stay," he replied as he waved and walked away.

As Don and I climbed back into our car, I looked over at Don and said, "I don't know about you, but I certainly wouldn't feel comfortable leaving my car and house unlocked."

"Me neither," Don replied as we drove up to the little house where we were to spend the next month.

The couple from Libya came out to greet us and help us unload. During the following week, while hanging out our laundry or sitting on the steps enjoying the warm evening breeze, our missionary neighbors shared with us what it was like to be missionaries in Africa. During their remaining days they showed us pictures of their church, the work they did there, the roads they traveled, and the strange animals they often saw along their bumpy dirt roads.

The next morning, as we stepped out of our apartment and onto the sidewalk we were surprised to see so many people already walking past us toward the church. Several of them looked up at us and asked if we were headed to church and invited us to join them. When we walked up the steps into the church, there were greeters standing at the door to welcome us.

After church several came up to us asking us to join them for coffee in the fellowship hall. They explained their church had three different types of adult Sunday school classes available if we wanted to attend. I was asked to participate in the opening of the children's Sunday school classes by teaching a song in sign language.

Our kids were welcomed by several of the kids their age. Everyone at this church seemed to go out of their way to make us feel as if we were part of their church family. We had never experienced such a welcoming church in our entire life!

Many adults and children gathered around us after Sunday school to invite our children to attend their vacation Bible school (VBS) starting the next morning at 9:00 am. Because everyone was so excited about having our kids join their VBS, our kids became excited, too.

Right after church, we attended the picnic at the nearby park. There were games for children to play and a lot of food. Many of the church members offered to make plates of food for us to take back to our little apartment so we wouldn't have to cook for a few days. We were amazed at how much these strangers wanted to take care of us. We felt as if we were already in heaven!

We were invited to return to church again after the picnic for the youth ministry and talent show at 7 pm. We were all very tired and I wasn't so sure it would be a good idea to return to church again in the evening with the unpacking and preparation to do before starting class the next morning. The day had already been filled with lots of fun and interesting activities and meeting so many people. I thought it might be better for all of us to go home and relax before starting the busy week that was waiting for us; but, we were talked into returning to church that evening.

Once again, we felt welcomed by several who came up to us and asked us to sit with them. As we sat down in a pew waiting for the program to begin, we heard drums and tambourines from behind us along with loud guitars and a keyboard. We were shocked as we turned around to see about 20 teenagers singing, jumping, laughing, and clapping their hands as they came dancing down the middle aisle from the back of the church up to the front singing, "King of Kings, the Lord of Lords."

We had never seen so many teenagers or anyone for that matter who were so fired up for the Lord! I had expected something more subtle, quiet and orderly like a piano recital, maybe even a somewhat boring evening. Then everyone in the church stood up joining the kids by clapped to the beat and singing along with them! We were stunned by all this joy occurring around us.

As my husband and our family walked back to our little apartment after the program, another young couple with kids about the same ages as ours walked behind us.

"We heard you are from Michigan," the man announced. "But whereabouts?"

"We live on the west side of the state in Muskegon, along the shores of Lake Michigan," I said.

"Hey, we are almost neighbors back home in Michigan! We live directly across the state from you in the Detroit area. How long will you be here in Seward?"

"One month," my husband replied. "My wife's here for training at Concordia to work with the Deaf and hard of hearing in a church back home. She starts class tomorrow morning."

"What do you and your kids plan to do while she's in class?"

Don laughed. "Looks like I'll be taking the kids to VBS for the first two weeks, and then maybe the library or anywhere I can find air conditioning. I am as not fond of the hot weather like she is."

"I'm glad you plan to have them join our VBS," the man replied. "The kids will have a great time. Our kids always loved going to the Bible school here. This will be their last year and they will only attend the first week." "We're moving back to Michigan after my graduation next weekend."

"We are really going to miss this church and all the activities for our kids when we return home. Tom has finished his studies here and we will be going home to wait until we get a call from a church," his wife said as she introduced herself and family.

"I have an idea," she said. "Why don't you all come over for a cook out tomorrow night after Bonnie gets back from class? We have a lot of food to get rid of and we would love to have you join us."

"That sounds great! We can bring over some of the leftovers we were given at the picnic," I said.

As we walked up the steps to our apartment we waved goodbye to our new friends who not only lived across the state from us back home, but just across the street from us here.

I turned to my husband as we entered our small warm apartment. "God has been so good to us. Can you believe all that has just happened? How everything has fallen into place for us to come here. It's like it had all been planned out for us. The kids will have friends and things to do this summer. It's like a vacation for you and our kids. I already love being here and feeling so close to God!"

"I've never experienced anything like this before in my life, either. I wasn't so sure how all of this could work for everyone when I agreed we would all go," Don said as he gave me a big hug.

We were all up early the next morning. After I finished dressing, I entered into the kitchen where Don was standing at the stove. "I've got oatmeal ready for you. I wanted to send you and the kids off this morning with a good breakfast. The girls aren't so sure they wanted oatmeal today, but they're eating it anyway."

"What are you going to do while the girls are in VBS?" I asked while gathering my notebook and pencils.

"I plan to stay at the church for a while with them. Then I think I'll walk around town and look it over. Maybe I'll stop at the library for awhile before going back to church to walk them home. I don't know what we will do after lunch. We will think of something. Maybe unpack and get organized. At least we won't have to worry about dinner tonight."

As we all walked out the door, I couldn't help but feel ecstatic with all God had provided for us. "Have a great day at VBS. I'll see you later this afternoon," I said as we all parted at the corner across from the church.

Concordia College was only three short blocks from our apartment. The gentle early morning breeze felt cool and fresh on my face and arms as I walked toward campus on sidewalks lined with beautiful pink, white, and dark blue pansies. The cottonwood trees and the awesome pink and green Macadamia trees seemed to move their limbs back and forth as if were waving at me and saying "Hello. Welcome and Good morning!"

In our welcome letter, we had been told to go to the chapel first thing on Monday morning where we would be meeting every morning before class for devotionals. After starting our days at the chapel, we would walk across campus to another building for our classes. My heart was dancing for joy as I walked into the chapel. I stood there a moment in awe looking at the beautiful wooden beams and alter. I felt so close to God with the sunlight beaming through the stained glass windows, the sound of the organ, and everyone smiling and being so friendly. I knew I was part of something exciting about to happen. I was ready to learn and excited that I had been chosen for this mission. *Thank you, God!*

"This is the day the Lord has made. Let us rejoice and be glad in it."[12]

Project Brothers' Keeper
Chapter 17

My first day of training had begun. After the brief chapel service and devotionals, I headed across the campus to our classroom. I arrived just as some of the other participants were beginning to introduce themselves.

Dan Marshal cleared his throat to get our attention. "It's time to get started," he announced while handing us a syllabus covering what we would be doing for the next month. He said there would be a lot to cover in a short time. "You will have to pay close attention because we will not be using our voices most the time."

Our first assignment during class was for each of us to stand up and finger-spell our name and if we had a name sign, to show that, too. Name signs are a sign a Deaf person gives to a person that shows something about that person as perceived by the Deaf person bestowing the name sign. The name sign can be associated such things as hair color, style, or length, their glasses, or some activity the person does such as "teach" etc. My sign name began with the manual alphabet letter B, the first initial of my name, then using the B draw a smile from the center of the lips to the ear. The Deaf person who gave me this name sign said, "It's because you always smile!"

After this exercise, we were asked to stand up once again and sign or finger-spell our travel directions from our own hometowns to Seward, Nebraska. Since I read the maps while my husband drove, I easily recalled the main toll roads and the cities we passed.

This was quite an interesting exercise, but the next part was much harder. We were asked to sit with another participant during lunch and learn about them, their family, their home town, and their directions to Seward, Nebraska. Once again we were required to stand and share that information with the rest of the group in sign language.

By the time the day ended, I knew I was getting better at finger spelling and signing. My eyes were tired and sore. I felt exhausted as I walked back home thinking about this entire day. I was so thankful our neighbors were making dinner for us. I needed some down time. I looked forward to hearing how our kids liked VBS and how Don enjoyed his first day in Seward.

When I arrived at our house, no one was there. My husband had left a note stating everyone had gone across the street to our neighbor's house and to come over as soon as I got home. I put down my notebook, changed into shorts and after drinking a big glass of ice cold water, I headed across the street to join my family and get to know our neighbors.

Don was already sitting at the picnic table playing chess with Tom and the older girls were playing Barbies with our younger ones. Alice was in the kitchen.

"How was your first day at Concordia?" Alice called out to me from the window over her sink.

"It was very intense, but fun. We got to know where everyone came from and what their life is like," I said as I walked into the kitchen and offered to help her with dinner. "Everything was in sign language and my eyes are feeling the strain of watching hand and finger movements all day."

We really hit it off with Alice and Tom and their children. I thought about them leaving at the end of the week and wondered how the rest of our stay would be without them as our neighbors.

After dinner was over and as the sun was setting, we said our goodbye's and started to walk across the street to get our kids ready for bed when Tom spoke up.

"Alice and I talked about this and decided we would like to offer you our family summer pass to the community swimming pool to use for the rest of the summer. We have only used it for the past three or four weeks but with VBS this week and leaving right after graduation this coming weekend, it will just go to waste. We thought your family might like to use it. There is also a playground at the same park with lots of activities for your kids."

"Are you kidding? We would be so grateful to have a place like that for our kids to enjoy while I'm in class," I said, overwhelmed again with another blessing. My family always loves going to swim at the lake back home, but I feel they would be so much safer at a community pool where there are lifeguards.

"We can't thank you enough for this," my husband said as he accepted the pass. "We don't have air conditioning in our apartment and today's afternoon heat got to me. Going swimming will be the perfect way to spend afternoons after Bible school and during the days after VBS is over."

The next day, our classes provided us an opportunity to take a deeper look at the sign language we each used, the variations in signs, and how interpreting scripture and songs could take on different meanings by the signs we might choose to use. We learned how important it is to first get a thorough understanding of the meaning of the song or scriptures before trying to interpret. I learned the difference from signing words versus concepts. For instance, the word run has three separate concepts (1) to run as to jog, (2) to run for office would mean to be put on a slate with a list of other candidates, or (3) run as a tear in nylons. This made a huge impression on me as I began evaluating the signing skills I had learned from the SEE language used in the schools.

Without first understanding the concept, I now understood how this could give the wrong meaning when communicating or interpreting.

In the afternoon, we opened our Bibles, started reading verses, and then talked in small groups about how the messages could be interpreted. After our small group discussions, we each stood up to sign those verses in the way that made the most sense for each of us individually. For the first time in my life, I saw so many variations of sign language and different concepts stemming from the same Bible verse. So who was right? We were taught the interpreter should first work with the pastor or person giving the sermon or speech prior to delivery to make sure the concepts signed are the ones wanted to be delivered.

We became aware of Deaf communities across the entire United States that were becoming disturbed with hearing people, especially those who worked in school systems, because they were changing American sign language to become signed words in English sentence structure. There was a huge difference, and I was beginning to understand the depth of this problem. As I thought back to the adult Deaf population who were involved with Deaf ministry, I recalled an older Deaf lady who laughed at my signing and said I was just a baby signer. I thought I was an excellent signer, but at that time, I did not realize how different exact English was from ASL, the language the culturally Deaf community used. When I first saw ASL being used, I didn't know that was what it was. My first impression was that ASL was a simple and outdated shorthand language. I was now becoming aware of how wrong I was and how beautiful and visual ASL actually is.

Most of the participants at Project Brother's Keeper were fluent in ASL, while I was fluent in signing exact English (SEE). I struggled through this change. Dan asked all of us to do as the Deaf often do, "Accept the language of those around you and expand your thinking". Because of so many variations and changes in their language, the Deaf also had learned to be flexible. Some were, but others were adamant about signing correctly, meaning by using ASL. I had learned from the elderly to accept and use their signs, but the some of the younger Deaf population in the Total Communication Program at school used whatever signs they saw being used. This often caused confusion to those interpreting.

Since my experience at Project Brother's Keeper, I have learned scientists have found young babies using the conceptual sign language (ASL) have a better understanding of the English language, even if they are not deaf! I have a family member who was born a few years ago with Down's Syndrome and a significant hearing loss. Yet, by the time he was seven months old, he could understand the concept of many words that were signed to him and could sign, cookie, milk, water, and a few other signs.

Our first week at Project Brother's Keeper seemed to breeze by way too fast. I was intensely absorbing all I was learning and felt spiritually like I was in seventh heaven. When I got home after class, I couldn't shut up. The classes and the immersion into the Bible were feeding my soul! Our family had been fortunate enough to do some sight seeing during the first weekend after Project Brother's Keeper had started. We had been given a four day weekend to celebrate the Fourth of July and decided to make a short trip to see the capital in Lincoln, Nebraska, then spend the weekend from Don's aunt and uncle in Missouri. While we were there, Don called a friend of his from high school who then invited us to come visit them in Kansas City before we headed back to Seward. His friend's wife worked in the state capital building and was excited to take our family on a private tour of the state capital and share the history of Kansas with us. I was pleased our kids had this opportunity and we could fit all of this in on one long weekend.

On Wednesday of the following week, Dan informed us of the reason he picked the dates for Project Brother's Keeper. "I found out there was going to be many Deaf, including Deaf ministers coming here to Concordia College for a regional conference on Deaf ministry and I wanted all of you to be part of this experience. The whole church service will be signed entirely in ASL with Deaf ministers preaching. There will be no interpreters for the hearing. I believe this will be an extremely important part of this training for each of you."

I started to feel scared, exposed, and ashamed that I was not good enough to be involved in this program. *What if I can't understand them? I don't know very much ASL! How will I communicate with them or understand the Deaf ministers if they all use only ASL?*

As these anxiety provoking thoughts started racing through my brain, two Bible verses flashed into mind: one from Exodus in which God reminded the Israelites, "I am the Lord, your God, who brought you out of Egypt.", [20] and the other was from Isaiah: "fear not, for I am with you, be not dismayed, for I am your God; I will strengthen you, I will help you..."[21] I swallowed my pride and decided to attend this service. I would meet and interact as best as I could with these Deaf ministers and others who were coming from all over the mid-western United States.

In preparation for this conference, we began to read through many songs familiar to us from our church hymnals. We began working in groups trying to determine how to interpret them. While I enjoyed singing many of these songs regularly in church, I was shocked to realize I had no clue about their meaning or the concepts. What a challenge this was trying figure out how to sign them with a visual meaning in ASL!

One of the first songs, "All Hail the Power of Jesus' Name", was a favorite of mine. I didn't anticipate any problem signing this song. That was until I started to sign the second part of that line. I stopped suddenly as I read the words "Let Angels prostrate fall." *How do I sign this? What on earth does the writer mean by angels prostrate falling? What is the concept?* That took a lot more than just a few minutes to rethink the meaning until I tried to picture this happening and realized it probably meant the angels were falling down before Jesus.

There were many lines in this song that caused me to stop, think, and rethink, ask, consult, and explore the meaning of the words. I wasn't the only one there having difficulty with this, but as a group we got through this song and onto the next one, which was "Come Thou Font of Every Blessing." I also loved this song, and as I read further down on the page, once again I was shocked by the words we sing without thinking of the meaning. "Here I raise my Ebenezer". *I've never seen an Ebenezer.* "Here there by thy great help I come. And I hope by thy good pleasure, safely to arrive at home." *What on earth is this writer saying? I can't imagine what he meant by raising an Ebenezer.* This was going to take a lot more effort to make visual than I had ever thought!

The entire week continued like this: very intense and focused on how to visually show church songs in ASL, while using as many facial and body movements as possible.

Friday afternoon, we met at the welcoming center to greet the Deaf pastors and other workers in Deaf ministry. We had just finished the past week which had been very difficult and challenging trying to understand and interpret songs in ASL. Once again, I felt anxious and uncomfortable at the same time being surrounded by so many who were fluent in ASL. I wasn't sure I should even try signing to those who were professional Deaf church workers. After all, I was just a volunteer who was trying to help out.

As we gathered in the multipurpose room to welcome the attendees to the Deaf Ministry Conference, I watched the signs they used and tried to pick up on what they were saying.

I could understand some almost completely, but others signed so fast I felt lost when they did not use their mouth to verbalize the words. Part of me wanted to slip away unnoticed, but my grandmother's voice saying, "He brought you here for a purpose. God has a purpose for you and someday you will know what it is," kept me there. Feeling inspired, I believed this was truly His purpose for me.

Sunday morning my husband took the girls to church while I walked over to the auditorium on campus where the Deaf were to have their own church service. I was shocked as I walked in 10 minutes early and found a huge crowd already there with almost no place to sit except for a few seats at the back of the room. Not only the Deaf ministers and workers with Deaf Ministry were there, but hundreds of other Deaf people had migrated here to attend this service. The sermon titled, "Becoming Sowers for God", was to be preached by a Deaf minister from Kansas.

Our instructor stood at the door handing out special programs for those of us in his class. He didn't mention he had included the sermon written in the ASL word order for us to follow. When I looked down at what was written, I put it aside because it didn't make any sense to me. The nouns and verbs were reversed and the sentences appeared to be so poorly written I thought Dan had accidentally copied someone's notes. However, as I found out later, it was typed exactly as the Deaf minister was to sign his sermon. Once I understood this, I realized how a hearing church service could be very confusing to those Deaf who try to read in English word order, but could understand only in ASL word order. I realized ASL was a reversal for me to understand, just like SEE signing was a reversal for the culturally Deaf to understand.

I struggled but was able to grasp the understanding of the sermon, partly because I knew the scripture verses and story. There was no voice or lip movement and the signing was entirely in ASL which at times seemed easier to understand because it was so visual. However, the quickness of the fingers, the signs of the hands, and body language was too new for me to grasp all at once.

At the end of the sermon, the gospel lesson, parable of the seed sower, was portrayed by Dorothy Sparks, a Deaf girl whom I thought was pantomiming. As I watched, I was awed by her movements and how well I could actually see this story without hearing any words at all. She was so amazing to watch. It was beautiful, but pantomiming wasn't new to me. When I was younger, my brother and sisters watched Marcel Marceau on the Captain Kangaroo Show just before I left for school. I enjoyed figuring out some of the stories Marceau was acting out. But later I found out Dorothy was not pantomiming. She was using pure ASL!

When it came time for all of us to join in singing and signing songs during the service, I was looking forward to signing some of the songs we had practiced in class, but none of those were listed in our bulletin. When the organist began playing music (for the hard of hearing in attendance), I recognized some of the other songs; however, these songs were also not in the same word order as I knew them. Dan had written the words of some of the songs for us in ASL word order to help us follow along. While I recalled the words of the songs from memory, I felt frustrated because the words I was reading were nothing like the words I knew in those songs.

During the fellowship hour following the service, I had an opportunity to listen as a minister (watch the minister as he signed) relayed what it is like for him to be the only Deaf minister in his state. I was shocked to learn that often the ministers for the Deaf have to travel a very long distance to provide services, sometimes they travel more than a day away. One minister said he was lucky to have a small parish of a 100 mile radius to travel every Sunday to share the Word of God. He was sad there weren't others to help in this ministry. Due to the time it took him to travel, he was often unable to get to his parishioners who were sick or dying when they needed him most. He said many times there were conflicts with someone dying in one part of his parish while someone else was dying in another part at the same time. Because of the demands on his time and the length of time it took to travel, he often ministered at funerals several days after a burial.

I walked out of the church service that morning thinking if God wants to use me to work with the Deaf, I had a long way to go. As I walked home, I felt inspired to become more involved with Deaf ministry even if it meant I had a lot to learn. I wanted to serve and thought about entering the seminary if women were ever allowed to become ministers.

The following Monday morning, our class reviewed what it was like for each of us to attend a fully Deaf worship service with a Deaf minister signing, without any voice or interpreter. Dan asked us how we felt about trying to sing or sign unfamiliar songs along with songs we did know, but were written in a different word order. I shared my thoughts about how this experience had helped me understand what it was like for the Deaf to visit a hearing church without an interpreter or any accommodations.

We discussed the effect of being Deaf in a world that didn't relate to those who couldn't hear. We understand the need for us to educate hearing people back home about what it is like for this population to live in a world that doesn't relate at all to them.

During the following week we made a trip to a nursing home where both the Deaf and hearing people live together. Although not purposefully excluding those with a hearing loss, we found this does happen as well as a huge difference in treatment. Those with a hearing loss usually missed out on what was happening with others around them in the home. They were often left out of such things as changes in daily planning of activities, or discussions among the residents or staff, television shows, announcements, radio programs, even music and games. Those who could hear were able to socialize with each other and were more aware of what was going on around them. While the nursing staff did not intend to do so, the Deaf and hard of hearing were forced into a world of silence. When we returned to class to discuss this experience, we learned there have been studies indicating Alzheimer's can be exacerbated when there is a lack of communication and interaction among others. We acknowledged the need to explore ways to help facilities like the nursing homes and hospitals to provide for equal access to communication.

After class one day during the third week, Dan came up to me and said he and his wife were talking about going canoeing on the Platte River. "Since you and your family are here, we thought of inviting you to join us for canoeing and a picnic this weekend. We thought you might like to see more of Nebraska instead of staying in this small town all weekend. Ask your husband and let me know by Thursday after class if you want to join us. We are planning to spend the entire day there on Saturday. Don't worry about food. We will take care of all of that, too."

"Wow Dan, that's such a nice offer," I said. "I'll ask my husband. I know he and the girls would love to go. I'm the only one who is not the camping and boating type. I can't swim and won't get into the canoe, but I'll enjoy sitting on the banks of the river to watch. I definitely won't hold them back from enjoying this opportunity."

"Don't worry. Everything will be fine. You'll like canoeing. Both my wife and I are good swimmers and will help with your kids."

So early Saturday morning, the week before we left Seward, Nebraska, Dan and his wife took us out in their canoe into the brown muddy swamp-looking Platte River. I was afraid of what might be in that muddy river so I was on a lookout for snakes in case we needed to get away quickly. I was cajoled into getting into the canoe with Dan, while his wife sat with Don and our family watching and cheering me for being so brave. We all had a great time taking turns on the canoe and eating hot dogs, hamburgers, and chocolate brownies his wife had made. We went home tired and very content that evening. It had been a wonderful time for everyone.

During our last week of class, Dan reserved a big table in the middle of a busy restaurant during dinner time, the busiest hour of the day. He had ordered ear plugs for us to wear and asked us to cover our ears with hair or a hat. He warned us that we were not to use our mouth or voices in the restaurant, no matter how hard it was for us or the wait staff. This experience was to enable us to gain a deeper awareness of what it is like for Deaf people to go out in public places. We were to converse only in sign language while in the restaurant. That also meant we would be ordering from the menu without using our voices. We were to take memory notes of what it was like and when we got home that evening we were write about our experience playing the role of a Deaf person in public. The next day in class we would discuss how we felt and the responses we received from others at the restaurant.

It felt strange walking into the restaurant and trying to inform the hostess that we had reservations. She looked very unhappy and perturbed that we could not talk. We made signs holding up ten fingers and pointing to each of us. Dan signed "table" by putting his arms on top of each other to look like a table. He signed phone, table and pointing to 6 on his watch. The hostess looked confused. The waitress looked at her list and said there was a table reserved for ten in the middle of the room for 6 pm.

She started to walk us to our table, and then stopped. "Would you like me to move your group to another area off to the side where you won't be bothered by others?" she asked. I wondered how Deaf people could be bothered by people around them. Or, was it the hearing people who would be bothered by the Deaf around them.

Dan looked at her appearing confused. We all copied this look of confusion as we looked at each other and acted as if we couldn't understand what was happening. I think she realized that either we did not want to move or that it was just too hard to communicate with us. She picked up the menus and then led us to the table in the middle of the restaurant.

Our waitress approached our table and began by asking if we all wanted water. We stared at her as if not understanding and looked down at our menus. She left and came back with a water pitcher and glasses. Then, she walked around the table offering a glass of water to each of us, individually.

While we were looking over the menu and signing amongst ourselves, customers sitting nearby stared at us. Sometimes it felt as if they were glaring at us, but we tried to ignore them and kept signing to each other.

When the waitress came around to take our orders, most of us just pointed to what we wanted, but not Dan. He asked in sign language for something he wanted fixed a special way for him. Since the waitress could not understand sign language, she brought over a pen and paper. When Dan got his order, he was upset about how they had made it and sent it back by shaking his head "no" and handing her his plate. The waitress was so upset that by the time we had finished dinner that Dan took our waitress aside and gave her a huge tip. Then he told her why we were doing this. We all learned how it felt to be different from others and the frustration of not being accepted or treated equally. We realized how much more we needed to educate others on deafness and accessibility.

The time had come for us to return home. Our month at Concordia College in Seward, Nebraska had come to an end. We packed our luggage, kitchen supplies, bedding, and leftover food for our trip home. Then once again, climbed into our old station wagon and headed out of town for our long trip back to our home in Michigan. I felt tearful leaving this small town that had been so warm and friendly toward us and helped us to make it our home. It had been a place of love and sharing I would never forget. I thought how much I would have loved to make this small town our permanent home, but we had family and responsibilities in Michigan.

I had never felt so close to God in my entire life as I did in Seward, Nebraska where we were surrounded with an enormous amount of Christian love. It was as if we had a little glimpse of what heaven will be like. Once again in my life, I experienced how God participates in our daily lives and the reality that He does have plans for us everyone who lets Him lead them. I couldn't wait to return home to share my experiences at Concordia with my grandmother and to see how God would allow this experience to continue to unfold in my life.

"I can do everything through him who gives me strength." [22]

Returning Home
Chapter 18

Upon leaving Nebraska, Don and I talked about stopping briefly along our way home if there were some historic sites or interesting places so the girls could learn more about history and their country to share when they returned to school in the fall. Our family had been very fortunate to do some sight seeing during our first weekend after Project Brother's Keeper had started. We had been given a four days to celebrate the Fourth of July and decided to make a short trip to see the capital in Lincoln, Nebraska. Then we headed to Missouri where we spent the holiday weekend with Don's aunt, uncle, and cousins. While we were there, Don called a friend of his from high school who invited us to come visit him and his wife in Kansas City before we started back to Seward. His friend's wife worked in the state capital building and was excited to take our family on a private tour of the Kansas State Capital and share the history of Kansas with us. I was pleased our kids had this opportunity and we were able to fit all of this into our schedule.

We were now on our way back home. We had been traveling for hours and it was very late by the time we finally found a place to stop. Although we knew we were somewhere in Des Moines, the capital city of Iowa, we had no idea how close we actually were to the state capital building until we stepped outside of our motel the next morning. The bright golden dome of the State Capital building looked like a huge space ship that was hovering above the treetops next to our motel. We stood outside on the deck and stared in awe at the beauty of the state capital's bright glittering golden dome that appeared so majestic, strong, and confident while the morning sun seemed to dance around it.

Even though it was very early in the morning, the temperature was hot and the air was so humid we could barely breathe. We took our luggage outside to the car, but no one was ready to climb back into the hot car that had no air conditioning. Don and I decided this might be a good time to take a break. We took the girls on a tour of the Iowa State Capital building, hoping that later in the day it would not be quite as muggy as it was in the morning.

By the time we arrived home, we were exhausted, yet very excited to share the highlights of our trip and our experiences with my family. I called my mother first, to let her know we were home safely and then mentioned I couldn't wait to talk with grandma about all that had happened.

"Oh, Bonnie Jeane," she said sounding as if she was sobbing. "I got a call from the nursing home just before breakfast today. They said grandma had passed away during the night or early this morning."

"No!" I cried. "I thought about her a lot while at Concordia and wanted to share with her everything that happened."

"I'm sure she does know and is looking down from Heaven with a smile. I know she was proud of you and so am I".

A few days later, after my grandmother's funeral, Don returned to his summer job. All was going well and we didn't need to worry about the money we would need for our kids school in the fall.

After we finally sat down to go through our finances. We made a list separating what we had spent from the donations for the cost of the workshop, and how much we had spent of our own money for the extras. There was an extra $500 left! The exact amount of the check Pastor Neisch had given to us for travel expenses.

I called Pastor Karl and Pastor Neisch shortly after balancing our budget to let them know we were back and how well everything had gone for us.

"By the way, I have a check for you," I told Pastor Neisch. "The $500 that was given to us for travel expenses was more then we needed or used. I'm going to return a check for that amount to give back to the church. We did do some sightseeing and had a nice vacation along the way. I am so grateful we had the money just in case, but I'm sure the church can use it. Please take it knowing how much we appreciated this."

"Well, I'm glad all went well and worked out for you and your family. Now that you are back, Pastor Barkley, from another school for Deaf in Michigan spoke to me about asking you to help with presenting a conference focused on working with Deaf and to train teachers, pastors, interpreters, and others who might be interested. We were thinking about doing that within the next two months."

"Oh, I'm not sure I'm that knowledgeable or skilled enough at this point to do something that huge! I'm still learning. I would feel like a hypocrite training interpreters, teachers, pastors or whoever else decided to come."

"You won't be doing this alone. Pastor Barkley and I will help and we will do the training on interpreting. But we want you to share what you learned and give examples of your increased awareness during your training there. We also need you to coordinate and help with advertising this event on your side of the state. You know a lot of interpreters in the area schools. This won't be for the Deaf population, but for anyone connected with them, including parents and teachers. Can we count on your help?"

"Of course," I said feeling scared and thinking I was way too inadequate to do it. "You know, Pastor, I just learned there are many other ways to sign than what I have learned."

"Yes, there are many forms of sign language, just like there are many dialects. Like the British English vs the American English," Pastor Neisch agreed. "You are in a good spot now to recognize that. As long as you are open to learning, you will go a long way in this field. I will let Pastor Barkley know we have your help and get back to you on the date. Thank you and God bless you. Say hello to your husband and let him know how much we appreciate him supporting you through this."

The summer of 1980 went very quickly. Our kids were back in school and our crazy life schedule began once again. We were all set for the workshop and many people came. I had feared trying to discuss the difficulty of interpreting the concepts of some of our church songs due to translation not having a concrete meaning. I knew the interpreters, who did this every weekend at churches across the state, would know more than I did. However, that was not my assignment. I was not to focus only on the needs of the interpreters. I shared what I had learned about how the Deaf feel ostracized and how we learned more about those with hearing loss and the need to educate the hearing population about this unseen disability. I also posed the signing of one or two difficult songs to my audience and let them take turns on deciding what the words meant and how they would interpret them. It was a great approach and the interaction and supportive recognition of the interpreters' skills was felt by everyone. Pastor Neisch said it was a great awareness of the things interpreters and church workers do, even pastors had to consider not the words, but what they meant when working with hearing as well as the Deaf.

That fall I started to share much of what I had learned at Project Brother's Keeper during my sign language classes. We were still meeting twice a month on Sunday nights with the Deaf for a potluck followed by a church service. Many of our parishioners were now able to communicate with the Deaf and were looking forward to the Deaf soon joining them on Sunday mornings during regular church. Yet, the Deaf were still not coming to the Sunday morning worship services as we had hoped.

We ended that year by those in my signing class joining with the Deaf to go Christmas caroling at nursing homes with Pastor Neisch joining us. Once again, it was beautiful to hear and see the Deaf and hearing standing together singing and signing Christmas songs. Yet, I continued to wonder, *why are they not coming to a regular church to worship on Sunday mornings?* I hoped this would change and prayed for answers.

"Therefore, I tell you whatever you ask in prayer, believe you have received it."[23]

Out of the Past
Chapter 19

Following the Christmas holidays and soon after the beginning of the new year, I approached Pastor Karl about starting a Sunday school class for the Deaf on Sunday mornings during their church's regular Sunday school time. This would be quite a commitment for me because it meant giving up Sunday school at my church and driving across town while my husband and kids stayed at our church to attend our church Sunday school. My husband agreed with my idea and as usual, supported me and my work with the Deaf ministry.

Pastor Karl was happy to find space for the Deaf to meet. Some of the sign language students from the church also agreed to join me to help out. We had four or five Deaf come weekly. Not knowing how much they knew about the Bible stories, and not having any special materials available for us, we used Bible verses read in church each week. At times it was difficult for me because I did not have the verses in advance to prepare for the class. As I think back to those days, it would have been better to have started with simple Bible stories. However, the Deaf who joined us seemed to enjoy our group and were open to sharing whatever we could with them.

One day, as we sat around the table chatting just before we started our lesson, one of the Deaf women in our group signed to me, "You hearing?"

"Yes," I replied smiling while shaking my hand with the yes movement.

"You interested Deaf, why?" she asked in sign language.

The first answer that popped into my mind was to tell her of the day I found out I was losing my hearing. But instead, as I was started to tell her about that, what came out of my mouth was entirely different!

"One time when I was about nine years old, a deaf girl came to my door and I couldn't talk to her I only knew her name," I responded.

"Girl name, what?" she asked in ASL.

"Martha," I voiced while I finger-spelled the name.

Her face lit up with broad smile. "Me" she tried to voice while pointing to herself and finger-spelling. "Martha. Me. Go your house!"

I was stunned as I thought about what she had just said. "Oh, it couldn't have been you, Martha," I voiced and signed. "The Martha who showed up at my door had a long black pony tail. She was tall and really skinny! She didn't look anything like you!"

"Yes! Me! Martha! Your house, I go." She looked as if very frustrated I didn't believe her as she continued to sign. "Picture me show you next week!"

She couldn't possibly be Martha! That would be too unbelievable for her to show up here! She doesn't even look like Martha. Although it's been twenty-five years since I've seen her and people do change, I don't think she'd change so much that I wouldn't be able to recognize her.

Although I felt stunned about what she said, I was absolutely sure she was not the same person. I had expected if Martha did find her school picture and if she did bring it back the next Sunday, it would prove she would not be the same person who had come to my door. After all, how likely could something like this ever happen?

The following Sunday morning, Martha showed up in our Sunday school class with a big smile and her school picture. I took one look at her picture and felt goose-bumps emerged all over my body. I felt my legs going weak as if I was going to drop to the floor in humble disbelief. Who would have believed this was the same Martha! I was in utter shock. I knew that this was not just a coincidence.

I could barely talk as tears started to flow down my cheek.

"It is you," I said as I threw my arms around her and gave her a huge hug. "You are the same girl who came to my door!"

I couldn't help but think, *how ironic this is that as a child, the very girl I could not communicate with in any language, was now sitting right here in my Bible class for the Deaf!* I felt overwhelmed by excitement and amazement as once again I recalled my grandmother's words, "God has a purpose for you and someday you will know what it is."

All the Deaf ladies who sat around the table watching us were surprised, too. They laughed and raised their hands waving (this is how they applaud when they like something). Some signed "friends" (by hooking their two pointer fingers together tightly and shaking them back and forth in the air) showing how happy and delighted they were we had finally found each other.

I drove home still not completely believing what had just occurred this morning. We had each gone our separate ways and so much had happened to each of us over the course of about twenty-five years. Now God had brought us back together for a reason. I wondered what would have happened if I hadn't started a Bible class or told Martha about the deaf girl. Would I have ever found out she was this same person?

Although Martha had been part of our Deaf ministry for two years, I'd never thought of her as possibly being the same girl from my past. Now, she was married with two teenagers. She had grown up at the school for Deaf in Flint. While other students went home to their families on Thursday afternoons for the weekends, Martha stayed behind in the dorm every weekend. I wondered if her parents had given her up because by making her a ward of the state, she could have a better life and education in a school where she could communicate with others. I felt sad as I thought how it must have been very lonely and maybe even frightening for her to be left behind on weekends and vacations when others went home to their families who were waiting to spend time with them.

Martha and I became much closer after this. My heart reached out to her and her family. I often picked her and her family up for church or drove them home from church. Sometimes I drove them to other events and sometimes I took her shopping or to appointments.

One day, I finally asked her, "Martha, why did you come to my house when you were younger?"

"Don't know," she would giggle.

"Had you ever seen me outside before you came to my door that first day?"

"Remember? Not," she signed back.

"I wonder what happened that you decided to walk up to my door instead of someone else's." I kept asking, but Martha would only respond by laughing, "Don't know. I'm clueless!" (Making an O with pointer and thumb and bringing that sign up to forehead).

I think God was giving me a present when he let Martha back into my life. In my heart I knew that as a child she was led to me for a reason. It was not a coincidence I opened a door to connect with her years ago. Now for a second time I was opening another door for her, or was she opening a door to me?

"Many are the plans in a man's heart, but it is the Lord's purpose that prevails."[24]

A Weekend Away
Chapter 20

Once again, spring had come and Sunday school was winding down for the summer. Our daughters were now 7, 9, 11, 13 and 14 and I still felt it was important to me to be at home with them during the summers. I made sure all five of them took swimming lessons at the lake three times a week every summer even if they were held at different times during the day. We enjoyed the time we spent at the lake and looked forward to it every year. They all were involved in softball practice and games in the late afternoons. Of course, they all chose to play on separate teams which meant we spent a lot of time at the park cheering for all the teams. Some of the other parents thought we didn't know much about the game because we cheered and clapped for both sides when the girls played against each other.

While my husband continued to work summers to augment our income, the girls and I grew and canned our own vegetables from our back yard. I also took the girls to pick strawberries and blueberries and Don joined us when we went cherry picking because we needed to climb trees or ladders. When we returned home with our buckets full, we made homemade jams and canned blueberries and cherries. Sometimes our daughters picked fruits to earn their own money for extra things they wanted.

When fall came, I returned to my volunteer position in Deaf ministry. I still enjoyed it, but something inside of me kept nagging at my heart strings. *Something is missing, but what?* I wanted to teach the Deaf in a better way so they could grow spiritually closer to God, but I didn't know how to go about that.

I kept searching for anything that could help to improve our program. I thought perhaps the problem might be my signing skill and the difference in the way I signed from the syntax of ASL. I had started to use signed English and pigeon language (a combination of ASL and signed English, but not exact English). I was learning from them and changing my signing to become more like the ones used by those who were culturally Deaf. I learned to drop the articles, adverbs, and adjectives that were not used or needed. I began to utilize different movements to indicate past and present tenses of verbs. The Deaf seemed to be fine with my signing. Of course, when I did make mistakes, they corrected me immediately.

Shortly after starting the Sunday evenings Deaf worship again in the fall, Pastor Neisch asked me to take a more formal part of the service leading in prayers and songs. At first I felt very uncomfortable doing this. I was still learning and struggling with interpreting concepts, especially in songs.

"You have the skills and talent," Pastor Neisch said. "God uses what is given."

Being a little hesitant, I agreed and found it felt good to be an active part of the church service. My heart was purring.

Shortly after the beginning of the fall session of Deaf Ministry, I received an invitation to the Convocation on Deaf Ministry to be led by Deaf ministers and some church workers. It was scheduled to be in Wisconsin on the weekend of November 21-24, just before Thanksgiving. I had been one of 200 church workers from across the country chosen to attend this national event. My entire expenses would be paid by the church. I felt thrilled knowing God was guiding me once again. I wished my grandma was still alive so I could share with her what was happening in my life.

I called Pastor Neisch and told him I had received an invitation and was sending in my reservation.

"I'm so delighted you want to go to learn more! There are not enough workers to reach out to this population. God is certainly leading you in this direction and you have a heart for this population. We are blessed to have you!"

I felt so validated, appreciated, and had a sense of peacefulness and joy just knowing God had a place for me in His plan.

"Thank you, Pastor. I do believe I am doing what God wants and I want to learn how to better serve and communicate with the Deaf in their language. They have been wonderful by accepting me as a hearing person into their culture. I feel very blessed by them, too. I am gaining a better understanding of my own language and idiosyncrasies. I'm especially becoming aware how hearing people, including me, are generally viewed by the culturally Deaf. I'm really excited to be invited and I'm looking forward to this conference."

The time was growing closer to the date of the conference when Pastor Neisch called me. "I have something to discuss with you. You may not want to do this, so please give this some consideration before you respond. Whatever you decide will be fine with this person and her parents. They are my friends and I know them very well. They live here in the Flint area and have a teenage daughter who is deaf. She is interested in participating in Deaf ministry and her parents would like for her to attend the Convocation in Wisconsin. Neither one of them could get off work to attend with her, nor did they want her traveling alone, especially when the flight from here stops at O'Hare in Chicago and then she has to catch another flight for Wisconsin. O'Hare can be a very confusing place, but even more so when there is very little time between flights and trying to catch another plane. She has never flown before and her parents are concerned about what could happen to her in such a big airport. Would you be willing to meet her at O'Hare Airport and help her connect with the flight to Wisconsin? You will both be taking that same flight from O'Hare."

"Yes, I'm willing to help, but I have never flown before either and I have never even been inside a big airport. It sounds like it might be really complicated to try to find a person I have never met before in such a huge international airport. Do you think it is possible for me to meet her sometime before we leave?"

"There is not much time for that, but I will talk to her parents and get back to you very soon. But it does sound you would be willing to help her but want to meet her first?"

"Yes. I will do this but think it would help to know what she looks like before I try to find her in a huge airport," I responded.

Later that evening, Pastor Neisch called back. "It doesn't look like it will be feasible for the family to drive to Muskegon. How do you feel about driving over here one afternoon during the week to meet her after-school?"

"I can't get away during the week with all the driving I do with our kids for their after-school activities. But, I would be willing to try to meet her somewhere in the airport, if we can work out how that could happen."

"I think we can figure that out. Tell me your airline flight number and schedule and I can work with her parents to figure out how the two of you can meet. Sometimes the airlines will provide an escort. I will contact the parents as long as you are still in agreement to do this. I know they will certainly appreciate all you can do help their daughter to have a safe trip and to be able to participate in this conference. It means a lot to them."

A few days later, Pastor Neisch called and said it was all worked out and the airlines would see that Sharon connected with me. We were all set.

The evening before we left there were reports of a heavy snow storm heading our way, but I was not at all prepared for what we encountered the next morning. Ten inches of snow had been dumped on us over night! We tried calling the airport early that morning, but only got a recording and nothing was mentioned about our flight or any delays.

My husband helped me pack the car and got the kids up to ride with us to the airport. It was a really special occasion since I had never flown before nor left my kids and husband alone for any length of time. Now, to be away from them for four days seemed like eternity. We were able to get our van out of the driveway and slowly make our way down to the main street. When we arrived at the airport, there were no planes to be seen. I began to feel scared and confused about what was going to happen. My negative thinking began to kick in. *Maybe God doesn't want me to go. Maybe it was just me who wanted to go so badly and God is saying "No" to me, now.*

The terminal was almost empty except for a few people standing around and one person at the desk. We walked up to the desk and asked the airline worker if there would still be a flight to Chicago. She said there would be as soon as they plowed the run way. She said they would call us when the plane is ready to board, but it could be a few hours. She said I could go home and she would contact me when the plane was ready to board. She also said I could stay there in the lobby and wait although she had no idea how long it could take before the runway would be cleared with the snow still coming down.

I found a phone booth and called Pastor Neisch to tell him about my flight being delayed due to the snowstorm. He then called Sharon's parents and then called me back to let me know what the new arrangements would be. "Her flight was on time. They are already at the terminal and she has just boarded the plane which will be taking off any minute. We will not be able to let her know what is happening at your end. We plan to contact the airline and have someone at O'Hare let Sharon know your flight will be later. Keep us informed."

My husband decided to take our kids back home, feed them breakfast, and then bring them back to see me off before my plane left. We were told it would be a few hours before that could happen, but a half an hour after he left, an announcement came over the loud speaker that my plane was now boarding. I quickly returned to the phone booth and called home. I asked my husband to call Pastor Neisch and let him know my plane was ready to take off. I was feeling really upset because I was not going to see Don or the kids before leaving and would not see them again until I returned on Sunday evening. I began worrying about Sharon and how we would meet at O'Hare. As I was getting more nervous about all of this, I felt a headache coming on, and began to feel nauseated.

When I boarded the plane, it looked entirely different from the big planes I had seen in movies. It only held about twenty people at the most. I looked around and the only seat left was at the very back of the plane.

Once I sat down I began to worry about how safe this small plane was. The motor was loud and hurt my ears. The entire trip was bumpy and I felt as if we were being tossed around like a basketball bouncing in the sky. The pilot announced over the loud speaker, "Please stay in your seats. We are hitting some wind pockets!"

Oh, how I wish my husband could have driven and attended this event with me. Another bump! *If this is what flying is like, I don't want to ever fly again,* I thought to myself.

It was a short twenty minute trip to Chicago when the pilot announced we would be landing soon. About ten minutes later, he came back on the loud speaker and apologized for taking so long to land. "Due to the ice and snow on the runway, we have been circling O'Hare for the past ten minutes. They are trying to get the snow and ice off the runway for us to land safely. It shouldn't be long now."

Ice! What if we crash? Please Dear God, keep us safe! What about Sharon and her flight? Please help us to connect in time and make it to our next flight.

Finally, the airline hostess said to stay seated and to buckle our seat belts. The pilot announced we were heading downward to land and would be experiencing a rough landing. He was right. The landing was very bumpy. All was well, except my headache, which was getting worse. By now, it was a migraine. I could feel my heart beating against my chest as I waited for the others in seats ahead of me to make their way to the front of the plane. I was in a hurry and needed to get off quickly to catch up with Sharon, but everyone was pushing their way out of the plane ahead of me.

Just as I was about to walk out the front door of the plane, I stopped to ask our flight attendant if he had any idea where the flight from Flint would be landing. He said he didn't know, but directed me to check with the desk at the terminal in the concourse. *What's a concourse?* I wondered feeling too embarrassed about my ignorance to ask. I decided I would just look for a desk when I entered the airport.

Luckily, there was a lady at the desk as I walked into the airport from the tunnel that connected from the airplane to the airport.

"Can you help me?" I asked. "I am to meet a deaf teenager who is arriving, or may have already arrived, from Flint. All I have is her flight number. Her parents did arrange for an airline escort to meet her here and help to see that we connect."

"I can help you with that. This is not an uncommon thing for us. Let me check her name and flight number. I will get right back to you." The airline attendant came back very quickly. "Sharon's flight has already landed and her airport escort is on his way here with her. Stay right here and they should be here in about five minutes." *Thank you Lord!* I said while taking a deep breath.

I watched and waited until I noticed a young teenager walking with an airport employee heading toward us. As they approached me, I stood and pointing to myself, signed my name, Bonnie. Her eyes lit up as she signed her name and continued to sign, "Thank God you are safe. I heard about all the snow you had before you left Muskegon. I was concerned you would not come. I didn't know what I would do if you were not here to go with me. Now, everything is fine. So happy you are here!"

The airline escort interrupted us. "You two will have to talk later, your flight to Madison, Wisconsin is now boarding. It's a long way to walk, but if you run you can make it!" He gave us directions to the concourse, which was now a term that made sense to me, and told us we would have better luck getting to our plane on time if went outside to a different part of the airport to catch our next plane. "It would be best if you two started running," he said as he turned around and walked back toward another concourse. "Good luck!"

I signed to Sharon that we had to run. We took off running down the long corridors, past the food stands, and stores to reach the door outside. I would have loved to have stopped to shop, or at least grab something to eat. My head was pounding as fast as my heart when we reached the terminal just in time to catch our next flight. We stopped to take a breath and then looked at each other. "Whew, we made it! What a morning!" I signed as I spoke. It was now afternoon and I was famished, but knew my stomach was too upset to eat or drink.

We took our seats in the plane and I felt much safer as I looked around and saw three seats on each side of the aisle. It was so much bigger than the little shuttle I had been on from Muskegon to Chicago. There were rows and rows of seats going so far back into the tail of the plane I couldn't count them. I figured there must be at least two hundred seats or more on this plane which also had restrooms! As the airline stewardess walked past me, I called to her. "I'm nauseated and have a tremendous headache."

"If you think you might get sick, we have plastic bags in the pocket of the back of the seat in front of you. Let me know if I can get you anything else."

We were ready for take-off and the stewardess showed us where the oxygen masks were located and how to put them on. Then she showed how to put on the life jacket. *I am not ready for this!* I thought as I interpreted the information to Sharon.

I could feel the roaring engine, the wheels lifting from the ground as the plane moved upward in the air. My ears felt as if I had just gone under water. I recalled someone saying to chew gum or swallow frequently when this happens. I never chew gum so I started to swallow repeatedly. Once in the air I tried to relax, but I was too nauseated and began to vomit.

It was a short flight to Madison, Wisconsin where we were to be taken by bus to the conference about two hours north of the airport. I saw several men dressed as ministers wearing black suits and a white collar around their neck carrying a sign with Deaf Convocation printed on it so we boarded their bus. Although I was feeling a little better, I informed one of the pastors and the driver I had a bad headache and feared vomiting on the bus.

We arrived at the conference center in time for dinner. I helped Sharon with registering, but soon felt confident she could do well on her own. There were many Deaf people mingling in the lobby and everyone was friendly and seemed to know sign language. I still had quite a migraine. Sharon said she would be fine if I decided to go lay down. I notified the welcoming committee that I was not feeling well and I headed straight to my room and climbed into bed.

Later that evening, I awoke feeling much better. I decided to venture out into the conference center to look around. I was delighted to see many Deaf ministers I had met the year before at the Mid-West Regional Conference on Deaf ministry in Seward, Nebraska. They were all aware I had not been feeling well and told me they had prayed for me to get better quickly so I would be able to participate in the weekend events.

I was happy that many remembered me and had even prayed for me. I sat down in a comfortable chair away from the activities going on at the tables where the Deaf and hearing workers were socializing and playing dingo (a card game the culturally Deaf community love to play). Suddenly, a familiar looking gentleman headed straight toward me.

"Dan! I didn't know you were going to be here. What an awesome surprise. Please don't get too close to me. I had a bad migraine after my plane had trouble landing in Chicago. I'm not sure if I have the flu or if it was just my migraine causing my nausea that made me very sick on the flight over here. If I have the flu, I don't want you or anyone else to get it."

"Don't worry about that. I suspect it was all the confusion with the flight. Many people have a lot of anxiety and get motion sickness while traveling, especially if you are not used to flying." He continued, "During dinner, one of the pastors told me one of my students was here from Project Brother's Keeper and was in her room not feeling well. We prayed for you to quickly get over whatever was keeping you from participating in this convocation. I know you will be feeling great soon and will be participating tomorrow. God needs you here!"

"I'm already feeling a little better. I just don't think I should eat anything, yet. I am still feeling very tired, but I wanted to see what is going on out here and if I knew anyone before going back to my room."

"I won't keep you, then. But, I did want to share with you that while we were in Nebraska, the little time my wife and I spent with you and your family, we were very impressed with how supportive your husband was for you and how well he interacts with your children. You are lucky to have such a wonderful husband and we are blessed he allows you to do this. Now get some rest. We have a lot to go over tomorrow. I know you will enjoy this convocation."

"Thanks, Dan. I feel very lucky and blessed to be here. I, too, am really looking forward to tomorrow morning. See you then."

As I walked back to my room, feeling excited but physically weak, I knew I was exactly where God wanted me to be and was excited knowing tomorrow would be a good day.

I awoke before the alarm and noticed the morning sun peeking in through the drapes. I got up and walked over to the window and opened the drapes to see my surroundings. I looked out over the yellowish brown grassy field dusted with frost and watched the sunrise. The beautiful red and yellow rays from the rising sun seemed to be reaching up to heaven as if praising the Lord. *It's certainly not like this in Michigan today. We have so much snow we can't see the ground,* I thought as I stood for a while longer and watched the sun move up above the horizon. Then I jumped into the shower, dressed, and put on my coat to step outside and get a breath of the fresh brisk air. I walked around the outside of the center enjoying the peace of the quiet early morning. Everything was so peaceful and fresh. I stood there thanking God for such a beautiful day, for taking away my migraine, and helping me feel so much stronger. I asked Him to watch over my family and keep them safe while I was away from them. Suddenly, I could smell the fresh coffee brewing and the smell of bacon coming from the cafeteria. I was famished and ready to go back inside to eat breakfast and start this day.

During breakfast I looked around for Dan and other pastors I had met the year before, but none of them were in the dining room. I didn't see any of the other pastors I had seen the day before and wondered where they all went. I sat down at one of the round tables and asked one of the Deaf gentlemen if he knew Dan Marshal. He said he did not know him, but had heard of him. I signed that had I met Dan at Project Brother's Keeper in Nebraska last summer and saw him upstairs playing Dingo and socializing before I went to my room last night. I had thought I might see him down here for breakfast this morning.

"Oh, maybe he's one of the presenters or is helping set up for the conference. Those who are working on the conference ate earlier than the rest of us," the man signed.

When breakfast was over, I went into the conference room a little earlier than others. I looked around for Sharon and whoever else was there that I knew and could chat with.

Sharon came in just behind me. She indicated she had a good evening and made new friends the night before. We soon got started in our morning session with both Deaf and hearing standing side by side signing and singing praise and worship songs joyfully to the loud music.

Following the opening prayer, a Bible verse was read and signed about speaking without love would be like a resounding gong or cymbal (author's paraphrase, I. Corinthians 13:1 NIV). And once again, we were awed by witnessing Dorothy Sparks vividly portraying this Bible verse. Her dramatic facial expressions, movement, and body language made this story come to life.

Following this dramatic presentation, one of the Deaf ministers read a story from Mark 7:32-34 (NIV) about a group of people bringing a deaf man to Jesus to heal. Jesus took him away from the crowd and touched his ears and tongue and said, "Ephphatha", meaning to be open as he opened the ears and loosened the tongue of the deaf man so he could hear and speak. (Author's paraphrase)

Next, one of the other Deaf ministers explained what Ephphatha really meant in this Bible verse. "Ephphatha means to be open," he said. "Jesus did more than open the ears of the Deaf man so he could hear." The minister continued to share the significance of Jesus touching the Deaf man's ears. "He validated all people who are deaf. Jesus was saying that everyone is important." He continued to explain, "To be open is not just to be able to hear, but to open our hearts for the Holy Spirit to enter into our lives. The Lord wants us to go tell others about Him and His love for us. After years and centuries of being shunned, ostracized, ignored, sent out from the cities into desserts and jungles just because the person was deaf, God was saying no one is worthless and I love everyone."

The minister continued to share an even deeper meaning. "Many can be deaf without any hearing loss; deaf to God's word, spiritually deaf, and deaf to listening to what God wants for them to do." He compared this to going through the day up in our heads, maybe reading a Bible verse and maybe thinking a little bit about God and what He wants from us, but not sharing with others what we know about God from our heart and not letting the Holy Spirit lead us."

That morning session was so powerful. Although I hated to admit it, I could see myself in his sermon. I, too, was often up in my head and not sharing God with others. Later that morning I heard, I mean, I watched in sign language, the Deaf as they began sharing their stories about hearing workers in churches who unknowingly try to take over and act like the Deaf can't do anything. Many of the Deaf participants got up to give examples in which they felt they were talked down to or felt hearing workers believed they were too dumb to take charge of their own Deaf church services. These Deaf said they often felt helpless, ignored, and unwelcome around hearing people in churches. They wanted to do more and be an active church member, but some hearing workers kept them from that. This really angered the Deaf community. They felt so belittled and treated as if they were little children. They believed there was no respect shown to them as being capable adults. People continued to stop and stare at them when they tried to voice words or use their hands to communicate. Many indicated these were reasons they did not attend hearing churches. Another reason noted was not having accommodations such as interpreters or sound systems for those who wore hearing aids.

I could identify with everything they were saying. I realized I had done similar things while taking a leadership role in our church services back home. I had never thought about how our Deaf group might perceive what we believed was helping them. I realized no one had ever asked our Deaf members if they would like to do so much as even take the offering or hand out bulletins. I didn't realize that by taking charge, we were making them dependent on us. I needed to hear this, even if it felt harsh. I knew we had to make changes as soon as I got back home.

As I pondered on all of this information, I knew this was exactly what God wanted me to hear and understand. He was opening a door for me to learn what was needed to help our Deaf group become an active part of their ministry and to grow in faith.

I had always been a caretaker, but these were adults and didn't need me to be their caretaker when they were on their path to a relationship with God. Perhaps I was getting in the way with my own agenda. I had to find a way to set new boundaries and redefine my role and those of our ministry team, while still encouraging the Deaf to develop their role in this mission. I knew this would be a challenge. It meant to do less for them while encouraging and supporting them to do more.

I reflected on the Deaf population I knew back home and thought about those who were deaf at this conference. It became apparent the ones at this conference were very well educated, middle, and upper class Deaf with professional careers. Some of them had graduated from Gallaudet, the Deaf University in Silver Springs, Maryland near Washington DC. There were many Deaf at this conference who were not just ministers or workers in the ministry, but some of them also had other careers such as journalists, authors, doctors, actresses or actors, artists, mechanics, teachers, photographers, or had technological or computer programming training. They had much more professional skills than those whom were deaf in my small hometown.

Back home, very few Deaf could find a full time job or had any professional career opportunities. Most of the ones I knew had problems finding any good paying jobs. Although some worked in a factory, most struggled to find full time employment. *Why is that?* I wondered. *What can be done to change that?*

That evening during dinner, I sat at a round table with about six Deaf attendees. I couldn't believe how fast they could sign and still eat! I felt helpless and left out of the conversation at first while watching them eat and sign at the same time. They didn't use their mouth to verbalize the words, which really is the Deaf culture way. I tried to join in the conversation, but I couldn't keep up trying to eat, use my voice, and sign all at the same time. They laughed and teased me about how awkward I appeared trying to communicate with voice and hands while trying to eat. But they quickly changed their mode of signing when they realized I was a hearing person. They did what is called sign switching. They slowed down their signing and started to use pigeon or signed English because that was what I was using.

This day had been filled with so much love, joy, and singing while interacting with Deaf people who knew the Lord and were filled with His Spirit. I hated to see this day end, but I knew tomorrow I would once again experience the joy of feeling the presence of the Holy Spirit and looked forward to being trained to carry out His work.

Sunday morning, the last day of our convocation seemed to come too quickly. Once again, upon awakening, I opened the drapes and gazed out at the beautiful rising sun and felt an overwhelming sense of excitement. I thought about the day ahead of me and getting back home tonight to spend time with my family, have dinner with them, and put our kids to bed. I looked forward to spending some private time alone with my husband tonight and sharing with him all I had experienced here.

I missed being with my family. While I felt compelled to be at the conference and to be involved with Deaf ministry, I also struggled with wanting to be home at the same time. *How can I keep my life in balance?* I questioned myself. *I wonder if others struggle with this too.* Although most of the attendees were men, I wondered if they also felt the struggle between family and career. Although I did spend time with my family, it seemed the time with them went too fast. It was important to me to be a good mom to my kids and also be a worker in this ministry. I loved both roles and decided I was really lucky to be able to be part of both in my life.

Once again, this morning's sermon was in ASL with Dorothy starting out with her skit. She portrayed what it would be like to meet St. Peter at the pearly gates when we die. She asked us to search our hearts and think about this. "Will he be standing there to welcome you into heaven or will he ask you why you had not done what the Lord had asked of you while on earth. What will you say?" *That is such a powerful question! I know God wants me to be part of the Deaf ministry and I am doing what I believe He has asked of me. I also want to be around my kids more often. Yet, they are in school and I am available to them a lot more than most other mothers are with their children.* As I thought about this, I realized

God was responding to my concerns. I could trust Him to help me keep my life in balance and do His will.

Then Dorothy continued. "We will all be leaving this convocation today and we will all be going in different directions: North, South, East and West. What will you take with you? What have you learned? Will it make any difference when you get back home?"

I had been thinking a lot about necessary changes during this weekend. I knew we had to encourage and support the Deaf to take an active part in their church services. I had been able to relate to their needs because I recalled my own need to be valued and how I felt as I took an active part in church. We had to help them feel valued, needed, and included as equal participants so they could realize that God could use them, too. I believed this would bring them closer to God and help develop their spiritual life.

After the church service, the closing session and a wonderful dinner, we said our goodbyes as our paths separated in different directions, just like Dorothy had said. There were two buses this time, one heading to the Madison, Wisconsin airport and the other to the Milwaukee airport. My bus was headed to the Milwaukee airport while Sharon was on the bus headed for Madison where she would transfer to a plane headed to O'Hare. Sharon's parents would meet her at O'Hare and drive her back home Sunday night. I was confident knowing she would be in good company with others who could sign and would safely direct her to the correct terminal once they arrived in Madison.

I was scheduled for a direct flight from Milwaukee to Muskegon. I would be home by 5:30 pm and I was very happy I wouldn't have to go through the O'Hare Airport, again. As I sat in the Milwaukee terminal, I began feeling very uneasy as my thoughts focused on flying over Lake Michigan. My mind was filled with "what ifs" again which was creating more anxiety the longer I waited.

What if the plane goes down in Lake Michigan? I recalled watching planes coming from Milwaukee flying directly over our home which was located between Lake Michigan and the landing strip at our airport. The planes flew so close to our house that birds were startled and flew out of the trees in our yard. When I was outside hanging up clothes, I often looked up and waved. I wondered if the passengers could also see me. I knew my kids would be watching the sky and looking for my plane to fly over the house this afternoon. Then, after my plane flew overhead, everyone would jump in the car and meet me at the airport as I landed. I couldn't wait to be home with them!

I checked in at the airport, found my terminal, sat down, and watched and waited for my plane to land. I waited and watched. Watched and waited and waited. It was getting late when I heard over the loud speaker my flight had been delayed for two hours in Detroit. I had really been looking forward to having supper with my family tonight. It was only a half hour flight over Lake Michigan and I would still be home before my kids' bedtime. It seemed every time I thought about flying over the lake, my stomach turned. I kept thinking, *what if the plane goes down in the lake?* To get my mind off the flight over the lake, I started walking, rather pacing, up and down the corridor, looking into the stores and shops in the airport. I found a restaurant and thought about getting something to eat, but wasn't sure I should. My anxiety was getting worse and I didn't want to get sick.

It was much later than the two hour delay we had been previously told when I heard another announcement over the loud speaker. My flight from Detroit was to be delayed even longer, but expected to arrive around 11:30 pm. The airport announced they were giving vouchers for food to be used at a restaurant-bar on the concourse. When I walked up to the desk to get my voucher, I asked what had happened that caused the plane to be delayed for so long.

"Just some engine failure that's taking longer to fix than they had expected," was the airline worker's response.

"Engine failure, are they sending us that same plane?" I asked in shock.

"Yes, it is the same plane, but that won't be a problem. They're fixing it. This is nothing unusual. Don't worry. We have this happen a lot, but the plane will be fixed and you will arrive at your destination safely."

Engine failure. It happens a lot? And, they're sending us that same plane that will fly us over Lake Michigan. Oh, dear God, I just want to get home to my family.

At 11:45 pm, we were told to start boarding and my group was the last one called. As I made my way to the back of the plane, I noticed near the last row, a priest I had seen at the conference. I looked at the seat number and my ticket and took my seat next to him.

"Deaf?" I signed with my pointer finger to my ear and lips raising my eyebrows to indicate I was asking a yes or no question.

"Yes, you were at the Convocation this weekend, too. You Deaf?" he signed back.

"No, I am hearing. My name is Bonnie." I finger-spelled and showed him my name sign. "What's your name?"

"Father Thomas Coughlin."

"Are you heading to Muskegon?" I asked.

"No, I'm changing planes in Grand Rapids and then heading for Rochester, New York. You? Going to Muskegon?"

"Yes, I can't wait to land! The plane will go right over my house once we reach the shoreline. I keep thinking about this plane we are on. It was delayed because of engine failure and now we are flying over Lake Michigan. I worry if the engine has problems again, and we go down, no one will ever find us. It makes me nervous just thinking about it."

"Don't worry. It doesn't do any good. God is with us. We are in His hands and nothing will happen. I promise. You can trust Him," Father Coughlin signed with confidence.

"I trust Him. I just don't trust this plane," I said with a slight smile.

"You say you trust Him, but why do you fear? You are safely in the palm of His hands and nothing is going to happen to you. He is right here."

"You're right. I sometimes forget that. How long have you been a priest?" I asked, trying to keep the conversation going and my mind off Lake Michigan below us.

"I was ordained about four years ago. I went to a Catholic seminary after I graduated from Gallaudet. What about you? What do you do?"

"I'm a stay at home mom most of the times, but sometimes I substitute interpret at the public schools in the hearing impaired program. We only use signing exact English, there. I also volunteer to teach sign language and help out in Deaf ministry at a Lutheran Church in Muskegon, along the lake shore." I pointed to the left side of the top of my left hand to show where Muskegon is located.

"How is that going? Are there many Deaf in your area?"

"We only have about eight of the Deaf who come to church regularly, but have about two hundred Deaf in our area. The older Deaf enjoy getting together with us, having a place to chat, and love to have potlucks. They do attend the church service sometimes with us on Sunday nights. We have a minister who works near the school for Deaf who comes and leads worship in sign language on Sunday nights.

"You have a Deaf minister?" He asked.

"No, the minister we have is hearing and comes over from a Lutheran Church in Flint on the other side of the state near the Michigan School for Deaf. Some of our Deaf members used to attend there."

"I know God will bless your ministry and what you have to offer. I will keep you in my prayers," he signed as we were interrupted by the stewardess, who announced we would be landing soon and we needed to stay seated.

I could feel the downward movement of the plane and cringed as the wheels hit the ground. My ears popped as the stewardess gave more directions to those staying on and those getting off.

"Thank you, Father Coughlin, for relieving me of my anxiety on this flight. I hope you have a safe trip back to New York."

"Goodbye, Bonnie. God Bless."

My husband met me at the airport and on our way home I shared some of the events I had experienced over the weekend. I came into the house, dropped my bags, and checked on each of our children, who were already quietly sleeping, except for the oldest. I thanked God for keeping them safe and bringing me safely back home to them.

As I crawled into bed that night, I thought about all I had learned and experienced over the weekend. The initial experience of feeling left out by being in a group of people who spoke a different language. The acknowledgment of how important I felt to be used by God and how important that experience will be for the Deaf when they begin to lead their worship services. I recalled my own anxiety and my inconsistency of truly trusting God at all times. I realized how much I acted like a hypocrite, one who says she trust God, but still allows fear to take over. If I only focused on what I knew in my heart, anxiety and fear wouldn't get a hold on me.

As I thought more about this I realized how much of a blessing it was that God gave me a seat next to a priest, a Deaf priest at that, instead of a stranger on my trip home over the lake. I felt safe talking (signing) with him which distracted me from my own anxiety provoking, fearful thoughts of crashing into Lake Michigan.

"When I'm afraid, I will trust in you."[25]

Author's note: About 28 years after this experience, while taking a class in Deaf History, at Lansing Community College, Interpreter Training Program, I read about Father Thomas Coughlin, whose picture I recognized in our textbook. He was the first Deaf Catholic priest in America and was listed as one of the famous Deaf persons in our country. The textbook had information about his ordination in 1977 at the Basilica of the Assumption in Baltimore, the oldest Cathedral Church in the United States.[26]

A New Plan
Chapter 21

It felt so good to be safely back home with my family. The following day was our wedding anniversary and we chose to celebrate at our favorite restaurant on the beach of Lake Michigan. I loved to go there and sit near the window where we could see tips of the waves rushing to shore while the snowflakes floated down from the dark night sky. Only, this year the snowflakes weren't coming down so gently. Instead, swirls of gusting wind with heavy snow pushed us into the warm cozy restaurant where we found a perfect place to sit near the fireplace and soak up the warmth from the fire and yet we could still view the snow and the waves.

It was a wonderful time to be together, to sit back and relax. As we reminisced over the past year, I couldn't help but focus on all that had changed in our lives over the past few years and how excited I felt about the way God was leading me.

"You know, Don, if we hadn't left the Catholic Church and joined the Missouri Lutheran Church, all of this would never have happened. I would never have gone to work at the school because I would never have met Leah and Harley at church. I would never have met the other interpreters, attend the sign language classes nor be invited to become part of the Deaf ministry. There never would have been a reason for me meet or become involved with the Deaf population. We wouldn't have been sent to Seward, Nebraska by the church; nor would I have been involved with this Convocation on Deaf Ministry in Wisconsin.

Since it was the Missouri Lutheran Church that sponsored all of these events, none of this would have ever happened if we had remained members of the Catholic Church. I can't believe we never thought to explore the Lutheran Doctrine, nor looked for a Lutheran minister to discuss their church theology with us before we were married. But, the way this all panned out, it seems to have been part of God's plan unfolding all along."

"That's true," Don said. "It certainly does seem God was leading us when we didn't even know it. In all my years at Catholic Central or attending the Catholic Church, I never heard anything about anyone in the church working with the Deaf or any Masses being interpreted for Deaf."

When I told Don about Father Coughlin, who sat next to me on the plane, he was even more surprised to hear there was a priest who was deaf. He was even more amazed when I told him of the different denominations represented by Deaf ministers at the convocation and how they all worked together to share God's message.

"How come we've never heard of any of this before?" he asked.

I didn't know the answer to that. "Perhaps we had just isolated ourselves from others who were not like us or could not hear, just like a lot of hearing people do."

After reminiscing about the events which occurred since our last anniversary, our thoughts brought us to the present and our plans for Christmas. Our schedule was going to be filled with band and orchestra concerts, piano recitals for each of the girls, getting ready for and attending Christmas programs, and Christmas caroling with the Deaf, plus squeezing in Don's and our daughter, Dawn's birthdays. All this plus shopping and wrapping gifts before Christmas!

It always seemed there was never enough time to get through everything the last four or five weeks of the year, no matter how far in advance I tried to plan for it. Yet, like everyone else, we managed. Certainly there was not much time for relaxation. The holidays and events had a way of taking up a lot of time and energy from everyone. I loved this time of year with all the singing, bright lights, and finding special gifts for everyone; but I was also very happy when January came and we could slow down, almost hibernate, before starting fresh again at the turn of the new year.

I didn't have much time to share what I had learned from the convocation with Pastor Neisch, nor anyone else, until our sign language group met again in mid-January. When I told them what the Deaf ministers and church workers advocated for at the convocation, Pastor Neisch, Pastor Karl and the Deaf ministry workers all agreed we needed to encourage the Deaf take more leadership with their worship services. However, the group had difficulty accepting what I reported the Deaf population said about how hearing people made them feel left out and ignored in churches throughout the United States. There were a few of our members who could relate to how that could happen, even though we were trying to show a welcoming, open and loving church.

A few of the group members discussed hiring an interpreter for the regular church services and then invite the Deaf to join us weekly on Sunday mornings. One of the members said he would get back to us after he looked into the cost of hiring an interpreter and explore how we could budget that service. He would then present this proposal to the church council.

Meanwhile, we continued our twice a month services for the Deaf and offered the opportunity for them to take charge and participate. The Deaf seemed to enjoy taking charge of handing out bulletins and taking collection, but not particularly by leading songs or reading from the Bible. I was now much more aware and able to understand their reasoning. English word order doesn't make sense to the Deaf who use ASL and reading the Bible would have been difficult for them. Most of those who were deaf at the convocation were professionals who had been educated in both their cultural language and the English language. However, while at the convocation, I had also learned there was a Bible written for the Deaf in ASL syntax, not English. When I returned home, I ordered three of them and gave them to the Deaf who were interested in reading the Bible for themselves. I hoped they would feel more comfortable reading from this version and signing the message in church, but they didn't.

Our winter that year continued to be exceptionally cold, snowy, and the roads were often very icy. It was getting more difficult for Pastor Neisch to make those long trips across the state after providing services to the Deaf in Saginaw, Pontiac, Lansing, Grand Rapids and finally Muskegon after preaching in Flint on Sunday mornings. Driving home across the state late at night was getting to be a challenge, even treacherous, with snow blowing and the icy road conditions, especially after a long day of preaching. But help was on the way.

God sent us a younger man just out of seminary. This man knew sign language and had been interested in ministering to the Deaf throughout his training. He would soon be ordained and have his own parish in Lowell, which would be much closer for him to drive to our church than for Pastor Neisch to drive across the state. Pastor Fremer would also be more available to the Deaf in our area when needed and it would be much easier for him to be regularly involved with our Deaf ministry.

After his ordination, Pastor Fremer joined our group for Sunday evening potlucks and church services. The Deaf were excited to have another minister interested in their lives and culture as Pastor Neisch was nearing retirement. Many of the Deaf were surprised when they learned how young Pastor Fremer was and that he was a hearing person, who really understood their language, culture, and their needs. Yet, they all still loved to join us when Pastor Neisch was able to come because they had a history with him.

Pastor Fremer stayed with us for the next three years. During that time, another ministry for the Deaf had started up in the Grand Rapids and was going strong. Some of our Deaf began to visit that church occasionally. We also became aware some of our Deaf were also attending another church in our area that had a regular interpreter on Sunday mornings. The interpreter, who signed weekly at that church, had grown up with many of these Deaf adults and already had a relationship with many of them. We were becoming aware there were also several other churches in area, including a Catholic Church, which were providing church services for the Deaf.

With so many opportunities available in our area for the Deaf to attend worship services, we were also aware there were still many other Deaf people in surrounding counties that did not have that same opportunity. There was a growing need for interpreters and ministers to serve them, too. Pastor Fremer questioned if it might be best for him to reach out to those in other counties who didn't have a pastor or church services available to them. When this idea was presented to our Deaf members, some said they enjoyed having two options for church services; one in the morning at the church with an interpreter and other Deaf friends and another available on Sunday evenings with a potluck prior to the service. After much prayer and discussion, a decision was agreed upon. Pastor Fremer would be leaving our group to develop a ministry to the Deaf in the Traverse City area. Our Deaf members knew if they needed him, he could still be reached and they did have several options available to them to worship weekly.

Although I felt sad and disappointed after our Deaf ministry came to an end, I was happy the Deaf had other choices where they could worship. I continued to be very close to the Deaf community and occasionally visited the churches that had interpreters signing during church services. As my own hearing continued to deteriorate, I realized how helpful it was to watch the interpreter when I missed part of what was being said. I was at peace with all that had happened and knew in my heart that God still had a plan for me.

"You will keep in perfect peace, him whose mind is steadfast, because he trusts in you."[27]

A Curve on the Path
Chapter 22

It seemed to be a time of change everywhere, not only with our Deaf ministry, but also in the school system.

Although it was now 1983 and The Rehabilitation Act requiring equal access for communication had been passed ten years prior, very few changes had actually been implemented. The Deaf were now merging together to take a much needed and stronger stance to advocate for their own rights. They were demanding the schools throughout the nation revert back to using ASL, instead of exact English (SEE), which was hindering communication within their culture and between the generations. They argued it was difficult enough for teenagers and parents to have the normal inter-generational conflicts; but using an entirely different language to communicate was creating too much havoc in families and between the generations. The cultural identity and habits of the older Deaf was being lost with this change and they were not going to allow that to continue.

In response to the protests from those who were culturally Deaf, the local school system contracted with the school for Deaf in Flint to evaluate all interpreters and workers of Deaf or hard of hearing within the school system. Since I was a substitute interpreter for Deaf, I was also required to have my skills evaluated.

The day finally came for my turn to drive across the state to be assessed. If I passed, no problem, but if I didn't, I could lose my job and working with the people I loved.

The test did not seem hard to me. The evaluation was based on interpreting many things such as stories, names of famous people and places, math problems, science terms, foods, sports and giving directions. I was confident with my vocabulary, but knew I had some problems with my receptive skills when I was tested to reverse interpret ASL for the hearing.

After taking the test, I drove home with mixed feelings. *I think I did good vs I don't think I passed*, kept running through my head. *What will become of me and my job? Will the Deaf accept me if I failed?* I was sure I didn't compare very well with the interpreters whose first language was ASL. In fact, I knew it. There was no sense obsessing about that test. Nothing would change it. I just had to wait and see.

The test had been videotaped and was to be sent to several evaluators around the state. It would take four to six weeks before I'd get my results back. The person who video-taped me said I would receive a written report summarizing the evaluation of my ASL skill level along with a numerical score. The report would provide feedback on what I did that was good and what I needed to do to improve my skills. It would be up to the school systems to either let go of those who failed, or find other work for them. I was hoping the school would provide more training in ASL for those of us who needed to develop better skills.

After feeling as if I was sitting on pins and needles for weeks, my evaluation letter finally came in the mail. I anxiously tore open the envelope and looked for my score, ignoring what the evaluators had written about my skills. My score was two points lower than the cut off for acceptable. I didn't pass! I felt sick to my stomach. I had been working so hard to pick up ASL by being around the older Deaf and yet I still had to use exact English at school. *What am I going to do now?*

As I began to read the report, I felt a little more hopeful. They were pleased that I had quite an extensive vocabulary, but indicated I often used signed English instead of ASL in sentence structure. My evaluators indicated my signing skills were at the intermediate level and suggested I work with someone using only ASL and then return in three or four months to retake this test.

I sat down feeling sad and humbled that I wasn't good enough. I was embarrassed about my low score, but hopeful if I retook the test, I could pass. *I don't know anything about the type of facial signs they said I needed to use. Who will teach me what I don't know? What's going to happen with my job, now?* My heart sank as I thought about the special education director finding out how poorly I did on this test. *My job will be eliminated!* I thought feeling very sad.

The following week I received a call from the school to once again substitute for an interpreter. Although I was sure by now that the special education director had also received a copy of my evaluation and recommendations, I was stunned I was still being called to substitute as an interpreter.

A few months later, while I was working in one of the schools, I received a message to contact the new coordinator of the H.I. Program immediately. I worried about her urgency and feared this would be the day I would be dismissed from my position as a substitute interpreter. I wished Harley was still with the school system. *If he was still here, he would be very supportive of me continuing to work with the deaf. He would find some place for me and direct me to where I could be the most useful.* But, I didn't have him to rescue me now.

As soon as school was out, I headed toward the office of the new coordinator in the administrative building. I felt devastated as I walked up the steps of the Administration Building expecting to be fired. I also felt ashamed I was still working as a substitute interpreter when I did not meet the recommended skill level by the evaluators.

When I knocked on the door of her office, the coordinator called for me to come inside. She was on the phone, but waved for me to come in and sit down across the desk from her. As I waited for her to put down the phone, my thoughts continued to focus on what I thought she was going to say about my evaluation and then tell me my job was over with the school.

"I understand you did fairly well on your sign language evaluation," she said.

Well? Her comment really threw me for a loop. *Did she even read that report?*

"I just missed the cut off by two points for skills expected for an interpreter," I replied trying to be honest and correcting her. "But, they did say I could return to retake the test to try to raise my score."

"Well, we think you did fine and since you are not a regular interpreter, your substituting here will continue. That's not a problem and we are very thankful we can call on you," she said. "The reason I asked you to come to my office is to explain another need we have in our school system. We often need substitutes in the physically and mentally handicapped program. We also have a few blind students who are being mainstreamed and need some assistance when their aide is out sick. Would you be willing to take on some other substituting positions as a teacher aide in addition to working with the Deaf and hard of hearing?

Instead of being fired as I had expected, I was totally caught off guard by this unexpected offer. For a few moments, I thought about the opportunity to make extra money and also what this might entail. *If I accept this position, I'll be working more hours. That means I'd be away from home more often. Although, for me to add on some extra work hours per week, it really wouldn't be a problem. As a substitute aide and substitute interpreter, I have the option to turn down a job should I have something else I wanted or needed to do. I wonder if this is God plan for me to work with other people who have a variety of disabilities,* I thought. *After all, I am familiar with this population and I did spend a good amount of time with those who had disabilities when I was a younger.*

"Yes, definitely!" I finally responded feeling grateful for being offered this opportunity.

The first day I entered the classroom to substitute for one of the regular aides, I looked around at all the kids. They reminded me of when I was ten years old and my parents forced me to attend Sunday school for the developmentally disabled with my brother. I recalled how I had changed from wanting to avoid them to getting to know them as people with needs and wants just like the rest of us.

As I continued to work with this population, I realized how much that earlier experience had helped me to understand these kids. Some longed to be like others and yet struggled with being able to accomplish simple daily tasks.

My job soon expanded to also helping teachers in over loaded regular education classes as well as special education. I loved being called to work in the classrooms with kids of all different ages, grades, and capabilities. I often recalled my dream to become a teacher someday. That thought kept popping into my head frequently while I interpreted, when I wheeled children with Spinal Bifida down the hall, or when I helped students with reading or math and while driving home after-school. Even if I wasn't the actual teacher, I had a lot of similar responsibilities a teacher has. By being in several different classrooms I had the opportunity to watch excellent teachers who strove to get the educational material across to the students. And, I watched some teachers who simply wrote the assignments on the board for students to work on during class time. I really wanted to work with students who were struggling and to help them in any way I could to learn and understand the material which was given. I believed if I became their teacher, I would make sure they completely understood what was taught. I was sure I would have been a great teacher if I had gone to college; but, being an aide in a classroom was the next best thing to that. I didn't have to write out lesson plans or prepare for the class, but I could still help the students learn.

While thinking back to those teenage years, I recalled the difficulty I had trying to go to college right after high school. *Money had been a huge stumbling block. I did, however, complete almost two full years before I got married. If I had had money or financial help, I would have completed my education back then. But perhaps working with the disabled would not have been my choice back then.*

Now, here I was, married for almost 16 years with five children, thinking about becoming a teacher once again. *How could I possibly afford to go back to school? If I could afford it, where could I go? The closest college I knew about was almost two hours away. I'd have to leave my children every day for a full day, five days a week to attend classes and then spend four hours on the highway driving every day. When I returned home from my classes, there would not be enough time to fix dinner, drive my kids to and from after-school events, or to do my homework. That idea is completely out!*

I really doubted I would ever be able to return to college. *After all, we would soon have kids going to college in three or four years and they would need our financial help.* I decided I would just continue as a substitute teacher aide. However, my desire was still growing.

"For I know the plans I have for you", declares the Lord", plans to prosper you and not to harm you, plans to give you hope and a future."[28]

Returning to College
Chapter 23

The following school year there were talks of federal and state grants being cut for special education programs. The school was in the process of eliminating many programs and letting go of teacher aides. I knew my job was no longer secure.

With all of our kids in school full time, I began to seriously reconsider this might be the right time for me to return to college to complete my teaching degree, even if it meant taking one class at a time. I was sure I wanted to become a special education teacher. I had a lot of experience, but I also knew somehow I needed to make plans to finance this goal. I had also been thinking rather than for me to start college, perhaps it might be better for Don to return to college to get his Master's Degree in Education or to complete the engineering degree which he had almost finished. Due to the lack of engineering jobs available when he would graduate, he switched his major to teaching during his last semester. Don loved teaching and working with kids at the high school. He enjoyed inspiring his students to pursue a mechanical, science, or a technical career. But, for us, raising a family with five children on a teacher's salary was challenging.

While I was working in the H.I. classroom at the junior high level, I had become close friends with one of the teachers. I shared with her my desire to become a teacher for the deaf and handicapped children, which I believed would provide me with better job security and a lot more money to help support our family. I was concerned about the cuts in education and told her if I could find any way to pay for it, I would return to college at least part time to become a teacher.

She advised me to talk to the local community college adviser about getting some financial aid and suggested I consider social work instead. "Although I'm sure you would make a good teacher, you have a heart for this population and want to make changes for the better, which is what a social worker does. I know you would do anything to help this population out and they need someone like you to stand up for them," she said. "Just consider it."

I knew I didn't want to be a social worker. I had heard the deaf talk about going to meet their social worker to get Medicaid and food stamps or fill out forms for other needs. That was not the kind of job I wanted to do. I really wanted to be a teacher.

I did take her advice and made an appointment with an academic adviser at the college. I told her about our family size, economic situation, and my desire to return to college, but also I questioned if it would be better for my husband to advance his education to gain a higher income rather than for me to return to school. I could still volunteer to work with the deaf if my substitute job was eliminated.

I was surprised with what the adviser had to say. "With today's statistics you have a 50% chance of becoming divorced! What would happen to you and your family if your husband left you or had an accident, died or developed a debilitating illness? He already has one degree, but your future could be quite dim if any of these situations happened to you, especially while raising five kids."

I did not expect that advice, but it was true. This was the mid 1980's and many divorces were occurring among many of our friends. *What would happen to us should my husband have an accident or die? How could I make enough money as the bread winner for our family? How could I support five children and afford the life I wanted for them and me?* I hadn't considered any of these situations before.

My adviser and I explored options of colleges with both teaching and social work curriculum's that were close to home. Then she reviewed my transcript from the classes I had completed at our local community college and at Central Michigan University. "I see when you stopped taking classes here in 1967, you only had three more credits to achieve your AA (Associate of Arts Degree). You will have to return here for one full semester to gain those credits back."

"What? Why would I need to take 15 credits when I only needed to get three more credits for the AA? Can't I just take the one class I was lacking?"

"No," she said. "Since you left, there have been several changes. The requirements for an Associate's Degree are different now. Some of those classes won't be accepted by other colleges. For instance, you took a class called Teaching Modern Math which is no longer a viable class. You will need a higher level of math now. How good are your math skills? Can you do quadratics? If you can, you might be able to waver out of the math requirement."

"Well, I had good math skills in high school, but it has been over seventeen years since I have done anything like quadratics. I've been too busy reading Dr. Seuss and changing diapers or driving kids to extracurricular activities, plus working as a substitute aide for special education, and volunteering with Deaf ministry. Those math problems have not crossed my mind in years."

She encouraged me to be the one to pursue my education. "If you start classes next January, you can complete your associates by May. After that, you can transfer to whatever college you want. Personally, I think you should consider Grand Valley State College. It's now an accredited college and it's close enough to your home that you could take classes during the day while your kids are in school. By the time they are out of school, you can be back home. They offer both teaching and social work curriculums. I'd like to set up an appointment with the Grand Valley adviser to help plot out your classes for you to take here and transfer there so you will be ready to start your junior year by next fall. How does that sound?"

"Great, but what's it going to cost? I can't afford classes on my husband's teaching salary."

"I plan to make an appointment for you with our financial adviser, next. She will be able to tell you if you qualify for a Displaced Homemaker Grant or if you need to apply for a loan. I suspect it will be a loan with your husband's salary, but you do have a large family and they may take that into consideration. There may also be some small scholarships available for you to check into."

I took her advice and enrolled in the winter semester of 1984 to finish my associates' degree with plans to transfer to Grand Valley College in the following fall, a thirty minute drive from home.

The ball was rolling. I met with the advisers and applied for a loan. I was required to take one additional class in child development during the summer to prepare me to start my pre-teaching assignment in the fall.

Here I am with five children of my own and I'm about to learn about child development! I thought. *How ironic is that?*

Little did I know this class was going to be an intense study of child psychology and educational theories, but I loved every bit of it as I read about things I knew and things I didn't know as a parent. I learned about Piaget and cognitive development in children, about Erik Erikson's stages of psychosocial development, of Sigmund Freud and his daughter, Anna's theories of the unconscious (id, ego and superego), and B.F. Skinner's theory of behaviorism and operant conditioning.

We studied the various theories of educating children such as the individual/independent learning theory of the Montessori Schools vs the Wilhelm Wundt Schools of Structuralism—two quite different ways of educating children. All of this was so intriguing and fascinating to me, I didn't want to stop learning or reading psychology books. I had outgrown Dr. Seuss and was ready for college!

I graduated with my A.A. in May 1984 and started my fall classes at Grand Valley with a full schedule. My pre-teaching assignment would be twenty minutes away at an elementary school. I was assigned there three days a week from 8 am until 3:30 pm. The other two days of the week, I would need to be in class on campus at Grand Valley by 10:30 am.

My list of "what if's" came back to haunt me. I didn't know how I was going to get our kids off to school on the days I was scheduled to be at the elementary school. Since Don left for work at 6:45 am, he would not be available to help me. I had lunches to pack, hair to brush, checking to make sure our kids brushed their teeth and were wearing appropriate outside clothing for weather conditions - all before rushing out the door on time. *Who would do that for them if I wasn't there?* I hashed this over and over in my mind wondering how this would work out.

I asked around, but couldn't find anyone to help me out at that time of day. I had one choice left. I put an advertisement in the local neighborhood paper and received a response immediately. There was an older lady, who lived about three blocks away and wanted to earn some extra money to go to Florida to visit her son and his family at Christmas. She said she would be willing to come over a little earlier than I needed to help out and stay a little longer if needed to clean up the kitchen, before she locked up the house and left. She was a Godsend and the kids loved her.

As I looked over all I had been doing for my kids, I thought about giving them more responsibility. I decided the kids and my husband could pack their own lunches every night before they went to bed. While it was a simple job of making seven sandwiches and packing fruit and a treat in their bags, the time it took every day, every week, every month added up to a lot of hours that I could use to do my homework or a more difficult chores around the house that I wouldn't ask them to do. This was something easy each one of us could do and it helped me with time management. We also made a list of chores and wrote them out on slips of paper and put them into a jar. Every Sunday night, the girls drew slips of paper from that jar to determine their chores for the following week. My husband designed chore charts for each week and put them up on the refrigerator. The girls had to make their own arrangements if they didn't want to do a job. Sometimes, they traded with each other, especially if the job was conflicting with an after-school event. Other times, one of them would take more jobs than another for one week and trade off a different week. It all worked out and I was able to be at the school in Grand Haven and on campus on time every day without any problems.

Grand Valley was another Godsend for me. Because the next closest college was so far away, I would not have been able to carry a full load. Nor would I have been available to spend as much time with my family as I did by going to GVSU. I felt God was telling me that now the time was right for me to return to college.

God had also provided an opportunity for me to continue to learn more cultural ASL. Although the school system had contracted with a lady to teach ASL in the evenings at the school for those who worked with the Deaf, I could not fit that evening class into my schedule. However, this same lady also offered classes in ASL on Tuesday and Thursday mornings near the Grand Valley Campus. I could attend her class and arrive in time for my classes on campus. When I asked the lady, who was already getting our daughters off to school three days a week, if she would be interested in coming on Tuesday and Thursday mornings as well, she was more than happy to help me out.

I learned a lot more than just improving my signing skills from this teacher. She used lot of positive psychology and often shared information about holistic health. The information she shared was something that came in handy the following summer when I was diagnosed with Epstein Barr (Chronic Fatigue Syndrome). When I phoned her to tell her of my diagnosis, she suggested I research books on immune psychology and natural healing. She recommended I relax, enjoy the summer, look for humor in everything and start taking large doses of vitamin C. Then she referred me to a book, "Anatomy of an Illness *as perceived by the patient: reflection on healing and regeneration*", by Norman Cousins. In his book, he wrote about how he struggled with a debilitating illness for ten years and after taking charge of his health, he survived for thirty-six years longer than his doctors had expected. It was an excellent book and I followed her suggestions after reading the book and researching the power of vitamin C and immunology. I learned about choosing to let the illness control me or to take steps to control the illness. I quickly regained my strength and energy and was ready to restart my classes in the fall.

One of this lady's frequent sayings has always stayed with me. She often reminded us "when you connect with your energy source, you will shine like a lamp connected to an outlet." Her words reminded me of the Bible verse "You are the light of the world. A city on a hill cannot be hidden." [22] For me, that source was God and I was already experiencing the joy and energy of good health and being His servant.

I really enjoyed my pre-teaching assignment I had taken my first semester at Grand Valley. I worked with first to third graders in the morning and fourth to sixth graders in the afternoon. I was particularly fascinated with learning the Schmerler Reading Program. The students were first taught the sounds of all the vowels and combination of vowels by voicing these sounds in a specific rhythmic pattern while clapping their hands to the beat. After learning the sounds of vowels and combinations of vowels, the consonants were taught later. I was amazed at how quickly the students learned to read, pronounce unfamiliar words correctly, and spell accurately after learning this system. Their reading skills soared! In a short time, they caught up with their peers in regular education classes. While I enjoyed teaching reading and math, I found I myself more interested in finding the reason for the children to be unable to settle down to learn. I wondered why they often exhibited negative behaviors and had difficulty following rules. I thought about Anna Freud's theory I had studied during the past summer and wondered if these children were exhibiting negative behaviors that were interfering with their ability to learn, were due to family issues or attention they got from negative behaviors. When the school counselor came to work with the students, I wanted to observe her sessions, but I was not allowed to attend them because I was not there as an intern in psychology. I did, however, try to understand each child individually and what positive rewards could be given to help him or her adjust to peers, learning, and cooperating. The teachers I worked with demonstrated mastery skills in all of these areas and I was so fortunate to be a student under their supervision.

I was changing as a mom, too, during this time. I started listening more to my own kids. I became more aware of their needs and not what I thought they needed. I was becoming more open to other parenting methods and shared them with my husband. We started utilizing more positive reinforcement and educational ways to discipline instead of the punishments we had been giving. But then, where had my husband and I learned our parenting skills? Like everyone else, we learned from those who had raised us. It was a different time and a different generation from that in which my husband and I had grown up. Values and customs had changed a lot between our generation and that of our children. By the time that semester was over, I had changed significantly.

I took more classes in child psychology and behavioral modification, offered through the special education program, but I was stimulated to learn more than this. I felt driven to take as many psychology classes as I could while I continued in the teaching program during that next semester. But, my heart kept telling me to drop these classes in education and to not continue in this field as I had planned. I chose to take an elective class in neuropsychology that spring and became obsessed with taking even more psychology classes. I kept telling myself, "If I take more psychology than the educational curriculum requires, I won't graduate on the time schedule my husband and I had planned." Yet, this didn't seem to matter and trying to mentally reason with myself wasn't diminishing my hunger for more psychology.

I tried not to listen to my heart. I kept trying to stay focused on the classes that would lead to a degree in teaching, not psychology. I had made an agreement with my husband to return to college for two years, complete my teaching degree, get a job and spend summers at home instead of working so we would be able to do more things with the family. That was my goal, his goal, and even the goal of my parents, who were so proud of me they were already telling everyone I was getting my teaching degree. I did enjoy teaching, but this internal conflict would not stop. I finished my junior year preparing to start the fall semester by doing my internship as a teacher. I didn't take any classes during that summer. The thought of starting in the fall to prepare for my final course work for teaching haunted me. I felt panicky. Whenever I thought about continuing in the teaching program, my heart seemed to beat like a red light flashing as to indicate I was off course.

Finally, I came to a decision. It was the last day for dropping and/or adding classes before the start of this semester. I had registered for all my classes before the end of the spring semester, but I still had a strong feeling I should drop all of those classes and sign up for psychology classes instead. I drove over to GVSU, walked around campus, walked through the School of Education, and then the Psychology Department as I thought about changing my career. I sat down on a bench outside the library watching others walking around the campus, wondering if they ever had this much trouble trying to stay in a program when their heart was telling them something else. After sitting there awhile thinking over my choices, I got up and walked into the registrar's office. I was going to change my career discipline. When I made my request to drop all of my classes and take other classes known to the registrar, I was told I had to first meet with the department head of the education before I could drop any classes. After that, if I wanted to change my major to psychology, I also had to meet with the department head of psychology or one of their advisors. I would have to do all of this today and it was already getting close to closing time.

When I met with the department head of education, he seemed more upset than I expected. He did not like my request to drop out of the teaching program without first consulting him months ago. He accused me of having cold feet about teaching.

"Have you even thought about this?" he asked.

"I have thought about this for about ten months now and I don't have cold feet, because I have spent a lot of time in various classrooms and worked with many special education students. I have a very strong feeling I need to do this. I also have considered if this doesn't work out and I change my mind, I can always return to get my teaching degree. If that happens, I will have a lot more understanding of behaviors and personalities to utilize in the classroom than I would have with just a teaching degree."

"I really don't like this. I think you would make a good teacher. I won't sign this drop slip until you meet with the department head of psychology. If he agrees and can get you into his program this late for the fall semester, then I will agree to drop you from the teaching program. You'll have to hurry as it is about time for us to leave today.

The psychology department head advisor happened to still be in his office and was willing to meet with me immediately. I explained what I wanted to do and why.

"Well, give me a little time to check some things out. If you switch to this program, I need to find an internship for you immediately because you are so close to graduating. You will need some hands-on experience. Come back in an hour so we can talk again. I'll let you know at that time if I can get an internship lined up for you. You will need to take more psychology classes along with an internship. Here is the list of classes you will need to take to graduate from this program. See what classes are open and if you can schedule those classes this fall and winter terms. I'll talk to you later, good luck!"

I went back to the registration desk and found all the classes were still available and I could sign up for them. I checked the classes needed for the winter term which would work with my ability to get to campus. I had decided that if I couldn't get into a psychology internship this year, I would do it when I could and then get the degree later. I was content with that.

When I returned to the psychology department head's office, the department advisor greeted me with a smile.

"I think I've got everything arranged for you now," he said. "How do you feel about working with the developmentally disabled population?"

"Not a problem. I have spent a lot of time working as a substitute aide in many special education programs for our local school district."

"Well, I have an arrangement with the lead psychologist at a center for the developmentally disabled and he is willing to accept you for an internship during the winter semester. If you are able to get into those classes I listed for you earlier, you will graduate in the spring."

"They're all available and work into my schedule," I said feeling relieved that this was working out so smoothly.

He signed the add classes form for registration. Then I left to meet with the teaching department head. He reluctantly signed my drop classes' form and shook his head, saying he did not know why I would do such a thing on the spur of the moment. I reminded him that it was not a spur of the moment decision, but something I had struggled with for the past ten months or more since starting my pre-teaching assignment.

"I just don't understand why you didn't come to talk to me," he said.

I responded that it was about me and I had to come to this conclusion on my own.

As I drove home, I thought about what my husband's response would be when I told him what I had finally decided. I hoped he would be supportive of my decision and prayed it was not something whimsical I was doing. In my heart I knew it was what I needed to do and felt confident I was doing the right thing.

"So, what kind of job can you get with a bachelors' degree in psychology?" he asked. "I had hoped you would be done in two years and we could travel and do things other families do in the summer. I doubt if you can get a job with only a bachelor's degree in psychology and suspect you will need to further your education."

"I don't know what jobs are out there. I just know this is what I have to do and I hope it is the right thing. They have an internship already set up for me to work with the developmentally disabled during the winter term and I won't have to drive all the way over to Grand Rapids. I can be home every evening."

"Well, I really hope this works out and it is what you want."

I felt at peace going to bed that night and looked forward to starting classes the next day.

"A heart at peace gives life to the body..."[30]

My Senior Year
Chapter 24

After dropping all my classes in the teacher education program, I signed up for a full load of psychology classes in preparation for my internship during the next semester. While I thoroughly enjoyed all of these classes and breezed through them carrying almost a straight A average, I spent a tremendous amount of time preparing and writing research papers. At times I found myself experiencing internal and emotional conflicts as I read what was considered normal or healthy while I also faced my own dysfunctional beliefs about the way I thought things should be. I recognized my own family of origin's dynamics, patterns of communication and family roles was not as normal (or emotionally healthy) as I had grown up thinking they were. I struggled as I looked back at my own past while realizing my husband and I had already created the same dynamics in our own family with our children. I began to feel like a failure as a parent. I was determined to take steps for our family to become less dysfunctional. Yet, I wondered how we could suddenly make changes in our family system that was already in motion. I knew I had a lot to learn.

I also recalled the words of my professor while taking an abnormal psychology class the year before. At the beginning of his first class, he made a statement that there was a tendency with new students to try to diagnose him or herself when studying the different mental illnesses and personality disorders in this class. He said it was common for some students to recognize the negative patterns and believe he or she may have one of the mental illnesses. He also stated if this happens, just remember there is a continuum of behaviors that ranges from minimal to severe and dysfunctional to functional dysfunction to some degree in every one of us. He further indicated that if anything continued to bother any of us or if we felt we needed to talk to him to just check out if we were normal or not, we were welcomed to make an appointment with him and he would be glad to reassure us we were okay or direct us to getting help if we needed it.

As you might guess, for peace of mind, before the end of the current semester and before I started my psychology internship, I met with this professor to discuss family dynamics. I shared with him my concern about what I was learning about the dynamics in my family of origin and my own dysfunctional patterns that were already emerging in our own family.

I told him about my childhood. "By the time I was ten years old, I had a five year old brother, a two year old sister and a new baby sister. My mother had been depressed most of my childhood, particularly because my dad was unable to find a steady job for many years after he returned home from the Navy during W.W.II. She was overwhelmed with finances and had difficulty accepting and dealing with issues surrounding my brother's mental and behavioral disabilities. I tried to make her happy. I jumped in to take care of my siblings and help with household chores. I had tried to be the best helper I could be for her with hope she would not be so sad and depressed. I also grew up knowing it was best to not ask or expect anything from my parents because it just stressed them out." I continued, "Yet, I have done similar things with my kids and have expected a lot from them, especially my oldest daughter. I have given each of them a lot of responsibility. By the time my oldest daughter was ten years old, I didn't understand why she wanted to go outside to play. I thought she should want to stay inside and do chores."

"Do your children have any friends or outside activities?" He asked.

"Yes, they have a lot of friends. In the summers they play soft ball and I take them to swimming lessons. During the school year they have music lessons and are in sports at school. They are also involved in church and youth group."

"Nothing too serious to worry about, then," he said with a smile. "Sounds like they learned to have a good amount of responsibility and they seem to have a balanced life. What is most important is for children to know they are loved and because you are concerned about them, I suspect they know that. But you may want to make an appointment with a therapist to help you change some of your thinking and the family patterns that worry you."

I was thankful to find out I was only a normal neurotic, as Freud would say. Before I left his office he had one more suggestion, "Why don't you stop by the library and see if they still have a video called "The Pinks and Blues". It is about how we train girls to be girls and boys to be boys, and how gender roles have been changing over the years."

I took his advice and picked up the video. I was glad I had watched it and could understand how my generation and generations past had been given roles according to their gender and how that could be changed.

January seemed to come quickly and it was time to start my internship to work with developmentally disabled adults. On my first morning there, I was introduced to my internship supervisor and many people at an interdisciplinary meeting, where professionals and staff were discussing diagnosis, treatment, and progress of those residents living there. As I left the meeting with the psychologist and walked down the hall, he explained the layout of the building, showed me the behavioral treatment rooms and talked about the behavioral programs. He explained the reason the dorm halls were locked with residents inside. Then he unlocked the door to the hall where his office was located. A short man stood just inside the door, as if monitoring who was coming in or going out.

"Hello, my name is Bonnie," I said with a smile as I put my hand out to shake his. He smiled back and extended his hand. He continued to stand there and watch as the psychologist unlocked and opened the door to his office to let me in and then closed and locked it behind us.

"Why did you do that?" he asked.

"Do what?" I asked.

"Offer to shake his hand."

"I don't know," I replied feeling confused about why he would ask such a question. "Why? Isn't that what you're supposed to do when you meet someone?" I said, with a nervous giggle.

"I just want to know if it was instinct or learned behavior."

"I don't know," I replied thinking this was such a weird question to be asked. "Probably both," I replied thinking this was such a weird question to be asked.

"Well, I should let you know. If you had not offered to shake hands, he would have tried to throw you down on the floor."

"What? You would let that happen to me?"

"No. I would have intervened, but you must be careful of this population. They are violent at times for no reason. You need to be on guard while here. Stay close to me or one of the trainers and you will be okay."

I did not expect that kind of answer nor the extreme negative behaviors I was about to witness. I was assigned a few residents to work with during my internship and spent a good amount of time studying their histories from the time of their birth and their mother's prenatal experiences. Many of the mothers had taken either legal or illegal drugs prior to or during their pregnancies. Many had stressful pregnancies and/or deliveries. Many of the residents had lived most of their lives as wards of the state in an institution. Many of their behaviors were unacceptable in public, such as biting people, smearing feces, head banging and screaming, to mention a few.

My job would be to write out behavioral treatment programs, starting with a baseline and implement step-by-step procedures to measure the success of changing behaviors which included a reward system. I found Pavlov's Stimulus-Response Theories and other Social Learning Theories I had learned about in my psychology classes were extremely helpful for me while working with this population.

Under the psychologist's direction, I tested residents on their daily living skills and used other psychological testing to assess their IQ and placement needs. All of this was very interesting and fascinating to me.

Toward the end of this semester, my internship supervisor asked me to help put information into a computer which was only available for this kind of use after the normal working day hours. He was evaluating the effect of long term medications on behaviors and needed to write reports for his presentations from the material he had gathered. I agreed to stay a few nights to help him complete his study. I enjoyed working with him and learning how some of anti-psychotic medications can have positive effects on behavior while also having negative biochemical effects on the body.

About four weeks before the end of the semester, the psychologist asked me to come back into his office to discuss his evaluation of my work. He said he had written a report to my academic adviser, who was also the department head of psychology at GVSU. He had to make a recommendation, but he wanted me to be aware of what he wrote and planned to say before he sent it. He said I also needed to write an evaluation of my own concerning my internship experience.

I was in agreement with all he had written about me and my work until I got to his final summary and recommendation in which he stated: "I recommend that Bonnie consider social work instead of psychology for her career goal."

What? I was stunned. *He had written a lot of good things about me, but he doesn't think I'd be a good psychologist. What did I do wrong?*

"Why are you not recommending me for a career in psychology?" I asked.

"You don't strike me as a psychologist. Remember the first day you came into this hall? You knew instinctively how to handle that resident."

"Yes," I said, "but what does that have to do with not becoming a psychologist?"

"You have a lot of intuition and empathy towards others. You search for <u>why</u> a behavior is such, and what the person has gone through to be that way. The way you do your work is much more like a social worker. You're ready to explore alternatives, which is what a social worker does. A psychologist is concerned about testing and typically doesn't look for reasons. We are concerned with test scores, medians, norms, deviations, etc. While you did well during your internship here, you are more focused on exploring the person's needs rather than the testing and measuring."

I took a gulp, feeling downhearted and not sure what I was going to do with that kind of recommendation. I wasn't sure if I would even be able to graduate with a Bachelor's Degree in Psychology with him stating I'd make a better social worker in his report. I didn't want to be a social worker. I wanted to listen to people and help them change. That was not something this population could do given their cognitive and physical abilities; but once out of the developmentally disabled environment, there would be people for me to help. I just did not want to be a social worker who would sit at a desk and help people fill out applications for financial assistance.

I cringed at the idea of meeting with the head advisor of the psychology department to go over the report from my internship adviser. I felt sad and upset when the day came to meet with him.

"How did you do with your internship?" he asked.

"My internship adviser said I'd make a better social worker than a psychologist," I said feeling very embarrassed and humbled. "I guess I didn't do as well as I thought I would do."

"I read his report and spoke with him. We talked at length and he spoke very highly of you. He is very confident that you would make an excellent social worker. He said he was impressed that you have a lot of knowledge concerning how people think and feel. He also said you are in touch with your own feelings and intuition. That will be something you will need if you choose to go into social work. GVSU now has an excellent Masters' Degree program in Social Work (MSW). I'd like to see you enter that program this fall."

"I don't really like the idea of becoming a social worker," I said. I thought about the plans I had made three years ago to go back to school for two years, get my teaching degree, and be done with school. If I decided to go for a Master's Degree in Social Work, I would have another two to four years of college. That would be more education than my husband has.

Once again, I thought, *if anyone should return to college for a higher degree, it should be Don. He is super intelligent, reads faster than anyone I know, and can troubleshoot anything very quickly.*

"Well, give it some thought and get back to me soon. There are still some spots open. I can see that you can get into classes when they start this fall. Give me a call back in a few days. If you decide to start this fall, make another appointment with me. Oh, don't worry about graduating. You did fine and the internship is a pass or no pass credit."

"Thank you," I said as I walked out the door thinking about the cost of more education, more time doing more research papers, more time on the computer, driving back and forth to Grand Rapids in all kinds of weather, and less time with my husband and kids. *What did I get myself into?* I questioned. *Maybe I should go back to the teaching curriculum.* But once again, something inside me said to go ahead and enroll in the social work program.

I called the head of the psychology department and told him I decided to enroll in the Master of Social Work program that fall. I also informed him I would only take two classes to give me time to think over and consider whether this was a career I might want. If by the end of the semester, it was not what I wanted, I would drop out of the program. He agreed and I got into the Master's Degree program very easily.

"Do not let your heart be troubled. Trust in God...."[31]

Growing Through Adolescence
Chapter 25

Although I really doubted I would stay in the social work program, I was open to exploring what it was about since I seemed to be directed into this career by others who knew me pretty well.

One of my first two classes in the MSW program involved the history of social work starting as far back as Moses. He was definitely a leader who during Biblical days made many changes for God's people as he led them out of bondage from the Egyptian Pharaoh. As we studied many social workers throughout history and how they worked to make changes for the better, especially for those less fortunate, I began to understand why my friends and many other people along my path had tried to direct me into social work. I had always been a helper and concerned about those who had difficulties or were underprivileged. I wanted people to have better lives and equal opportunities. I wanted people to get along with each other and to be happy. As my interest in social work grew, I became excited about entering this career. I realized God had been putting all those people in my path because this was where he wanted me to be.

The other class I took had to do with different cultures and behaviors in a variety of social environments. This class provided me with a deeper awareness (from a psychological and developmental perspective) of my how my own life evolved and was still evolving.

During our first session in this class, the professor asked us to choose one of Erik Erikson's eight stages of life from his theory on the stages of psychosocial development.[32] The professor began asking each of us according to the alphabetical order of our last names, to choose one of these eight stages of life to work on for the entire semester, climaxing to a one hour presentation in class at the end of the semester. I had already studied all of these stages in a previous psychology class and had found them all very interesting. As I listened as each person made his or her choice, I had difficulty determining which stage I would like to work on for the entire semester. Because no one had made the choice to work on the stage of adolescence by the time the professor got to the end of the alphabet, there was only one other student left to make a choice besides me. So, he assigned that stage to both of us.

I thought this would be an easy assignment for me considering I already had three teenagers at home going through this stage. Little did I know how much I would personally be impacted by this assignment.

As I gained a deeper understanding of the dynamics which occurred during this stage of adolescence, I couldn't help but think back to my own teenage years, as well as what my own teenagers were currently going through psychologically, socially and emotionally. I had been totally blind to the importance of this stage and ignorant to what adolescents actually have to work through before reaching adulthood. I was oblivious to the extent parents impacted their own child's identity and maturity as their teenager progressed toward individualization. Although a difficult period for both parents and teens, I knew conflicts between the generations were considered to be normal. I was aware teenagers wanted to be different, especially from their parents and the generation before them. Yet, I never had a clue as to why this occurred, nor the depth of importance this stage had on one's entire life.

I grew increasingly aware of the many issues and the internal conflicts adolescents had to face progressing from their childhood into adulthood. It was the time in their lives for setting goals and making many choices for their futures such as their careers, families, and friends. They would be developing their own identity and building relationships, as well as accepting their own physical changes and growth.

According to Erikson's theory, the teenage years were full of ups and downs. Those who did not have a strong sense of self by this time in their life would be unsure exactly what their role in society would be and would have difficulty trying to fit into groups. They would feel confused and lost about what they wanted in their future, their relationships or career. It was often a time of trial and error as they tried to understand what they wanted but often doing what others expected of them. Many of the teens in this group would do anything to be accepted by their social group. In the worse scenario, some would go against their family values or society norms to please their friends who also had these same issues. This group would tend to develop a negative sense of self. Unfortunately, for some in this group, their choices often led them into gang activity where they could find acceptance with others who were also looking for acceptance.

Those who had developed a stronger sense of identity by this time would become industrious, ambitious, and trustful. They would be more confident about themselves and their goals in life. They would welcome the chance to take on responsibility as they matured and entered into adulthood.

Erik Erikson also mentioned if the stage of developing identity was not resolved during the teen years, a second opportunity would reappear again during middle age (approximately between the ages of thirty-five to forty-five years old). This would provide the individual with another opportunity to resolve their internal conflicts, develop their identity and mature.

I felt stunned as I studied this theory as I thought how close this was describing me. Although I was very mature at an early age, and had been pretty much the perfect teenager by never caused any trouble and never daring to ignore my parents' rules (that is until after I was nineteen years old and began dating my future husband), I really did not develop my own identity. I did just as my parents had said. I got married and took on the role of wife and mother as they had expected. I didn't have the needed support to allow me to explore any other goals for my life. I was obedient and respectful of them since they were my parents. I did as they said and became the caretaker I thought girls were supposed to be. Only now I was stepping out of that role and into a role I hadn't planned. When friends began to ask me about taking college classes and my career plans, I often laughed and I said, "I still don't know what I want to be when I grow up".

But here I was sitting in this class still wondering what I really wanted. I was forty years old and just now struggling through my own identify crisis! I felt sorry for my poor husband who had to deal with his wife and three of his daughters who were all going through this stage with the same emotional ups and downs of trying to find out who they are while not knowing what they wanted to be. I felt it was not by coincidence I was assigned this stage of life to study in depth for the next three months! *What is my actual career goal?* I wondered. I decided to leave that in God's hands and let him continue to lead me.

My moods had been like a roller coaster as I was torn between my deep desire to learn and have a career while trying to be the mother who was involved in everything with her kids. Three years prior, when I returned to college, I had made a difficult decision to change my life and our family lifestyle. I was going to be a teacher. I felt like a trapeze artist who either had to hold on to what was behind her or reach out to grasp what could be. I had gone too far to turn back. I not only had to complete my education because I had student loans to repay, but because I had spent the past three years seeking a career to help our family financially. Whatever I chose to do, I couldn't hold on to what was. I could either stop, drop of out of college, and get a job or move forward with my education and enter a career I liked.

All of our kids were in school full time by now. Our youngest daughter was in fourth grade and our oldest daughter had just started college. Our second daughter was in her senior year of high school with plans for college, too.

Now that I was a student, my life was so much different. Unlike my past, of sleeping in on Saturdays or doing whatever I wanted as I wanted, I was spending most of my days focusing on writing papers while our kids were practicing music, doing their homework, cleaning their rooms or spending time with friends. As much as possible, I worked my studying around them and their schedules. My weekdays and evenings were also quite different. Sometimes after class or late at night, I drove over to the high school parking lot where I sat in my car studying while waiting for our daughters' school bus to return home with their team after an away game. On Sundays we went to church as a family and after a big Sunday dinner we spent time together often visiting our parents or other family members. Although I was not always available, I tried to attend most of our kids sporting events and concerts. Our weekday evenings often found us all sitting around the dining room table doing our homework together. Even my husband sat with us correcting papers or developing his lesson plans.

As I sat in class recalling what life was like, I began wondering, *Who am I, really? I feel like a student, but not a mother anymore.* It seemed I had lost my place at home and began to feel very sad and alone.

I wondered how others perceived me. *Maybe I am like the adolescent who is looking to be what others expect of her,* I questioned myself as I reflected on all the people who directed me into this program including the psychology adviser who thought I would make a good social worker. As I thought about all of this, I recalled one of my professors who encouraged his students to never let anyone else define you. I sat there feeling more confused and lost since I couldn't define who I was.

I finally decided the best thing I could do for myself, at this time was to accept where I was in my stage of life and what I was experiencing now. I decided to continue to let God lead me. I believed too many things had happened that was part of His bigger plan and prayed I was doing the right thing for me and our family.

Kathy, who was my partner in researching and preparing for our joint class presentation, had already been working with adolescents and dysfunctional families in the area of substance abuse. Although she did not have any children of her own, she knew so much more than I did about adolescent negative behaviors and experiences.

There is an old Buddhist proverb that says, "When the student is ready, the teacher will appear." Kathy was that teacher for me. She was a mentor and another Godsend. She listened as I shared some of my history and concerns about the difficulty teenagers have going through this stage of life. We talked about all the different family dynamics that either hindered or helped them navigate this stage so they could successfully make it into adulthood.

I found myself feeling disturbed at times as I grew more empathetic to my own children and others going through this stage. I could understand the impact this stage could have on their futures if they didn't develop a healthy sense of self. I was also grieving the loss of my own lost childhood and felt confronted with guilt for not feeling like I was a good enough mother. I wished I had been better equipped to understanding the needs of my teenagers earlier in their lives.

After sharing what some of my childhood and adolescent years were like with Kathy, she expressed her thoughts that my parents might have had some sort of addiction.

"That's absurd!" I'd respond. "My parents were not alcoholic! They forbid drinking and wouldn't allow any alcohol in our home. They talked negatively about anyone who even drank one glass of wine or beer. My dad would not allow that because his dad was an alcoholic and his parents divorced because of that. His dad died at an early age because of his drinking. My dad had to quit high school and go to work in the celery fields to support his mother and siblings until he joined the Navy in World War II. His mother remarried a man whom I believed was abusive and whom I feared when I was growing up."

I continued to share with Kathy my mother's reasons for not using alcohol. "According to my grandmother, my maternal grandfather played in a band at bars, drank heavily and was a womanizer. My mother had to grow up without a father because my grandmother divorced him when my mom was a toddler. Because my grandmother had to work full time, she wasn't around my mom much. My mom was raised by a very strict old-fashioned aunt who was very superstitious. When my mom was a teenager, her mother remarried. My mom never liked her step father because he drank too much and eventually left my grandmother for another woman."

No matter how much I denied alcohol or any other addictions in my family, Kathy continued to believe I had grown up with family dynamics which were similar to those in a home where addictions existed.

At the end of the semester, after we completed our presentation, Kathy handed me a book to read titled, "Adult

Children of Alcoholics and Dysfunctional Families" by Janet Woititz. "I think this book will help you understand yourself. Read it over Christmas break. It is only about100 pages and it's very easy to read. It's my present to you for being such a good partner in this class. I know you have personally struggled but grown through this stage of development. Let me know what you think when I see you back next semester."

Classes were coming to an end and I was completely convinced this was the career for me and was sure I wanted to work with teenagers. During Christmas vacation I read the book Kathy had given to me and cried through most of it. It seemed as if the author had written this book about me and my family.

I realized Kathy was right. One did not have to be an alcoholic or have any addictions to exhibit those same patterns of family dysfunction they had experienced while growing up. I knew I had so much more to learn, but before I could help others. I needed to work on changing myself first. I had to learn to establish interpersonal boundaries, and that often meant learning how and when to say no to others. I had to learn to do things in moderation. I was ready to start making those changes and found a therapist who guided me through that.

In January, I started the second semester of the social work program with a class in cultural diversity. In this particular class we were divided into small discussion groups after our lectures which focused on creating awareness of people of different cultures, behaviors and lifestyles. This was part of our social work training which would help to broaden our perspectives as we learned to accept and develop tolerance of others who may be different from what we were familiar or expected. We were learning to view people through the eyes of our creator and to try understand others from their viewpoint, not just our own perception of them. I loved this class and had a deep respect for a couple of the men in my study group who were understanding, caring, and empathetic of others.

About halfway through the semester, our professor announced, "I am going to do something different with our next presentation. I am asking all of you to say nothing today about what you are about to hear. This is the true heartbreaking story of two people you already know in this class and it may take a few days to absorb what they have to say." She then introduced the two men from my group.

I was stunned when these two men announced they were homosexuals who struggled with their identity for years. When they finally came out of the closet, their family, church, and loved ones turned their backs on them. They didn't fit in anywhere. They had tried many ways to change their feelings, thoughts, and behaviors, but nothing helped. No one accepted them. Nor could they really accept themselves. They withdrew from church. Suicide seemed to be the only way out, but that didn't seem like the answer they really wanted. Soon they began to find others going through a similar experience and started a support group, focusing on validating the skills and talents they did have. As more and more people joined their group, their self-esteem and self-worth grew. They were no longer alone. As others were "coming out" and announcing they were also gay or lesbian, more straight people were also becoming more willing to accept them.

I sat there feeling shaken as I listened to them speak. *Oh, I can't believe what I am hearing! These two men have been awesome in our study group. If I needed a therapist, I would choose one of them. If they had committed suicide, the world would have been at a loss for them and others like them. They are so caring, gentle, and empathetic as they speak about things they disagreed with in our group discussions.*

One time during our group discussions, the thought occurred to *me if I was younger and not already married to my best friend, the man I adored, and who had the same qualities as these two men, I could easily fall in love with either one of them. But, how could I accept them now? How could I not?*

I was taught according to the Bible that homosexuality was a sin. It was contrary to God's plan and they would not be accepted into heaven because of their sexual orientation. Now I had to think about this and be ready to discuss this issue in class later this week with these two men present. I wondered how this new knowledge about them would change my perspective and relationship with these two classmates. I didn't know if I could accept them. Except, I had already accepted them and admired their skills and abilities!

I understood why our instructor did not want us to discuss this in our study group for a few days. We all needed time to digest this shocking news. I had mixed feelings and was sure others in the class did too. We had to come to some conclusions ourselves, before discussing this in our group, in which they were also participants.

I thought long and hard about this and my own values, at least the values I had accepted growing up. I wondered what the Bible actually said. Were they really going to Hell for their homosexual behavior? Was it or was it not their choice to be homosexual? Was it psychological? Did they miss having a father or maternal image while growing up? Were they abused? I had recalled hearing of mothers who had a son instead of a daughter, dressing their sons in frilly dresses and treated them like little girls instead of boys. There also had been a lot of reports in the news during the 1970's about hormones being put into our livestock which then gets into our bodies. I wondered if this could also affect homosexuality in some people. If so, homosexuals couldn't help what happened to them. But if that was true, why did it happen to only a few people and not everyone? All these questions made me think of what I had learned growing up about God's love for all of His children. I took out my Bible to search for answers and take notes.

Here are the verses which helped me put this issue into perspective regarding our beliefs about someone else or their behaviors not measuring up to acting like a Christian.

- "If anyone of you is without sin, let him be the first to throw the stone..."[33]
- "There is no one righteous, not even one..."[34]
- "...Anyone who speaks against his brother or judges him speaks against the law and judges it. When you judge the law, you are not keeping it, but sitting on judgment on it...But you, who are you to judge your neighbor?"[35]

The next verse was so powerful: "If you really keep the royal law found in Scripture, 'Love your neighbor as yourself', you are doing right. But if you show favoritism, you sin and are convicted by the law as lawbreakers. For whoever keeps the whole law and yet stumbles, at just one point, is guilty of breaking all of it."[36] Throughout the Bible, we are reminded to not judge. So, what the Bible is telling us is that we are condemning ourselves if we choose to judge others. As Christians, I believe we are to strive to be like Jesus and to focus on seeing others through the eyes of love, not hate. "...The Lord does not look at the things man looks at. Man looks at the outward appearance, but the Lord looks at the heart." [37] This verse seemed to hit the nail on the head for all of us and brought me back to the first verses I had read that we are all sinners and that means we are all ungodly." "...Christ died for the ungodly."[38]

Throughout the Bible, we are reminded to love others and not judge. So, if we choose to judge others, the Bible makes it clear that we are condemning ourselves.

So, what is it we should be doing instead of evaluating, judging, or accusing others of not being worth our Savior's grace?

As Christians, I believe we are to strive to be like Jesus and to focus on seeing others through the eyes of love, not hate.

I recalled repeatedly hearing in church that Jesus came into the world while we were in darkness to save us, not condemn us. "But, God demonstrates His own love for us in this: While we were still sinners, Christ died for us." [39]

The more I read, the more relieved I felt. I had come to my final conclusion, which meant I was to strive to become more loving toward others and show acceptance for all God created. It was not my place to judge others. I understood the need to step back and to let God be the judge. This freed me to focus on my own relationship with God and His commandment to "..Love thy neighbor as thyself." [40] We need to stop and think before we judge because we are told we will be judged in the same way. [41]

I did not read anything about salvation depending on what we do, but instead, it was what Jesus did for us. Even when we did not know Him, even before we were born, He gave his life for us. I was determined I'd focus on these Biblical truths and try to exhibit them in my own life.

In this class I had been learning to not expect others to have the same values or beliefs I had. Now I had come face to face with that exact issue. I was put to the test. I was not God and so I decided to let God be God and I would be whom He wanted me to be. That was all there was to it. I felt peaceful coming to this conclusion. I would share love and be accepting of others as He asks us to do. Although others, especially those reading this book, may not agree with me, I was beginning to understand how to become a stronger Christian, more Christ like and to let go of what I viewed and deemed to be not good in others. I would try to see others through Christ's eyes.

"For God did not send His Son into the world to condemn the world, but to save the world through Him." [42]

Unexpected News
Chapter 26

The third Sunday of the following January our pastor gave a sermon on the matter of Right to Life. There was a lot of support mentioned in the sermon for those who had a child out of wedlock. When church was adjourned we were given brochures from local chapters of Muskegon Pregnancy, Planned Parenthood and Right to Life.

After we returned home and while I was putting dinner in the oven, the phone rang. Don picked it up and I heard him say he would leave right away.

"Who was that?" I asked. "Is something wrong?"

"Our daughter. She said she and her roommate made a quick trip to visit her roommate's family in Grand Rapids. They were on their way back to college this morning when something didn't sound right with the car. She decided to head over here to have me check it out, but was worried she shouldn't drive it any farther. They pulled off at the Fruitport exit. She called to ask me to meet her there. I'm going to drive over there to find out what is wrong with her car. Go ahead and put dinner on the table for the kids. I'll eat when I return and maybe she and her friend will have time to come here to get something to eat before heading back."

About 20 minutes later, the phone rang again. It was Don. "Can you bring me my toolbox from the garage?" he asked.

"What? You didn't take your tool box with you?" I suspected something wasn't right because it was highly unusual for my husband to not carry his tools with him.

"I have one of my tool boxes with me. The other one has the tool I need in it. Just get it and come out here as soon as you can."

"Okay. But, where exactly are you?"

"We're in the lumber yard parking lot, just off the exit. Thank you!"

When I arrived, our daughter was sitting alone with her dad in the front seat of his car. There was no one else and no other car around. As I looked over toward her, I noticed she had been crying. She looked devastated and scared. My stomach turned over. I felt something was terribly wrong.

My husband jumped out of his car and came to sit with me in my car. "Don't get out yet. I need to talk with you alone."

"What's wrong?" I asked. "Where is her friend and her friend's car? Were they in an accident?"

"No, it's not that! I didn't tell you this before, but I couldn't sleep last night. I got up to read for a while and about 2 am the phone rang. I thought it might be a wrong number and since you were sound asleep, I picked it up before the ring was completed.

After I found out it was our daughter, who called, and the reason she called, I didn't want to wake you right then. I didn't want to say anything this morning about that call in front of the kids, because I wasn't sure how to handle what she told me."

"Handle what? What has happened?" I asked suddenly feeling sick to my stomach and expecting something awful had happened.

Don explained that when he answered the phone, he could barely hear her. He said he kept asking her if she was all right and what was the matter. "She was sobbing as she slowly said, 'Daddy, I'm so sorry.'" He said he asked her why she was sorry, but she didn't answer right away. Then she said she needed to see a doctor and soon. He said he wondered why she didn't make an appointment with the doctor on campus. Then it occurred to him she might be pregnant.

"When I asked if she was pregnant, she started crying and said she was." She said she had gone home with her roommate to talk to her mother who was a nurse and ask her what she should to do. She stated she was scared and felt that she had disappointed us. She knew we had plans for her to get a college degree, but now believed having a child would change all of that. She didn't want an abortion, but didn't know how she could support herself and a baby unless she dropped out of college and went to work. After she told him this, he said he asked her to come home today after church so we could discuss this together.

I felt heartbroken for her and what she was going through. I began to cry as I looked over at my daughter who was also crying as she watched us from the window of her dad's car. I got out of my car, walked over, opened her door, and hugged her.

"I love you," I said as tears ran down her cheeks and mine. "Don't worry."

I looked back at my husband. "We need to talk for a while and I'm not ready to go back home with all her sisters listening in on this conversation. Let's stop at a restaurant on our way home, get something to eat, and discuss this."

When we got to the restaurant, I called home to tell her sister we would be coming home in a while and everything was okay. She was fine with clearing the table and cleaning up the kitchen and watching her younger sisters until we returned home. "I hope we can see her before she goes back to college", Dawn stated as I hung up the phone and I returned to our table.

"Have you talked to anyone on campus about this," I asked, "A doctor, nurse, adviser or anyone at all?"

"No I haven't. I was afraid they would kick me out of the dorm if they found out."

"Okay, but what about the baby's father?" I asked. "Is he willing to help out?"

"He doesn't want anything to do with this," she said as she looked down at her lap. "He said it was all my fault."

"You said you did not want an abortion, is that correct?"

"No, I don't want to have an abortion, but what choice do I have?"

"If you will stay home a day or two, we can get you into a doctor to get you on prenatal vitamins while you take some time to calm down and thoroughly think about this before you make a final decision. Have you considered adoption?"

"I have," she said with tears rolling down her cheeks. "But that would be too hard."

"So would the abortion," I said. "Whatever you decide will stay with you forever. One option I have heard about recently is open adoption. The birth mother stays involved, similar to an older sister or aunt, but not the person the child calls his or her mom. You and the adoptive family would decide when and how much time you could visit the child. There are other possibilities to explore before making such a lifelong decision. Are you willing to explore those options?"

"Yes, but I have to be back in class tomorrow. I can't take time off or it will affect my grades," she replied while looking for more Kleenex to wipe her cheeks and nose.

"Let's make an appointment first thing in the morning with the doctor. I will call your school adviser to inform him you came home sick and we are taking you to the doctor. I'll let him know we will bring you back when you are feeling better. I'm sure the doctor will write an excuse for you to miss classes. Does that sound okay?"

She agreed and her school adviser said he would take care of things and make sure she was excused from classes until she returned in a day or two day.

During the following month, our daughter made the decision to keep her baby and found resources to help her financially. That summer we were thrilled to welcome our first grandchild into our family. She just had one more thing to do before returning to school in the fall and that was to have her son baptized. I was happy she knew how important this was as part of being in the family of God when she asked me to go with her to talk to the pastor to set up the baptism.

"Yes, we can baptize him after church on a Sunday of your choice," our pastor said.

"Baptize him after church?" I questioned feeling stunned. "Why not baptize during the service? That is when everyone else gets baptized."

"Well, this is a touchy situation," he said. "The child is illegitimate and our baptisms include both parents. Is the father available or will he agree to attend?"

"No, the father doesn't want anything to do with him. It's just me," our daughter said as she wrung her hands.

"Well, I don't know if our deacons will approve of this. It's not the normal way we handle this kind of situation."

"Are you saying this child is not part of God's church family because he is illegitimate? I can't believe you are saying that after giving a sermon about seven months ago on pregnancy and the Right to Life. It sounds like you're saying a child who was not aborted cannot be baptized because he is illegitimate. I personally believe all of this is contrary to God's teaching." I was feeling very angry as I got up to walk out.

"I'll call a meeting with our deacons to see what I can do," the pastor said apologetically.

I could not believe that a pastor would say or think this way. I decided that if our church deacons did not agree, I was ready to move on to a more loving and accepting church.

A few days later the pastor called and said the deacons did not have a problem with having the baby baptized during the church service. Furthermore, the deacons agreed this rule needed to be changed for future situations like our daughter's.

"Thank God!" I said. As I put down the phone, I couldn't help but think that it was not just a coincidence that the same day we heard the sermon about agencies to help support pregnancy, our daughter called seeking help for her pregnancy from us and how this all had played out with changes in our church and our life.

That fall, our daughter moved into family housing on campus, and enrolled our grandson in the college day care center while she attended college full time.

I often drove up to Big Rapids after my Thursday night graduate classes in Grand Rapids to stay and help her out on Fridays. Sometimes I stayed through Saturday afternoons so she could complete her homework and lab work for her classes.

In 1990, both our daughter and I graduated from college. She received her Bachelor's Degree and I earned my Master's Degree in Social Work.

In my journey, God had prepared me to not judge but to show love. She was my daughter and I couldn't bear to think of turning our backs on her when she needed us the most.

I had grown up thinking we had to be "perfect" to be a Christian and for God to love us, but my knowledge of the Bible and my training as a social worker had been preparing me to become much more compassionate and less critical.

I believe God wants all of us to do as Jesus would do and to become more like Christ in our interactions with others. My classes had opened my eyes and heart as I explored and let go of my own list of "shoulds". I was learning what was really meant by being a Christian.

But, God wasn't finished molding me. He would use this experience again in the future for me to help others who found themselves in similar situations. I was to continue to grow from this experience He had just put before me.

"Love bears all things, believes all things, hopes all things, endures all things."[43]

Internship Experiences
Chapter 27

During the final semester of the Master's Degree Program in Social Work, I was assigned an internship in a psychiatric unit and an out-patient program. I begged my adviser to place me in a school system because I wanted to work with children and I wanted an opportunity to become a school social worker. However, the professors who chose the internship for me denied my request because they believed working in the area of mental illness was a better fit for me with my skills.

I totally disagreed and reminded them I had worked in the school system and treatment programs for developmentally disabled and with those who were cognitively impaired who also had behavioral problems. I argued I had those very skills which supported me working as a school social worker. I also made a comment that I wasn't sure I even knew what was "normal" and would not make a good mental health social worker.

My professors replied, "You are where you need to be." After my professors refused to change my internship to a school setting, I finally accepted the internship position to work with psychiatric patients.

I learned quickly how to diagnose patients, write up treatment plans, lead group therapies, and work with some of most severely mentally ill who had disorders such as schizophrenia or borderline personalities. I also worked with those who were suicidal as well as some of the patients who lived on the streets or had very low cognitive abilities.

During the second half of my internship I worked in an outpatient partial hospitalization program. While there, I continued to lead outpatient individual and group therapy and loved this experience. Upon discharge from the in-patient program, some of the patients were transferred to the outpatient program which provided support to these patients as they returned to their homes and families at the end of each therapy day. During this program, they were also being monitored for medication management and evaluated on their ability to cope once back in their environment.

One day, my supervisor indicated she was assigning me to a young man who was suicidal and facing court for charges on child sexual abuse. I stared at her for a moment then replied, "I can't work with him! It would be too difficult for me to work with anyone who sexually abused a child."

My supervisor refused to back down from assigning this person to me. "Bonnie, you don't get to choose your patients in real life. I think this case will be an excellent one for you. You will come across many who abused or were abused and find themselves in this situation. Having this opportunity to work with this type of client will be very helpful for you in your career. I'll be here to guide you as usual. You will meet with him this afternoon at 2 pm for an intake into our program. I'll talk with you tomorrow after you complete your intake assessment."

I didn't perceive any value of trying to understand this client. After all, he made a choice to hurt a child. My mind was made up. I was sure I was not the one who could give him the help he needed at this time.

As I began working with him, I learned about his family life and history. I listened to what had happened to him as a child. My heart opened up and I became empathetic to him. He had been repeatedly sexually molested at a very young age by a family member. He continued to be a victim of emotional, physical, and sexual abuse throughout his life. As I began to empathize with him and told him what had happened to him should never have happened to any child, his suicidal thoughts became less frequent. He began to break down and cry about his own painful experiences and slowly realized he had violated another just as he had been violated. By the end of treatment, he went to court. He was ready to face the consequences of his acts and to speak up against those who were still alive and had abused him. Once again, I had been put to the test and recalled what I had learned in my diversity class about becoming non-judgmental, especially in this field.

While working with him I had gained a deeper understanding of those who molest, as well as becoming aware of my own strength as a social worker.

When I met with my supervisor after he was discharged, we were both glad I had accepted this patient as part of my training. She also informed me that studies showed those who abuse were once abused themselves. However, out of the entire group of people who were abused, only a small percentage actually became abusers.

A few years later, when someone I knew had been charged with child molestation, I realized how much my experience during my internship had prepared me to emotionally be able to deal with that situation as a Christian and a social worker.

"I will instruct you and teach you in the way you should go; I will counsel you with my eye upon you"[44].

Starting My Career
Chapter 28

Before I had completed my internship at the hospital I was hired by an outpatient therapy agency to begin working as soon as I finished my internship and graduated from the MSW program. I was thrilled and felt honored to be considered for this position.

A few days after my graduation, I took one of my daughters to lunch to celebrate having her braces taken off. As I walked into the restaurant, I noticed a large group of people sitting at a table in the middle of the room. One of the men stood up and started walking toward me. I recognized him as the director of the agency that had just hired me.

"Well, hello. I'm certainly glad to see you here! We are having a staff luncheon and I'm sure the rest of the staff would like to meet you. How about joining us for lunch?"

"I'd love to," I replied. "But I promised my daughter I'd take her to lunch today."

"Well, then come over and at least let me introduce you to our staff," he said as he led me and my daughter over to the table. "Staff, I'd like you to meet our newest therapist. She will be starting with us next week."

Therapist? Did I hear that right? He called me a therapist! I felt my face blush. *Wow, A therapist!* I couldn't stop rehearsing this in my head. I had walked in feeling like just a mom and suddenly I had another title. I was not used to thinking of myself as being a therapist. Although I had done some therapy and led therapy groups during my internship, I had not been referred to as a therapist before today. I was always referred to as a social worker at the hospital. All this was going through my mind as the director of the agency proceeded to introduce the staff to me.

I was fortunate to be hired to work for only thirty hours per week as a contractual employee with the ability to have flexible hours and days. This was very important to me because time with family had been a real crunch during the past six years while being a college student. With such a flexible schedule, I could now be more available to my family, attend my childrens' after-school events, and perhaps also become involved in day time events at school with my younger children.

The mission statement of this agency was to learn to balance mind, body, and spirit. As I learned how to balance my own life and to manage my stress by practicing relaxation, meditation, diaphragmatic breathing and progressive relaxation techniques, I taught others. I learned the extent to which relaxation and breathing techniques could actually decrease headaches, asthma, impulsive behaviors, and help to manage other problems such as digestive disorders, and pain. Many doctors referred their patients to our agency specifically to learn these skills to reduce medical problems such as hypertension, anxiety and phobias.

I really fit in with the other therapists in this agency and felt right at home with them because many of them had a lot of experience in various ministries. One therapist was a retired minister. Another one was a youth minister, who had also been trained as a Christian youth counselor, and my direct supervisor was also a pastoral counselor on staff at a local hospital. Our staff meetings and supervision hours were always Christian and spiritually focused. I felt so happy, content, and excited working with other Christians and knowing I was doing the work God had planned for me to do.

One fall day, about four or five months after I started working, I sat mesmerized by the colors of the fall leaves dancing around in the wind outside my office window when my secretary stepped into my office.

"While I was out to lunch, we received a call from one of the insurance gatekeepers who has a referral for you. I called him back, but he would not give me the name of the person or the reason for therapy. He wants to speak to you directly."

That seemed very odd to me since referrals were dispersed to each one of us in turn as they came in. The fact that this gatekeeper was asking for me specifically made me curious and a bit nervous. I wondered if I had done something wrong or if someone had made a complaint against me.

When I called him back he explained he had a female patient on his caseload that had been in and out of psychiatric hospitals and had exhausted all of her in-patient benefits. He wanted to know if I would be willing to try to help her in outpatient therapy.

"Why has she been in the hospital so many times?" I asked, feeling unsure of myself as a new therapist and concerned I was not the right therapist to accept a new patient who was so mentally ill that she needed frequent hospitalization.

"This woman has had several suicidal attempts following several abortions," the gatekeeper said. "I know this is a heavy assignment. Other than outpatient individual therapy, she doesn't have any other benefits available to her at this point. I can authorize two or three appointments per week or even every day if that is needed to keep her out of the hospital. What do you think? Are you willing to help her?"

I took a breath and hesitated a moment before I replied. "I would like to first meet her to get a better understanding about her situation and her willingness to work with me".

"I can arrange that for you. I would really appreciate it if you would accept her as a client. I will be available to you for consultation if you need it. Or, if you decide you can't work with her, I will transfer her to someone else. She needs a female therapist and I simply cannot find one available who has had as much experience with suicidal or borderline patients as you have had. Can I have her schedule with you today or tomorrow?"

I was a little nervous, but I knew I had been trained well and had my internship supervisor available for a consult should I need that from her. I also had a Ph.D psychologist available in our office if I needed supervision or more help. Knowing I had the support from all these professionals, I agreed to see this woman for an initial intake session. I would contact this gatekeeper afterward and let him know if she and I had decided we could work together.

Shortly after I hung up with the gatekeeper the office phone rang. This woman had called to make an appointment and came in that same afternoon. She was barely twenty years old and looked much younger than I had expected. She appeared very thin and very scared. She cried as she told how she feared losing her boyfriend, his family, and her church family if anyone discovered she had become pregnant out of wedlock or found out she had abortions to keep her boyfriend and their secrets. This had been going on for the past three or four years. Her boyfriend had promised he would marry her someday when the time was right. Meanwhile, she had the abortions so she could continue the image of her being a perfect Christian girl who was worthy of the love from those who were most important in her life.

While listening to her story I thought of my own daughter who could have been sitting here a few years ago if she had not had the support of family and friends. I knew whatever I did to help this woman, I had to do it slowly and gently to gain her trust and to help her feel loved and supported by me.

During the next week after our session, I was surprised to get flier, which came over our fax machine, inviting me to join a new training program called Project Rachel. It was a program to train therapists to help heal those with post abortion stress. Project Rachel was being promoted by the Catholic Church. However, other denominations had also been invited to join this project and training with the goal of reuniting those victims of abortion and to know they were forgiven with the goal to lead them back to God and the church. I got goose bumps as read over the material. I knew this was not a coincidence. Only God would have known I how much I needed this resource at this time. I filled out the forms and faxed them back immediately. After coming home that evening and telling my husband I had signed up for this training, I later overheard him telling one of his friends he was married to a perpetual student. I agreed, "Yep. That's me!" I said with a smile.

I started training for the Project Rachel Program and began working with pastors, priests, and nuns offering my support to those whose actions were considered by others to be unforgivable. This became a spiritual journey for me and the participants, whom I often offered therapy free of charge when they did not have insurance coverage.

The program began by teaching us to understand these women from their experiences and their reasoning for making this kind of choice. I watched as many of them changed from self-abusive behaviors to attaining a higher level of self-esteem as they learned to listen to how much God loved them and to not focus on what others thought or said about them. Some of the fathers of aborted children also wanted to participate in the program and be forgiven. We helped them acknowledge their pain and grieve their loss along with their parents who would have been grandparents. We listened, supported and offered prayers for them as they reconciled with God. What a ministry!

Many women, who had chosen to abort babies earlier in their life, became depressed or had nightmares years later, especially on the date of the abortion or what would have been the date of their child's birth. All of them had similar feelings of being unloved, ashamed, guilty, and living in fear of God's wrath. Some of them chose to come to confess what they had done and attend prayer vigils. They lit candles as they named their aborted babies and during a ceremony offered them in prayer back to God for Him to raise them in Heaven.

There were still some who could not accept God's forgiveness for the choices they had made. For them, the only hope therapists had was to let go and let the Holy Spirit do His work at His pace until these individuals could forgive themselves and accept God's forgiving love. That was the tough part for me. It was sad knowing Christ was standing at the door with His arms stretched out to these women who continued to turned their backs and walk away because they could not accept themselves for what they had done.

I was blessed to watch the woman, whom I had seen at her insurance gatekeeper's request, accept God's forgiveness and change her life around. She eventually left her boyfriend and changed churches. A few years after successfully completing therapy, she married a man who really loved and respected her. I have since seen her and her husband enjoying their children in public places. It warms my heart when she notices me and comes up to me with a big smile to give me an update of her family.

About the time I was nearing my second year of working, I was informed, along with others, that our agency was merging with another agency. Our manager warned us many changes were to be expected and those who worked for the other agency would be given the first priority for jobs when the merger was completed. I ignored this at first, but little by little I realized my position would be also eliminated. Reluctantly, I began applying for social work positions in the area.

By August, my position had been eliminated and I had found another position working with families going through divorce. It was only twenty hours per week and much less pay than I had been receiving. Although I had never personally experienced a divorce, I learned a lot about the families, changes in lifestyles, and the trauma children experience during their parents' divorce. I learned about the cycle of love versus cycle of hate which was found to be common in marital conflicts. During my presentations on a good divorce, I always encouraged the divorcing couples to review their marriage and the impact of the divorce on their lives and the lives of their children before continuing their plans to divorce. I often advised, "If, after reconsidering everything, and divorce is still your choice, then move ahead with this."

During one of our supervision sessions my supervisor reminded me, "You know your job here is to help couples have a good adjustment to their divorce?"

"Yes," I said, feeling confused as to why she made that statement.

"We are noticing many of your clients are considering reconciliation," she said with a laugh. Yet, I felt pleased to hear so many were taking my advice to rethink their choice to divorce.

Throughout my sessions, I had found out many of those who were going through divorce were themselves victims of their parents' divorce. In group sessions many often expressed feelings related to their own childhood experiences. The dynamics of their own families of origin was being reincarnated and their subconscious drives of family dynamics as well as their needs to resolve their past issues were evident from the damage I had seen these adults bring with them into their own marriage. I often thought that before anyone gets married we should offer premarital classes to focus on these issues which would eventually emerge. Unfortunately that would not be something two people in love and anxious to marry would choose to consider.

I enjoyed providing divorce adjustment group therapy for kids and adults, as well as working with individuals and couples in therapy. Although, working part-time was nice at times, and I had more free time, the income from part-time work made it difficult to have spending money after making payments on my school loans. I needed to find more work to meet expenses, so I prayed for help and hoped my part-time job would open up to full-time employment.

My prayer was answered one night when my internship supervisor from the psychiatric unit called me. "I'm aware your position was cut last year with that merger and wondered what you are doing now."

"I'm working part-time in family and divorce counseling," I said, as I told her about my current job.

"I don't know if you are aware that I left the psych unit and started my own practice," she continued.

"No, I did not know that. Where are you located now?" I asked.

"I have an office in town with a play therapy room and some extra space for another therapist. I thought about you since I heard about the merger and that your position had been cut. I'm wondering if you might be interested in joining me part-time in private practice."

I was really excited about this offer, but had some concerns about starting private practice. "Yes, I would like that, but would you continue to provide supervision? I learned so much from you before as a student and this would give me an opportunity to continue to learn from you."

"Of course, I value supervision time and am glad that is important to you, too. We all need to learn from those who can mentor us. Would you be available to meet with me sometime this week at my office? I'd love to show you around. We can talk more then."

I could hardly wait to see her office and the opportunity to work with her. I really admired her skills and was thrilled and honored to be asked to work with her. When I arrived at her office, I was amazed at how large her office space actually was. Besides a waiting room and two separate offices, the play therapy room was huge. She had already filled it with many bean bag chairs, a doll house with little people, and lots of other therapeutic toys. After seeing this, I was ready to begin.

She explained she had just opened her office when she discovered she was pregnant. "After the baby is born, I want to take at least three months off. Then I'll return to work part-time for about a year after that. That means you would be working alone for a while and building you practice, as well as keeping mine going."

This seemed reasonable to me. I would work about twenty-five to thirty hours a week at her office and stay with the family therapy job for twenty hours a week until she returned after those first three months.

As we talked, she also shared that most of her clientele was not the common clients normally seen in outpatient therapy, but the more severely diagnosed with dissociative disorders commonly known as multiple personalities. Some were or had been involved in cults. Some cut themselves instead of verbally expressing their emotional pain. Others couldn't sleep at night because of their history of traumas and abuse. She said she felt God had called her into this field as a mission and had led her to work specifically with this population.

"Bonnie, you are someone I feel I can depend on and trust to work patiently and spiritually with these women. Do you want to give it a try?"

"Yes!" I was ready for more challenging work. She began to teach me more than I could ever imagine about dissociation, and more than I wanted to know about cults and satanic worship. She gave me a book to familiarize myself with the satanic and cult rituals and their calendar schedules so I would understand what was going on and could be prepared ahead of time for those having a need to be seen in an emergency or crisis.

While she was still on maternity leave, there was one strange incident which occurred while working with one her patients who had been involved in cult activities. The client had called the office one morning stating she was in a crisis and needed to be seen immediately. Since I didn't have any openings that day, I agreed to see her during my lunch hour. She arrived just after our secretary stepped out for lunch. Because there was no one else in our office during lunch hour, I locked the office door behind the client. Then we walked into my office and I shut the door behind us and invited her to sit down. As she began to vividly describe the experience she recalled at one of the rituals, I began visualizing what she had seen. Suddenly, the room became freezing cold and I began to feel as if I was experiencing the very same trauma she had witnessed. All of a sudden, we heard a loud crash as if the five drawer steel filing cabinet had fallen over outside my door. I opened the door and rushed out to see what had happened, fearing the secretary had returned and the file cabinet had fallen on her; but she wasn't back yet and our filing cabinet was still standing upright. I checked the other rooms of our office and walked out into the hall to look around although there were no other offices on our wing of the building. I walked around inside the building and looked out windows to see if there had been an accident outside. Everything was quiet. Nothing looked abnormal. I walked back into my office and looked out over the parking lot from my window. Everything appeared to be fine.

Thinking how strange this was, I felt frightened as I sat down to continue our therapy session. Just then a memory verse from the Bible came into my mind, "...fear not, for I am with you..."[45] I immediately recalled a biblical picture of the apostle Peter stepping out of a boat when he saw Jesus walking on water toward him. He held out his hand as he climbed out of the boat and began walking on water toward Jesus. Suddenly he realized he was also walking on water and became afraid. Jesus reached out and caught Peter as he began to sink[46].. *This is happening to me right now*, I thought. In that brief second, I recognized I had let fear control me as I felt pulled into experiencing the frightening event the client had seen. I took a deep breath and silently prayed asking God be with us and to send his angels to protect me and my client. I felt relieved and began to feel the room getting warmer as we continued our counseling session. I had forgotten I was not alone in this line of work and to trust that God was with us.

I never again had such an alarming experience happen to me. I also learned I would be in a better position to help others if I did not get caught up into their experiences and if I keep stronger emotional boundaries between my client's emotional experiences and mine.

When my supervisor returned to her practice later that year, she told me she had applied for a grant for me to work with children who were abused. She indicated that while sitting in her private room adjacent to the play therapy room, she could overhear my voice as I spoke with children. "Bonnie, you don't realize the gift you have for working with these children or how warm and soothing your gentle voice is to them. Many of them have been through so much abuse and have never heard anyone talk so soft and caring to them," she said. "I really hope we get this grant so you to continue working with this population."

Unfortunately, she didn't get the grant. Not long after that she decided to move to a smaller office to cut overhead costs. We would have to share space and alternate scheduling times with our clients. That arrangement didn't work out very well for me and caused limited therapy sessions and scheduling problems. I decided it was time for me to move on.

After submitting my resume to several agencies I was contacted by an out-patient Christian agency to work part-time. Two weeks after I was hired I received a call to work full-time with children and adolescents who were mentally ill and/or incorrigible at another agency. Because we had three children in college at this time and could use the extra money, I accepted this job in addition to the one I just started. I worked full-time during the day and two evenings a week in outpatient therapy. I liked working both positions, but the strain of working emergency services after-hours with severely acting out children and teens was exhausting. I often was called away from a quiet evening at home to evaluate a child or teenager, who was suicidal or homicidal.

Although I really enjoyed the challenges of working with children, teens, and their parents, as well as with other social agencies, doctors, the juvenile court system and psychiatrists, I was getting tired of the middle of the night calls. At this same time, my mother was dying and my father, a brittle diabetic, was having problems controlling his blood sugar. They were both in need of more care. It was not unusual for me to return home from a work emergency, and then return to the hospital emergency room for a family emergency.

After attending a series of trainings specifically on the Deaf substance abuser, I assisted a group of social workers in getting an Alcoholic Anonymous program for Deaf started in another city and then began to think about ways in which to utilize my skills locally. I began asking substance abuse treatment agencies what they were doing to help this population. One of the substance abuse organizations was interested in what I was sharing with them about addictions and the needs of the Deaf for treatment. They offered me a position for less pay than I was making, but I would not have to take after-hours emergency calls. I would have every Friday off and never work on weekends.

They said they wanted me to start working on a grant to help the Deaf get treatment. I was so excited to accept this job and looked forward to helping the Deaf to get these services, that I overlooked researching the credibility of this organization.

I hated the idea of leaving the mentally ill population and the supervisor there from whom I had learned a great deal, but I was at survival level with too many demands on me. I believed by taking this job, there would be significantly less stress in my life and I would be able to open the door to help those in the Deaf population who needed help with addictions. Because I had been on a team to help start a 12-Step Program for the Deaf who had addictions, I knew what to do and how to start it and who to contact for help if I needed it.

Unfortunately, after I was hired, my new position became very disappointing to me as the opportunity to provide services for Deaf was not of significant importance to this agency. After starting to work there, I found that most of those working in this agency were recovering from one form or another of addiction and many did not have a college degree. I became concerned about some of their practices. However, when I tried to address these issues, they did not want to hear what I had to say. I felt as if I was an outsider to this group. I realized this was not the place for me and planned to start looking for another position elsewhere.

By this same time my mother had died and my father had become totally in need of daily help and supervision. He had recently fallen in the bathroom and had broken a rib. It was alarming to discover he repeatedly burnt himself by dropping his cup of hot coffee when he tried to set his cup down on the table or cupboard. He left food cooking on the stove and would forget to turn off the burner. He began eating TV dinners high in salt and sugar, which was not good for his diabetic problems. When his blood sugar dropped during the night, or when he fell out of bed, I was the one who received calls and had to get up out of bed and drive across town to check on him, or meet the ambulance and paramedics at the emergency room. With all of this happening, I felt drained of the energy I needed at work the next day.

My first most important task was to find a safer place for my father. Since the agency I was working for did not have family leave time, I decided this was the time to quit. I planned to search for another position once things settled down with my dad and after I had given myself time to readjust and to re-evaluate what I wanted to do in my career.

Although I trusted when the time was right God would lead me to a more satisfying position, I was uneasy leaving a professional position without another position waiting for me. I wondered if a future employer would even consider hiring me since I left my job after working only a few short months. Yet, I knew I had to do this to help my dad and keep my own sanity. I would trust God to lead me.

"When I am afraid, I will trust in you. In God, whose word I praise, in God I trust; I shall not be afraid. What can mortal flesh do to me?"[47]

A Step in Faith
Chapter 29

After quitting my job and after finding someone to come into the home to stay with my father until we could get him into an assisted living center, I contacted the director of the Interpreter Training Program at Lansing Community College and requested an evaluation of my skills for placement in their training program. During my college years and throughout my career, I had been keeping up with conferences and educational trainings for the Deaf and interpreters. I continued taking classes in ASL taught by Deaf teachers and thought by becoming an interpreter for Deaf and combining my sign language skills with my Master's Degree in Social Work, I would be a rarity and this would be a real asset to my career.

I reflected on how God had worked in my life before I even knew there were interpreters and how my life had unfolded around the Deaf population during the past thirty years. I believed God still had a purpose for me with this population. I didn't know if or how I could take classes half way across the state from my home, but out of curiosity, I wanted to explore what possibilities might be available for me and if this was the direction I wanted to go.

After evaluating my signing skills, the director of the interpreter program indicated I had a large vocabulary and could communicate with a variety of Deaf using the various forms of sign language I already knew, but to be certified, I had to pass the state QA (Quality Assurance) test. She said I used a lot of signs that came from various parts of the United States, like dialects. "While that will help you, eventually, if you want a state QA certification, only ASL signs familiar to the majority of the Michigan Deaf will get you through that test."

She suggested I start with level three classes in ASL, a class in Deaf History, and a creative signing class. "Those classes should get you into an internship which would take another year full time or about two years part-time. Classes are offered here in the evening and on Saturday mornings. If that works for you, you can start in January."

I was interested.

When I returned home to share this information with my husband, he was reluctant to have me return to college. "I know the frustration you had with that last job and I understand all that was going on with your dad has been very stressful for you. But, do you realize it has been over a month since you stopped working and now Christmas is only a month away? We still have three kids in college and you still have student loans to repay. We don't have your additional income to depend on now. I don't think we have the extra money to spend on furthering your education at this time. Have you given any thought to looking for a job?"

"I have been thinking about those same things. I'm glad I took the time off and believe I did the right thing by taking a much needed break. I know we don't have as much money to spend on Christmas, but this has given me time to think about my future and enjoy getting ready for Christmas with the kids coming home from college. I do plan to start looking for a job right after the beginning of the New Year," I said. "I just don't think I want to work in this area. I'm tired of feeling a lack of professionalism from what I have experienced in some agencies. I really liked my job working with emergency services, but I was too exhausted with that part of my job after working all day with kids."

I poured myself a fresh cup of coffee and sat down across the table from him. "I think working in Grand Rapids might be better for me. There are several colleges there offering fresh ideas with lots of educational and professional support and training opportunities. There is also more accessibility and opportunities available for the Deaf and you know how much I care and enjoy working with that population.

"So, what is your plan of action?" He questioned.

"I've been thinking about picking up a Grand Rapids Press the first Sunday after New Year's Eve and begin searching for a job over there."

My husband was satisfied with that, but said he hoped I would hold off starting the Interpreter Training Program until things were more settled with me. He said he also would prefer I had a job before I added more stress to our budget.

I bought a copy of the Grand Rapids Press after the first of the year and began searching for a job just like I said I would. To my surprise, when I opened the paper to the listing of professional jobs in the mental health section, there was an advertisement for a case manager to work with the mentally ill and physically disabled Deaf population. The job description indicated they were looking for a candidate who would have a Bachelor of Science Degree in Social Work or related field, experience working with the mentally ill, and could use sign language fluently.

"I can't believe it!" I yelled out loud. "This job was designed for me!" There was so much excitement in my voice that my husband put down the newspaper he was reading to find out what I was talking about.

"I have all the requirements, but they are looking for someone with a bachelor's degree instead of a master's degree. I wonder if they would accept someone with a higher degree. I did some case management with some of my mental health clients and I am fluent in sign language. I'm sending my resume and we'll see what happens."

My hands were shaking with so much excitement that I could barely type out my resume and cover letter. I ran to the post office, just a short distance away, slipped it in the mailbox the very next morning.

On Tuesday, just after lunch, I received a phone call from the director for support services for Deaf. "So you have a master's degree in social work and can sign?" he asked.

"Yes, that's true," I said feeling quite surprised I had received a call so soon after submitting my resume. "I have a hearing loss and started signing about twenty years ago. I also have several culturally Deaf friends."

"Well, I 'm ready to offer you the job right now. I never dreamed I would get a response from an MSW when I sent out this request. I was hoping to find someone with some college and some signing skills, but you have everything I was hoping to find. Were you looking for a part-time position as advertised, or would you prefer full-time employment? I can request a change in the job and job description if you want full time. I'm sure I won't have a problem with that when I show them all your credentials."

"For now I would like part-time," I said. "But, if you need me, I can be flexible and work more hours."

He indicated that he wanted to set up an interview as soon as possible. He said they had Deaf people on staff and he wanted to include them in the interview since I would be working very closely with all of them as a team.

"I can come over any time. Just let me know," I said. I was feeling so much excitement that I was sure he could hear my heart pounding through the phone line.

When he called back, he informed me the interview would be done totally in sign language and he would have an interpreter present.

"Do you think you can handle that?"

"Yes! That won't be a problem. I have interviewed before with an interpreter."

"Great. We will have three case managers at the interview. Two of them are totally Deaf and will be participating in the interview along with an interpreter. I will give you a call in a day or two after I can arrange the exact time when we can all get together."

The day came for my interview and just as he had said, it was done completely in sign language. It lasted about two hours. I answered questions focusing on the type of clients and experience I had with a variety of mental health patients. We discussed my own hearing loss, my involvement with Deaf over the past twenty-two years, and my work history. After the interview I was asked to sit outside while the three case-managers, the supervisor and interpreter discussed my responses during the interview, what they thought of my signing skills, and made a final decision on whether or not to hire me. I had felt very comfortable with these people and was confident I would become part of their team.

Finally the door opened and the director invited me back into the room. "We want you to start working as soon as possible." Everyone was smiling while waving their hands in the air to welcome me.

"I would like to start right away. However, I have sinus surgery scheduled for two weeks from now. Can you wait that long?"

"Take care of what you have to do and call me back when you are ready to start. We'll be talking again soon. Good luck on that surgery. I hear the recovery is not so pleasant."

It was a month later when I was actually able to start work and as I expected, I loved my job working alongside Deaf case managers. I met with our Deaf clients to monitor their mental health progress, establish and work on their goals or assist them with doctor appointments, job interviews, or on the job training. I led some social/educational groups and weekly fun activities at the end of the day.

After being hired, I started taking classes in the Interpreter Training Program. Every Saturday morning I drove over to Lansing to attend a class in Deaf history. During the week I shared with our Deaf educational group what I had learned in my class about some of the famous Deaf people.

One day while doing an assignment in my Deaf History and Culture class, I was surprised to read about the first ordained Catholic Deaf Priest, Thomas Coughlin.[48](This was the same man whom I had met twenty years prior at the Convocation for Deaf Ministry in Wisconsin and had sat next to him on my flight home. I was also surprised to learn of a man by the name of John Brewster, who could be in my family tree. He was a famous deaf artist in New England and in 1817, at the age of fifty-one, he became one of the first deaf students at the first school for deaf in America. It was then called The Connecticut Asylum for the Education and Instruction of Deaf and Dumb persons. According to Gannon, his art work is still hanging at that same school which is now called The American School for Deaf and he also has another painting still hanging at Gallaudet University in Silver Springs, Maryland.[49]

While doing some genealogical research on Brewster, to determine if we were related, I found another book entitled, "A Deaf Artist in Early America: The Worlds of John Brewster Jr." by Harlan Lane. According to this author, John Brewster was the great-great-great-great grandson of Pilgrim Elder Wm. Brewster of the Mayflower through his son, Love and grandson, Wrestling. Since I am also a descendent of Elder Wm. Brewster through his son Love, we were related as cousins several decades back in history! After reading about him, I wondered if there was a genetic connection between our hearing loss and interest in sign language.

Shortly after I started working with the Deaf in Grand Rapids, we welcomed the birth of our fifth grandchild. I loved to watch her she smile and enjoyed holding and cuddling her. But a few months later, the unexpected happened. After her mom took her to the doctor for her three month well baby checkup. The doctor said she was very health and proceeded to give her several immunizations all in one day. She died three days later of SIDS while at daycare.

I was staying late after work that day when I received a call to come home immediately. Most of the staff had already left the building when I told the secretary about the call I had just received. She called my supervisor who contacted me right away.

"Just go home, don't worry about your notes or anything left undone. I will take care of that for you. Let me know in few a days when you are ready to come back."

I drove all the way home shaking in disbelief. By the time I got to the hospital, everyone was standing outside the emergency entrance looking stunned and asking each other how could this happen to a healthy baby? What went wrong? Although it was hot outside, we were shaking and cold from this shock. It was one of the worse days of my life. Why did God let this happen? Her mom had just graduated from nursing school and was preparing for her state boards. Her father had an excellent job and adored her. She had everything waiting for a wonderful life full of love.

I longed to help my daughter and son-in-law deal with this grief, but I was grieving my loss, too. I couldn't say or do anything to help them. I felt so helpless. I knew I had to take care of myself before I could help someone else. A few weeks later, my daughter and I decided to join a grief support group together. She wanted her husband to come with us, but he just couldn't talk about their loss. For Tracy and me, it helped to know we were not alone and to openly share our own feelings without trying to control or change how or what the others thought or felt as they talked about their losses.

A few months after I returned to work, our supervisor decided we needed a staff development day to get away from our serious business and take some time away from work to reconnect as a team. We told jokes and stories. I learned a lot about how the Deaf view things and their humor. I came away with a deeper understanding of why hearing people do not enjoy the same humor as Deaf people. For instance, one of the stories was about a young deaf man who just got his first car. As he drove down the street to his home, everyone looked up and pointed at him. Some covered their mouth or ears with their hands. He felt very proud of his new car as everyone looked up to notice him driving down the street. He began waving to everyone and smiled. When he arrived home, his mother ran outside yelling at him and shaking her fist. He was shocked and wondered why she came outside yelling at him.

"You dummy!" she shouted as she signed. "Your horn is constantly making a loud noise. It's hurting everyone's ears!"

There were several other stories and humor shared from hearing people's humor to Deaf humor that afternoon and we all walked away feeling a lot more connected, lighthearted, and relaxed. I really appreciated the time away from work to spend having an enjoyable afternoon and reconnecting with my co-workers after returning to work following the mourning of our youngest granddaughter.

"He heals the brokenhearted and binds up their wounds."[50]

The Coalition Challenge
Chapter 30

One morning while working at the Deaf support services, we were surprised to have a representative from an advocacy group come to visit us. He worked closely with a state office in Lansing for those who were Deaf or Hard of Hearing (DOHH). The purpose of that agency was to advocate for Deaf rights according to the law. I had already become aware of the depth of the American Disability Act and the Law[51] giving equal rights to equal access of communication in schools and all public places including doctors' offices, hospitals, employers, nursing homes, and all government agencies.

I had experience with this law in the school system and our program director also had shared these legal requirements with me prior to when I started working there. However, when this man spoke, he explained how difficult it was to implement this law and how hard it was to get information out to those who needed to hear it most. He was traveling across the state looking for volunteers to help educate various agencies on how to make the changes to become compliant with the law and also to help the deaf in their own home town areas to make sure they were getting the accommodations necessary for their needs.

"Because this agency is doing so much to help the deaf in this area, we really need someone to represent your agency as part of our coalition. You have set a good example of providing for the deaf who need mental health help and cannot get it because of lack of available services. I understand your services also help them with job training and integrating into society. We need to let other communities become aware of these needs and services that can be available to them as well. We have monthly meetings in Lansing to bring our concerns about violations to be addressed and to help the employers understand this law. We also acknowledge and support those agencies, like this one, providing services to this population."

Our supervisor was excited about this, but dolefully responded, "We are very busy here with psychiatric and neurological visits, medical doctor appointments, job training, counseling sessions and sometimes working with the law with some of our clients who get into trouble by not understanding what they did wrong. I don't see any way our workers could take time off from work here to become part of this group."

Then our supervisor turned to us and asked what we each thought about this proposal and his response to our visitor. Everyone agreed it was a worthwhile cause, but the needs here were far too great for any of us to leave our clients to take time off from work to drive to Lansing to spend an afternoon. Plus, this would also mean a day without pay once a month.

Feeling the call to help, I spoke up. "I don't think this would be a problem for me. Since I only work part-time here I can arrange my work hours to attend those meetings and report back here. I don't have to be home until late afternoon or by evening on most days and I only work two evenings per week in my outpatient office. I would love to become involved with something like this which is so close to my heart. I can represent our agency if that would be okay with everyone else."

Everyone agreed and said they would happy to have me to represent our agency in Lansing.

"We would be so pleased to have you on our advocacy team!" the representative said. "Your degree in social work and experience here is exactly what we need. We have a deaf social worker and a deaf psychologist already, but adding a hearing person would balance our discussions."

"Actually, I am hard of hearing and I do wear hearing aids," I said. "But, I have been hearing most of my life and am considered a hearing person."

"Since you also have a hearing loss, that makes it all the better! You will be a great asset. I'm so happy you are interested in taking part in this coalition. We meet the third Wednesday of each month at 9:30 am until 11 or11:30 am in Lansing. We take a short lunch break and work on issues before we adjourn. Will you be able to join us for the next meeting?"

"Yes!" I was so excited to be part of such a wonderful movement. Once again, I felt affirmed I was exactly where I was supposed to be and it was not by coincidence all of this was happening.

It was almost the end of my first semester at Lansing Community College and was sitting in my office sharing with my Deaf co-worker my plans to take another class in ASL during the summer when my supervisor stepped in.

"I couldn't help but overhear you talking about taking a class in sign language. If you plan to take a class with the goal of using that skill as an interpreter, we will reimburse your tuition," he said. "At the end of the semester, when your class is over, just let me know and I will get you the forms for you to have the college fill out."

"Really? I asked. That would be wonderful! I'm planning to take my next class on Thursday nights after work. I wonder if the agency would also pay for the class I am currently taking? Tonight is my last class."

"All we need are your final grades and transcript sent to us and we will reimburse you."

"That's wonderful!" I said feeling very surprised. Everything seemed to be coming together for me and I couldn't wait to share this with my husband. *It seems when you are on the road to where God wants to lead you, things that could cause road blocks simply have a way of working out,* I thought to myself on my way home that night. I was glad I had waited until I had a job to pay for the classes and even more thrilled the agency I worked for would pay for the classes I took.

That summer I decided to take two classes because they were scheduled back to back. One was in advanced ASL and the other class was Creative Sign. I loved both classes. Telling stories and interpreting poems and songs in ASL was both challenging and exciting. I learned not to use just words and facial expressions but also body language to make the songs or stories come more to life, visually. To do that, I had to learn to let go of inhibitions and move out of my comfort zone. I had to become the person (or even an animal) in the story or song and act out the feelings by sometimes exaggerating facial movements, body posture, and physical actions. I envied the younger students, who were just out of high school, and seemed to move about freely without thinking about any physical inhibitions.

On our first day of the Creative Signing class our instructor had passed around a sheet of paper and asked us write down the name of a song we liked next to our name. She said she would get back to us about the song before the end of summer, but she never said anything more about that during our classes. However, when there were only three days of classes left, she announced our final assignment and final grade would be based on signing the same song we each had written down on our first day in class. She requested us to sign the song using ASL and to do our best to enable the audience to see, feel, and understand the meaning of the song.

I felt doomed. I had chosen the song, "For Those Tears I Died" because I had heard Marsha Stevens sing this song a few years previously at a concert and had thought it was such a beautiful and meaningful Christian song to be shared.

There were parts of this song that were very symbolic. I struggled with words that did not have a sign. I tried to understand the meaning in some of the verses such as "from earth's humble shores". This phrase and some of the others were beyond what I could describe in a short movement and keep in rhythm to music. My stress level hit the ceiling as I worked on this over and over for two nights; memorized the song and making choices on how to create signs that expressed the meaning visually in such a short time.

The day arrived for me to stand up in front of my class and sign my song. I was scared and felt nervous thinking everyone would make fun of me. I was sure I was going to fail this class.

As I watched the younger students signing so gracefully and beautifully, I thought about how I had interpreted my song. I was concerned it was not what the teacher wanted and was not sure I wanted to get up in front of everyone to do all the miming and body movements I had chosen for this song. But, I did it anyway. Afterward, I returned to my seat still feeling very awkward for using so many dramatic body movements instead of specific signs for my presentation.

At the end of our class, the teacher announced she had made video tapes of each of us and after she had reviewed all the video tapes she would give us each a copy of our own video with our grade attached. When we returned to class for the last day, I was stunned to see that I had received an A for my rendition of the song! Her notes were so positive I left class that day feeling more confident about my signing skills.

During the previous year before I took this class, I had attended a few weekend workshops for interpreters and Deaf with my co-workers. On Sundays, I always left feeling impressed by watching those who led church services or signed songs, but never thought I could ever sign scripture or songs as vividly as the interpreters and Deaf could do. After receiving the encouraging note from my instructor, I had the confidence to start signing Christian songs occasionally at church.

Although my sister wasn't deaf, just before her death from Lou Gehrig Disease, she told me the words of that song I had signed meant a lot to her. She said she would be truly grateful to me if I would agree to sign that song, "For Those Tears I Died", at her funeral. I agreed, but when the time came, I had a hard time signing while holding back my tears. When I finished and sat down, I was shaking, but glad I had developed the confidence to sign it as she had requested.

For the next two years, I was intensely involved with advocacy issues for Deaf, working with the mentally ill and emotionally impaired Deaf, and attending classes at Lansing Community College. As I became more and more aware of the needs for Deaf, I realized there was not the availability or community services to the Deaf in my own hometown like those services to the Deaf in area where I was I was working, especially for those in need of mental health services. I knew there weren't enough interpreters in my home town to provide for equal access to communication. Nor could the Deaf receive the same information and/or support as hearing persons.

I decided something had to be done. Having worked as a social worker in the mental health field, I decided to make a call to one of my previous supervisors to share my concerns with her.

"I know we have some Deaf in our area, but they don't usually request our services," she replied. "Since I have been here over the past several years, I only know of a very few who have ever contacted this agency for services. For those who have contacted us, we depended on the school interpreters. We don't have anyone else to call."

I surmised the Deaf individuals wouldn't come for services, because there was no one available to communicate their needs. By agencies requesting interpreters from the school during school hours, this would leave those Deaf students who needed the interpreter without communication assistance. Although this wasn't a good answer, it was the only answer for services to adult Deaf individuals that was available.

"How many Deaf do you think there are in our County?" she asked.

"I personally know almost two hundred who utilize sign language," I said. "I'm sure you know statistically one out of four (25%) of the population experience depression at any given time and also 10% of the general population have a hearing loss. That could mean there is a significant number of the Deaf population who don't have access to services when needed."

"That's a sizable number! I'm really interested in what you are sharing and would like to discuss this further when I have more time and have done some research on what services are offered to the Deaf. I'll call you back in a few days."

A few days later, after spending an afternoon working with a suicidal Deaf person, I wondered what would happen if a Deaf person was suicidal in my hometown. Would they be able to get help if they tried to call the hotline? Who would help them? I decided to find out.

When I got home from work, I went to my TTY and dialed the hotline number. No one answered. I called again and again over the next few days, typing "HELP, I need help!" Although I left my phone number for someone to return my call, no one ever responded. Luckily, the TTY also had a print option and I kept the tape for proof that no one responded.

I called my previous supervisor. "I thought you should know I've been trying to contact someone from emergency services using my TTY, but no one answered or returned my calls."

"Do you need help or was someone with you who needed help?" she asked.

"No, I was just testing the emergency call line in case a Deaf person decided to request help. I have a print out of my calls showing the dates and what I typed but I never received a response."

"Are you kidding?" she asked, sounding very alarmed.

"No, I'm not," I replied.

"No one responded to an emergency call? I will look into that right away. I appreciate you letting me know. I'll take this information to my superiors and we will get to the bottom of this!"

She called back the next day and indicated that she had discovered why no one had answered the TTY. "Apparently the TTY was put away because no one knew how to use it. That will be taken care of immediately!"

"Meanwhile," she continued, "I have been talking to our assistant director and he would like to meet with both of us. He wants to go over what you have shared with me about the lack of services for Deaf and what the other counties are doing to provide therapy for them. When are you available?"

We met the next week and I went over what I knew was the Law for Accessibility for Equal Access to Communication. I talked about why the Deaf had not been using mental health services and many other issues related to providing services to this population. I shared with them what the agency I worked for was doing. We walked through step-by-step the procedures that would be needed to be put in place to make those services more accessible. When we finished, the assistant supervisor said he would be taking the information to the board of directors and then was going to find out what the state was recommending for services to this population whose needs were apparently not being considered or provided.

A few weeks later, I received a call from the assistant supervisor stating that everything I had said was absolutely true and they needed to get busy to be in compliance with state and federal laws for accessibility needs for the Deaf. "I appreciate your concern for bringing this to our attention," he said. "Will you be available if we need your help as we put together this project?"

"Of course I will. I am so glad you are going to do something to make the services available. Just let me know if you have any questions or want me to find out anything that can be helpful to you," I said. I felt very content knowing they had listened and the Deaf would be able to get help when they needed it, just like those who are hearing. As time went on, I developed power point presentations to train outpatient mental health workers and therapists on mental health issues and Deaf culture along with the related issues on the law and the Deaf.

"Do not neglect to do good and to share what you have, for such sacrifices are pleasing to God."[52]

Accepting the Call
Chapter 31

One day toward the end of my second summer working with support services for the Deaf, our supervisor announced that he had received a flier with information about a Deaf attorney who was working as an advocate to help Deaf people navigate the legal system. The attorney requested an opportunity to come to talk with our Deaf community to enlighten them on to how to get equal access to communication from agencies that continued to be unaware of how to apply the law to their population.

"What do you think about setting up a time for this attorney to come here and do a presentation for our clients?" he asked.

We all came to an agreement this information would have a greater impact if it could be shared not only with our Deaf clients and their friends, but also with the Deaf from surrounding counties. We all thought it would be best to invite everyone interested in this need and also to invite agencies which would benefit from the information on how to provide appropriately services to Deaf.

One of our case managers suggested since we were having such nice weather and because the Deaf loved potlucks, we should have a picnic and make this a fun event. We knew we could get support for this event from the interpreter resource centers around the state and open this up to the entire community instead of limiting it to only our Deaf. We all liked that idea and agreed to start making plans for this event.

While most of the Deaf knew the law had changed to open their communication barrier, many agencies still failed to provide for their needs. Yet, those same agencies were making costly structural changes for blind. Most of these agencies were often at a loss as to what kind of resources were needed and how to provide those services to the Deaf or hard of hearing.

Most communities did not have enough local interpreters so it was easy for them to ask the Deaf person to bring someone with them to help with communication or paperwork. But, the law strongly forbid that. Too many times the friend or family member was not familiar enough with the legal language or the medical terms they needed to interpret effectively. More times than not, they did not know the sign language well enough to clarify the information that needed to be understood by the Deaf person. This was often less than desirable for a Deaf person who may have a serious or life threatening illness or may not want his or her family or friends becoming aware of his or her private business and due to issues of confidentiality.

Several agencies joined us to support our plans for the picnic by donating food, gifts, and volunteers to help with games, prizes, door prizes, and even clowns and magicians for the kids to enjoy. We had all worked together to make this a special event and our Deaf clients were filled with excitement as they looked forward to this event.

Although the day was a beautiful late summer day and a perfect day for outside activities, I had mixed feelings about going to the picnic. Part of me wanted to stay home with my husband and get caught up on household chores and yard work before he had to start back to school.

While ruminating over this, I finally decided I should stay home. *After all, my Deaf clients won't miss me with all of their family and friends surrounding them*, I thought. Then the phone rang.

"Hi Bonnie, this is Bobbi. I'm just calling to see if you plan to come over here today for the picnic. It's going to be great afternoon and presentation. Many people are here already and waiting to hear about what the attorney has to say and what the law says for the Deaf. I'm just wondering if I will see you here today."

"I would like to come, but there is so much to do here at home. I don't even have a dish prepared to bring to pass," I replied feeling guilty knowing that she was right and I was letting my clients and co-workers down by not showing up.

"Don't worry about that," Bobbi said. "Just come on over. There is more than enough food and your Deaf clients would love to see you outside of the work environment. Bring Don, too. Can I let them know you will join us a little later?"

"Okay. I'll head over in a little while. I need to finish a few things here. I'll see you in about an hour," I said, feeling better about going over to the picnic even though I had a lot of other things to do at home. I turned to my husband and told him that I had just changed my mind and would be going over to the picnic for a little while.

"Would you like to take a break and join me?" I asked.

"Oh, I see what you're up to! First you get me started on yard work then you take off leaving me here alone to work while you go have some fun!" He said teasing me.

He knew how much I was focused on the needs of the Deaf population and the struggle I often had balancing my own life around the Deaf, my family, household chores, and him.

"Well, you are welcomed to come with me. I'd like that and you know Bobbi and some of my Deaf friends."

"No, it's okay. You go and enjoy yourself. If I get tired of working outside, I can always go inside and start working on my preparations for school."

When I arrived at the picnic, Bobbi was already interpreting. I always admired Bobbi, whose first language was signing. I loved to watch how gracefully and eloquently she used concepts instead of just signing the words. Watching sign language also helped me catch up when I missed hearing words or parts of sentences. Sometimes I felt as if I lived in two separate worlds: that of the hearing but also being part of the hard of hearing world that often benefited from watching an interpreter.

I heard Bobbi announce while signing, "We will soon be taking a break while everyone gets something to eat. We will continue this presentation after lunch. While eating and socializing, think of some legal questions you would like to have answered by this attorney. Maybe you have had a problem getting services or perhaps you have had incidents happened to you and you want to know what you should have done or can do according to the law." Then, they both stepped down from the platform and Bobbi walked over to me to give me a big hug.

"There's such a nice turnout here with so many more people than I thought would come," I said. "I'm glad I decided to come over. It's much better than staying at home doing house and yard work!"

"Can I talk to you in private?" Bobbi asked. "I only have a short time before the attorney goes back to the stage and I have to return to voice for him. Let's step inside this shaded area under the steps and away from others for a moment."

"Wow, Bobbi, this sounds serious. What's up?" I asked, wondering if something unusual was brewing under all this wonderful activity.

"I'm wondering how you would feel about working with 150 deaf kids."

"What? Are you kidding?" I blurted out without thinking. I was so excited about that question my heart began to take leaps as I questioned, "Where?" thinking she had found a social work position for me in a school somewhere in the area.

"Well, I know you are involved a lot with your family and are active in a lot of activities, but how do you feel about mission trips?"

"I'd love to go on a mission trip. I wanted to be a missionary when I was younger. Where is the mission trip?"

"Jamaica."

"Jamaica?" I repeated while questions began to flood my mind.

"Yes. There is an orphanage and school there that needs our help to work with the Deaf kids and several building projects."

"You're asking about a mission trip to work with Deaf kids in Jamaica?" I asked. When is this trip?"

"In February," Bobbi replied.

"What? A mission trip to Jamaica in February? Are you kidding? With our cold snowy winters here? What an opportunity! Yes! I want to go."

Bobbi explained that we would need to get pledges for money and prayers for our safety. Kingston, the capital, which was not far from where we would stay, was under political unrest and there was a détente going on. Bobbi said if Don and I were interested, she would get more information for us. Her husband was also planning to go with her and she thought Don would like to go, too. "There are so many needs on this mission trip and a lot of technical and building work that needs to be done. I think Don would be a perfect asset to have with us on our team," she said encouraging me to ask him.

All the way home I kept thinking about the trip. I had a strong deep inner feeling I was definitely going and so was Don. Running into the house and finding Don at the computer, I couldn't hold back all that Bobbi had shared with me.

"So, you're planning to go on a mission trip this winter?" he asked.

"Oh, you're going, too!" I said with confidence.

"I'm afraid that will be impossible. Unless you forgot, I work full time as a teacher during the school year. I can't take time off work for a mission trip or I'll lose my job."

Somehow I knew my husband would accompany me. I knew he was needed, too. I couldn't explain it, but I'd had this same kind of feeling before on other occasions; for instance, when I was invited to Project Brother's Keeper in Nebraska in 1980. I had learned to trust that strong inner feeling of knowing it was going to happen.

"No, you won't lose your job. I know you are coming, too. Just ask for the week off."

"I signed a contract with the school system to be there the entire year. I can't go, but you can go."

"I know you are going. Your help is really needed there. You have all the skills we need. Just ask, please," I begged of him again.

"You seem to know so much about how I could help, what exactly is it you think I would be doing there?" he asked sarcastically.

"Are you kidding? They are building a big house for missionaries and a home for a young Deaf couple that needs to be finished. They have a school that needs a new roof since that hurricane hit them a few months ago. And, they need help teaching the Deaf. I know you have more than enough skills that could benefit them."

After much urging, Don finally put in a request to the administrative secretary.

"Well, don't let me stop you!" was the secretary's response and then nothing more was heard from her for months. During that time, Don accompanied me to all the meetings at the mission's headquarters where this mission trip was being organized. We received more pledge cards than we expected and the money kept rolling in. We donated the extra money to the general fund to help those who still needed more in their account so they could go. We met often to pray for guidance, learn about the customs and culture of Jamaica, and to discuss what might be expected of us.

As the time grew nearer to the date, and after we got our passports, it was almost time to pay for our plane tickets. However, the school administrator had not responded to Don's request for permission to take that week off. I urged him to call the secretary again to find out the status of his request.

"Oh, you really are asking to go on a mission trip during the school year?" the secretary asked when he called the office after-school one day. "I thought you were kidding! But if that is what you want to do, you will have to fill out a time off request form as soon as possible and submit it to the superintendent."

"Okay, I'll get down there tomorrow after-school to fill out my request," Don said as he turned to me shaking his head as if to say it's not going to happen. "Don't count on me getting time off especially asking at this late date."

"Don, you haven't taken any personal time off like other teachers. You haven't been sick, or had any family leave time. You must have more than enough sick days built up over the years. I think they will give you the time off. Just think positive."

A few days later, he came home and sat down in disbelief. He had received a letter indicating his request for time off to go on a mission trip had been granted!

"Looks like I'm going with you on this mission trip. I can't believe I was granted the time off during the school year!"

"I knew it would happen!" I said. I was overwhelmed with joy and relief. I quietly said a prayer of gratitude and thanks for allowing Don to join us.

Now we just had to finalize our plans and get our immunizations. Time was growing close and we had to get everything ready at our end.

"Until now you have not asked for in my name. Ask, and you will receive, and your joy may be complete."[53]

Blessings Received and Shared
Chapter 32

Our excitement continued to mount as the days grew closer to leaving for Jamaica. Prayers were offered by our church, family and friends for God to watch over us and keep us safe on our journey.

I was excited about being on this mission trip, but also looked forward to heading toward a warmer climate where we would be getting a break from the cold, snowy, Michigan weather during the month of February. This would be a pleasure we had never before experienced. We were filled with both excitement and anxiety as we thought of our destination into an unknown third world country, not fully understanding their culture or knowing what exactly would be expected of us.

The morning of our departure finally arrived. We needed to be at the airport very early and were blessed to have our son-in-law offer to drive us over to the airport in Grand Rapids at 4 am to save us the cost of parking fees. When we got out of our car, he took our winter jackets to keep in the car with him until he returned to pick us up eight days later.

As we walked up to the concourse, I could smell the aroma of fresh coffee brewing from the Starbucks Cafe. Not knowing when we would have another good cup of coffee again, Don treated me to a cup before joining some of our team members who were already standing around on the concourse half-awake as we waited for the rest of our team to arrive and to have pictures taken before we boarded our plane.

After boarding the plane, I sat down next to Don, who was looking out the window next to his seat. I looked over his shoulder to see the sun peeking up just over the horizon while the engine of the plane started to roar and the airline hostess began to instruct us on the use of our oxygen masks.

Suddenly, fear got a strong grip on me. I thought of the recent 9-11 terrorists attack in New York. "What if our airplane crashes? *What if our plane gets shot down and we never return? What if something happens while we are in another country and we never get to see our kids and grandchildren again?*

As the plane lifted off the ground, I became overwhelmed with all those negative and fearful "what if" thoughts while trying to feel brave and not cry. I felt very insecure and helpless as I thought about leaving my country, home, and family. So much could happen to us or our family in those eight days.

The plane tilted after take-off. I grabbed the armrest with my left hand and my husband's arm with the other. I looked up just in time to see my friend, Larry, who had turned around and was looking at me with a big grin. He noticed I was almost in tears and appeared uneasy. "Remember, you prayed for this!"

Just beyond Larry, I got a glimpse of the sun shining brightly through the window, almost blinding me. It was like the warm sun was laughing at me along with Larry. I chuckled after hearing his comment and took a deep breath as the plane turned once again and tipped to the other side. I let out a scream as it leveled once again. Then I caught a beautiful peaceful view of pink, orange and reddish rays beaming from the sun against the light blue sky which seemed to be saying calm down. All is well and going to be okay.

I sat back and recalled my last plane trip when I sat next to Father Coughlin who questioned me why was I afraid if I trusted God. I felt a deep sense of peace as I thought of his words again and sat back in my seat. He was right. I needed to let go and trust

God. *God has brought me this far. He will not let anything happen that He did not plan for on this mission trip.* However, I continued to pray for our safety, especially with each and every bump I felt as we flew through some turbulent wind clouds.

After a short time, the plane leveled and we were told we could get out of our seats and move about. I joined a few of the Deaf members of the team, who were walking around in the aisle, chatting, and getting to know other members of our mission team until the airline hostess announced we needed to return to our seats. We were flying over Cuba and would be landing very soon.

It was mid-afternoon by the time we actually landed at Montego Bay. As we exited the plane, the warm fresh ocean breeze softly surrounded us like a warm blanket while we could hear Calypso music in the distance. As we walked into the small airport, we saw native Jamaican women who were dancing and dressed in bright yellow ruffled dresses with red trim and large bright multicolored flowers in their hair.

I stopped to watch and then began shuffling through my carry-on bag searching for my camera and video tape recorder. Suddenly, I felt a hand grabbing my arm. Our mission guide was standing next to me looking very scornful as she spoke. "Don't do that! It is against their (pagan) religion. They forbid pictures to be taken because they believe their souls will be taken from them. If they see you take a picture, they will confiscate your camera and demolish it. Then you will not have any pictures at all to share when you get home."

I was shocked and very disappointed that I wouldn't be able to have a picture or video of these beautiful dancers. I wanted to share everything I was experiencing with family, friends, and supporters back home. Yet, I did understand. I needed to first respect the culture and the religion of those in this country.

After picking up our luggage, we gathered outside in the parking lot waiting for what seemed like hours for our ride to come from the other side of the island. I desperately needed to use the restroom and started to head toward one when our guide stopped me. "You can't go in there alone. I'll go with you. It is very dangerous for tourists here." Then she asked our husbands to stand guard around the outside of the restrooms while each of us took turns going inside two by two.

The director and some of the staff from the mission finally arrived to greet us. "I want you all to know, your team is the very first mission team we have ever had come here, where everyone knows some level of sign language. I am really impressed to also have five Deaf members of your team joining us! This will be something our school has never experienced before. I welcome all of you. It will certainly be good for the children to have all of you here."

He continued to inform us, "In this country the Deaf have no rights whatsoever. They are ostracized. They are not allowed to work, drive a car, or get a visa to leave this country. You are very fortunate that your country has equal rights for the Deaf."

Soon the trucks and vans from the mission finally arrived and we piled in for our long trip around the mountain to the southern side of Jamaica. Some of our men climbed into the back of trucks to guard and protect our luggage, while the rest of us took a seat inside the van.

Along the way, we saw things we had never seen before except maybe for pictures in books or movies. Women walked alongside the road with baskets and jars balancing on top of their heads. Men rode bicycles down the middle of streets along with heavy traffic and cows meandered alongside and down the middle of the roads. There were potholes everywhere and all the roads were in dire need of repair.

"Watch out!" I shouted to the driver without thinking. "There's a cow in the middle of the road and he is coming right toward us!"

"Yes, do cows have more respect in this country than the Deaf," replied our driver.

Being concerned with how fast it seemed we were driving, especially around S curves on the side of mountains, I tried to not be critical, as I spoke up. "I don't see any speed limit signs. How do you know how fast you can drive?"

"No, we don't have speed limit signs. Everyone drives at their desired speed. We don't have any drivers' education programs like you do in your country. It is very easy to get a driver's license here unless you are deaf."

As I looked over the side of the mountains I could see damaged cars hanging on trees or left where they had stopped rolling. The driver said the cars were left there because there was no way to get them out safely.

"We don't have big trucks or equipment to lift them out of the side of the mountains like in America. The roads are too narrow and steep. It would be almost impossible to remove the cars. There would be no way to warn oncoming traffic of the need to stop and that would cause more accidents. So, we just leave them."

"You could put signs up to slow down," I said.

"Many people, who have driver's licenses here, do not know how to read."

I certainly didn't feel very comfortable hearing any of this. However, I did feel my heart pounding with anxiety as we continued up the narrow, bumpy, mountain road that wound around cliffs without any rails. I thought if I had known about all of this, I might have not decided to be on this mission trip. Each time another car came around the mountain toward us, our driver would move closer to the mountain side to let the vehicle pass (in Jamaica they drive on the opposite side of the streets than we do in America). Sometimes, I wondered if there was enough room or if the other car would crash over the side of the mountain while trying to get past us.

I looked up toward the front window again and saw a huge semi-truck suddenly appearing from around the curve. "Watch out!" I screamed. Then closed my eyes thinking it was over for all of us.

Larry, who was sitting next to me at the back of the van, put his hand on my knee and once again teased me. "Didn't we pray for this?" He laughed and then continued, "Better be careful what we pray for next time!" When he stopped laughing, he looked serious as he said, "I, too, thought we were going to be pushed over the cliff instead of moving closer to the mountain."

As we neared Mandeville, we saw little huts along the road that reminded me of small fruit stands along country roads in the rural areas of Michigan. Next to them, stood eloquently designed adobe houses with varnished wooden window shutters and doors with beautiful designs carved in them. Tall black wrought iron fences surrounded these homes with black wrought iron bars protecting their windows and doors from intruders.

I mentioned to our driver how odd it was to see little shacks standing near the roads in front of these large beautiful houses. He told us that these shacks, which could barely protect someone from rain and wind, were for the poor to use as family homes.

"The rich and poor live close together, here. The rich have to use strong fences to protect themselves and their belongings from thieves. That is why they have high iron gates and bars across their windows and doors."

We finally entered a long winding driveway into the mission, passing the red brick pillars at the entrance, and pulled up to what they referred to as the "Big House". It had been used as a dorm at one time, but now it housed missionaries. It didn't have any air conditioning and our driver warned us to not drink the water from the faucets inside. At one of our team meetings, prior to coming to Jamaica, we had been prepared for this and each of us had packed a suitcase full of bottled water. There was one large room in the Big House where we could hold our meetings and have our team's daily devotionals in the mornings and evenings. There was only one bathroom for all twenty of us with a sign-up sheet outside the door for when we planned to use the bathroom.

We were told how to conserve water while taking showers. First we were to rinse ourselves off, then shut off the water and lather up before turning the water back on again for a quick final rinse.

"Those of you who are married, can double up in the shower to also help conserve water," our guide said.

"Sounds like fun to me!" my husband whispered in my ear as he nudged me and I responded by looking up at him grinning with a little chuckle.

By the time we unloaded our luggage it was dinner time. We were starved since we had not eaten a real meal since leaving our homes early that morning.

After a jerk chicken dinner, we stepped out of the dining room into the warm evening breeze of the courtyard where we were surrounded by children who were laughing, jumping rope, and playing basketball. We spent time getting to know their names and joined in their games until they were called to go inside to eat dinner. Their custom was for the guests eat first and then the children were allowed to eat afterward.

We used the time while they were eating to walk back up the hill to the Big House, where we unpacked and made our beds using the pillowcases and sheets we had brought from home. By the time we had finished that, we walked back down the hill to the courtyard as the children were coming out of the dining room and headed toward their auditorium.

The director led all of us up the stairs of a building that looked like a pole barn to join the children, who were excited as they reached for games from the shelf. It was Saturday night and that meant time for fun. Before starting to play games, one of the staff members asked each of us to stand up tell them our names and share something about ourselves using sign language. Following this, the children led us in a short devotional and signed a few simple songs. When they were finished, some of the children and staff wanted to hear more about where we were from and what our country is like while others enjoyed playing board games or cards. We stayed until the dark starry sky told us it was time for them to go to bed and for us to go to back to the Big House for our evening devotionals before we retired.

After devotionals, our guide announced we had to be up early the next morning for our trip into Mandeville where we would attend a hearing church. "Breakfast is at 8 am and the bus will be leaving at 9 am, so make sure you are all done with showers and preparations on time."

Although my husband slept very soundly beside me, I tossed and turned. I was exhausted, but couldn't sleep. Our bed was just a mattress on the floor and our pillows smelled dusty. I watched as cockroaches seemed to crawl out of nowhere and ran across the floor. There were no shutters or screens covering the windows, only wrought iron bars. Feeling very uncomfortable in such a setting, I watched for geckos or whatever else might crawl in through the window. In my prayers, I reminded God of my need to feel safe and to help me get over my fear of cockroaches, lizards, and geckos, which seemed to be abundant around here.

The next morning, at breakfast, our guide and her husband announced our group would be teaching Sunday school to children at church that morning. She didn't have a clue what the lesson would be or how many children to expect, but said we could always improvise.

All of us knew many Bible stories and most of us had some experience teaching Sunday school at one time or another, but this was impromptu and we were all feeling confused about which lesson to share. I wondered how this was going to work out with so many of us asked to teach. We prayed that God would lead us to do what we needed to do.

Once inside the church, we were seated with the Deaf off to the side, separated from the congregation that sat in main sanctuary of church. At first, I felt awkward being in an unfamiliar church in another country and not knowing the customs. However, I soon began to relax as we sang and signed familiar songs we knew such as "Because He Lives" and "The Power of His Love".

After the church service we were led downstairs to the Sunday school classroom where there must have been at least 80 kids of all ages waiting for us.

Our team took a few minutes to decide which story to tell and then we each took part sharing pieces of that Bible story. When we finished the Bible story, we still had a lot of time left before class would be over. We sang a few songs. Then one of our team members, who was a school teacher, taught some interactive games to cut down the noise and commotion that often occurs when there are many students in one room and there seems to be a lack of guided activity or unplanned free time.

Sunday afternoon after dinner we spent relaxing and visiting. Later that day we were introduced to the staff and given a tour of their classrooms. The children were excited to show us what they were studying and many of the crafts they had made.

Most of the elementary classrooms were very much like our own, except several of the books and materials were worn and some outdated. The high school students were proud to show off their technical wings and where the girls took cosmetology, sewing, and cooking classes. There was a co-ed classroom for computer skills and the boys took classes in auto shop, welding, woodworking and mechanics.

"In this country Deaf people are considered to be worthless and often left alongside the road at a young age to fend for themselves," the teacher said. "We started this Deaf School to find those kids, take them in to educate them, and share Christ's love with them."

Two of the high school boys stepped out of the industrial arts wood shop classroom as I walked by and waved for me to come inside. They pointed at several doors and headboards for beds leaning against the wall. Each door or headboard had either praying hands, the face of Jesus, angels, doves, crosses or other biblical pictures with Bible verses carved into the wood. I stood there feeling awed by their creations. I couldn't hold back tears as I looked at these high school boys who were standing there, rightly proud of their work, and staring at me for my reaction.

My heart ached as I thought about their parents, who had given these boys up because they couldn't hear. They would never see these awesome carvings that they had made and never share the pride of having sons who could create something so beautiful. I wondered if the outside community ever have an opportunity to see this kind of work of art, would they still overlook these boys' valuable skills just because they were Deaf?

I became so choked up I couldn't verbalize the words, "beautiful, awesome". It was a relief that I could sign those words to them.

That afternoon my husband had found his way up to the computer classroom. The teacher was having problems with the computers, and since my husband taught robotics, office skills, and many programs in an adult education program, he sat down and fixed all the computers in the classroom.

Later that day the auto shop teacher talked to my husband about the problems they were experiencing with their tractors and machines. My husband stepped into the shop and helped the teacher and students fix these things.

Sunday evening we returned to the Big House for our devotionals and to prepare for the next day when our true work at this mission would begin. Our guide and her husband went over what we would be doing starting very early the next morning.

"Breakfast is at 8 am every day this week. Make sure you have everything you need, gloves, hats, and water to start working immediately when you're done with breakfast. Some of you will stay in the kitchen to clean up and wash dishes. Others will start clearing the ground of rocks and rubbish, while others will be bending rebar to reinforce steps, clearing rubbish for the land, mixing cement for an addition to the house or finish laying tiles in some rooms that had already been started by the previous team."

I woke early after my first full night of sleep without any anxiety about the creepy, crawling creatures getting me. After breakfast, I was assigned to start bending re-bar. Don started working on clearing the ground for the new addition.

I had thought being on a mission trip was going to be like VBS where we taught from the Bible and shared Jesus with the children. Or, perhaps I would be helping teachers in the classrooms. I didn't anticipate twisting re-bar when I signed up for this mission trip, but I was willing to do what was needed to be done.

One evening during our team devotionals I became aware of how God had chosen each of us to be on this trip. One of our team members stood up to give a testimonial. He told how hard it was to be a Deaf person in a hearing world and trying to fit in with others. He felt left out most of his life and started to do whatever he could to fit in with other teenagers. He tried to find jobs without luck. Eventually he started drinking and using drugs to be like other teens, but that got him into trouble.

Then someone shared Christ with him and helped turn his life around. Since then he said he has been trying to help other Deaf people to know how much God loves them, too. He said fitting into society is no longer his goal. Instead, doing things for Christ gives him a much more meaningful life.

His story was so powerful that we all stood up to hug and pat him on the back. We encouraged him to share this story with the kids, too.

Later that week, he met with the children at the mission and shared his life story. Young faces listened to him as he told about his experience of being an outcast in society. Every one of the kids could relate to him and some of his experiences as none of the rest of us could, regardless of whether we could sign or not.

By the end of that week our team had built an extension on the Big House using cement, re-bar, and bamboo. We had pushed stones over the mountain. We had carried two buckets at a time of cement up to the second floor until Don made it easier by making a simple pulley. We took turns doing each job for an hour or two so we did not get bored or tired. It was hard work, but fun as a group. The children often came out of their classrooms during their breaks to help us and talk with us while we worked. When I say "talk," I mean using sign language. The kids had fun with us, too. Sometimes we took a few minutes to bounce their ball or jump rope with them. They often offered to help us by running errands or getting us some of the purified water from the kitchen area while we worked.

One day I was asked to paint the ceiling of the new apartment that had been built for a Deaf couple who were recently married. I knew I was not good at painting, but when I tried to paint the ceiling, the paint from the roller dripped down all over my face, hair, and clothing. I looked like a clown! Everyone laughed and agreed this was enough painting for me. I returned outside to help build the cement steps on the back side of the house where it was much cooler due to bamboo trees surrounding that area.

When it came my time for kitchen duty, I was stunned that they did not have hot water or sudsy dish detergent for washing dishes. I wondered how safe it was to eat using the utensils, but I realized it was too late to think of that now. I was also shocked to see so many cockroaches the size of silver dollars crawling around on the kitchen floor. Since we had already been eating here for the past few days, I thanked God everyone was still okay.

After lunch on Thursday, the director called us all together. "You have all worked very hard and finished the goals ahead of schedule. We now have to wait for the cement to set. Get into some play clothes and bring your swim suits and towels. We are going on a trip to Ocho Rios, near the ocean, to visit Dunns River Falls."

I had never heard anything about Dunns River Falls and didn't know what to expect. But, I went along with the crowd hoping not to see bigger lizards or other creepy crawling things.

Once we arrived at Dunns River Falls and unloaded the van, we walked past many palm trees and flowers as we took the steps down the hill to the ocean. For the first time in my life, I saw a huge cruise ship anchored close to the beach. It amazed me how large the ship was and how close to the beach the ship had docked.

I immediately fell in love with this place surrounding us with a warm moist breeze and the most beautiful light blue-green water with palm trees shading us. Along the beach were little tiki bars where we could buy food or drinks and listen to the music which reminded me of several Jimmy Buffet songs I had heard back home.

I laid my towel down on the sand next to Don's where we could hear the music. I leaned back to soak up the sun and relax when suddenly others from our group called to us as they rushed over grabbing and pulling us toward them. They said we needed to climb the falls with them. I was really hesitant about climbing up the falls and wanted Don to come too, but he wasn't feeling very well and wanted to just relax and read a book he had brought along.

"Hmm, climbing the falls? Is that safe?" I asked our leader as we walked closer to the falls which flowed into the Caribbean. When we got to the foot of the falls, I stood there for a moment looking up. I could see the water rushing down over huge boulders and lots of people climbing upwards while others took the steps along the catwalk next to the falls. I felt relieved to see these falls were not like Niagara Falls in Canada. But, I was still unsure about climbing the 600 feet of these big gray boulders while warm clear water washed down over me. I was afraid I would slip or lose my balance and feared falling and getting hurt.

"I'll be right behind you if you need help," one of the men from our group, said, as he handed me a rope that was connected to the top. "I've been here before and climbed these falls several times. It's not hard, but if you get tired or want to stop, I'll help you out so you can walk the rest of the way up on the catwalk."

At times the rocks got slippery and other times, I had to put my full foot deep into a crack between the rocks. I cringed as I thought of all kinds of creatures that might decide to nibble on my toes, but there was not one bite and nothing hurt except my hips from my weight and stretching my legs and body as I scaled the rocks that got bigger and bigger toward the top of the falls. Although it was so much more fun than I had expected it would be to climb these rocks with warm water splashing over us, I got about three fourths of the way up when I couldn't stretch my legs anymore.

"Guess I'd better stop here," I said. The gentleman behind me helped me off to join other tourists, who were walking up the steps alongside the falls. Once at the top, I looked around and saw the most breathtaking scenery with beautiful flowers and unique huge tropical flowers everywhere amongst the palm trees and other awesome exotic plants. It was like visiting paradise!

That afternoon was an especially wonderful and refreshing experience at the beach, but it was soon time to return back to the mission and have dinner. Don said his stomach was still too upset from eating too much jerk chicken the past few days and didn't want dinner that night.

As I was finishing dinner, Don walked into the dining room asking for a piece of toast and came to sit next to me. The director caught a glimpse of Don and walked over to our table. "I'm glad I caught you both, here. I want to meet with you (Don) and your wife in private later this evening while the others are outside with the children." Then he turned and walked back to the table where he had been sitting.

"I wonder what he wants to talk to us about." I asked.

"I don't know, but we will soon find out," Don said as we finished and got up to walk out of the dining room.

A little while later, we returned to the dining room to meet with the director. "I'm glad the two of you came back to talk. How are things going for you, here?"

"Fine," we both said in unison, still questioning the reason for this meeting with the director.

"I suppose you are wondering why I invited you to talk with me. Well, I have heard good reports from our staff about your work and I've noticed your skills," he said while looking at Don. "I've heard you are a teacher back home, but I wonder what else is in your background?" he asked.

"I have a lot of mechanical experience," Don replied. "I had an engineering scholarship at Michigan State University, but the field of engineering was full when I was near graduation. I tried a semester of student teaching in an industrial arts program where I could utilize my education and skills in building, electronics, wood shop, automotive and several other areas I enjoyed. When the Industrial Arts program was eliminated a few years ago in the school where I worked, I was transferred into the adult education program and taught computers, robotics and office skills. I had some previous experience in college working with Fortran computers. I gained experience in computer repair while working in adult education."

"You know, we could use someone like you here. I heard how quickly you fixed our tractor and made carrying cement up the steps easier by designing that pulley and the computer teacher was overjoyed to be able to get her students back online again. I know this might be a difficult question for you, but what would you think of coming here to work and live?"

My heart took several flip flops as I looked at my husband, trying to figure out what he was thinking. I was also trying to figure out how I was feeling—happy and excited to be working with Deaf as a missionary or sad and depressed to leave my family back home.

The director continued, "Of course we would pay you, but your salary would be nowhere near what you are getting back home. However, we would provide free housing and living costs, too. There wouldn't be much you would need here. We would also arrange for a three month furlough home every year."

My heart was still doing flip flops. When I was younger, I had envied the lives of missionaries I had met. But, now, with kids and grandkids back home, I didn't want to leave them. Even if we had three months off to return home and do nothing but visit them, which three months would we take? Would it be Christmas or Easter? Or the summers that I loved back home near the lake? But then, we'd be home for only three months a year! We would miss out on a lot in their lives and activities; but it wasn't me he asked to stay. It was Don.

"Let me think about this and talk with Bonnie," Don said. "I'll let you know tomorrow,"

"That's fair enough. But please do give this some thought and prayer," he said as he patted Don on the shoulder and shook my hand. "I'll look forward to hearing your decision tomorrow."

By Friday noon, we had finished everything. After lunch the director told everyone to take a shower and grab their bags or wallets. He was going to take us down to the market near Montego Bay. He warned us to not touch anything unless we planned to buy it. "The native custom here is, if you touch it, you own it."

We walked around for hours looking over the craft work and items that were all made by hand and searching for souvenirs to take back home. On our way back to the mission, the director said he had arranged for another surprise for us this evening. He was taking us to the Big Tree for a cook out.

He was right to call this the Big Tree. I had never ever seen such a huge monster of a tree! The branches wrapped themselves around the main part of the tree as if to create a place for many people to sit or sleep.

The director had brought some dough he had made for this picnic. He showed us how to make wraps by putting the dough on a stick to roast like marshmallows. When the dough was done, we filled it with Guava jam and peanut butter. It was so good.

Then he brought out hotdogs the staff had purchased for us to eat at our cookout. As we ate while sitting around the Big Tree, the director told us the history of Jamaica. He shared his dream to build a village where Deaf adults could live after they graduated from their school and mission.

"It could be a place for the Deaf to live, work, worship, have families, and live like the rest of us in the hearing world." He then appeared sad as he continued to share more about his dream village. "Money, time, and materials prove to be the stumbling blocks for this to happen. Sadly, when our Deaf students graduate and leave our mission, they cannot find work. Their lives change, but not for the better. Some hang around the school during the day looking for ways to be useful in exchange for something to eat. While America provides social services for their deaf, Jamaica does not provide anything." He looked down almost in tears. "I haven't given up hope. I ask you all to pray with me that someday God will answer my prayers to create this village that I so deeply want for our Deaf adults.

Although it was hard after hearing this, Don and I had agreed that living this life full time was not for us. We met with the director alone when we returned back to the mission. Don told him we were very sorry but we could not take the job he was offering. We had several obligations and family commitments back home and didn't feel this was to be part of lives at this time. Don thanked him for offering this opportunity to us and prayed he would find the help he needed from someone without so many strings holding them back. Luckily, the director understood what we would have to give up. He told us that he had to give all that up when he came to Jamaica, but he was much younger without a family and had not settled into a lifestyle that would require much from him.

That night when we returned to the campus for our final game night and devotionals with the children and teachers, we would be saying our final good-byes to all these people with whom we had developed a relationship and enjoyed being with them during the past week.

Unlike our previous game nights with them, the students were extremely full of energy and excitement as they directed us to certain seats where they wanted us to sit. The older children performed a skit of a young man looking for love and doing anything he could to get it. He headed down the wrong path, but finally met Jesus who showed him a much better way to live.

Finally, the young man knew the feeling of true love. We knew this skit was about our team member, who had shared his story earlier during the week with us and then with these kids.

Next, the Praise in Sign group of children entertained us by signing several songs such as "Shout to the Lord". We could hear the words from a CD while their teacher directed them in sign language from the back of the room. The last song brought tears to my eyes when they signed "Thank You" by Ray Boltz.

I felt blessed with the opportunity to have spent this past week with them and to watch them sign such beautiful songs for us on our last evening with them. We would never forget such a wonderful gift and experience. I hoped we could return again someday.

Everyone on our team was quiet as we walked back to the Big House together that night. Each of us focused on our own thoughts about our experiences during the past week. We had grown so much spiritually as a team and individually. We had fallen in love with the children, some of whom were orphans in search of caring people like us, to take them back home and to bring them hope for their future.

Saturday morning came too early. We were tired and sad. Yet, we were excited as we looked forward to our trip back home to our country and families. As we journeyed down the mountains and passed palm trees, cacaos, coffee, and banana trees, we spied the Caribbean Sea at a distance from over the tops of trees on the mountains below us. It was such a beautiful sight to view from the mountain tops. We finally arrived at the airport where we said our goodbye's to the drivers and staff who had accompanied us. As our team sat waiting quietly for our plane, we talked about all we had done and seen in this third world country and the kids who had stole our hearts.

We boarded the plane much quieter than we did before we left the states. We each took our seats feeling tired and sad. We were leaving behind kids who were in search of families to take them home, love them, and give them opportunities like our kids had. As the plane began to take off, I watched out the window as we passed little grass shanties lined up in a row with palm trees surrounding them along the runway. Once we were in the air, I looked down over Montego Bay and the shoreline of Jamaica. I took one last look of the beautiful bluish green, almost clear Caribbean Sea with the coral reefs I could barely see below us. We were on our way back to the safety of our warm homes with television, electrical appliances, and our family and friends who loved us. Oh, yes. I almost forgot, and snow.

Will we ever return to this Jamaican mission again? I wondered.

As I continued to watch the coastline of Jamaica fade away, I pondered over this entire mission trip and the people we had worked with. I would miss the joy of the kids' smiling faces when they came to see us every day offering to help us as we built and repaired their school and dorms. I would miss their excitement of being able to communicate with us in sign language and their longing for us to take them back with us to a country where there would be opportunities for them.

I reflected on what I had learned and realized being a missionary was much different than I had expected. Being a missionary was not about preaching or teaching, nor like I had expected. It was working side by side with each other to help carry their burdens and love them like God loves us without judgment. It was being kind, listening to them, and being open to understanding their world and their needs. It was so important to accept them just as they are while not trying to change them. Our goal as Christians was to make their lives easier without taking over. Just being there and showing we cared meant so much to them. This was all that God was asking from us. I also thought about my training as a social worker and the similarity of that to being a missionary.

God had provided Don and I an opportunity to serve Him. As I sat there thinking about and struggling with my feelings of wanting be a missionary and also wanting to be at home with my family, I wondered how God viewed our decision to not stay in Jamaica as missionaries. Would we be able to return to this mission again, someday? Yet, I also knew that if God wanted us to come back or go elsewhere to do His work, He would make a way for that to happen. We just had to put our future in His hands.

"Trust in the Lord with all your heart and lean not on your own understanding."[54]

Expanding Horizons
Chapter 33

It felt so happy to be home in our own country even though we were greeted with snow, and an extremely cold and blustery wind. Our son-in-law was standing in the airport holding our warm winter coats for us just as he had promised when he had dropped us off. We would soon return back to work and our daily grind. Yet, the memories would be with us forever. We couldn't help sharing our experiences with everyone. We were asked to do presentations at our church and at a meeting for DeColores en Cristo, an interdenominational spiritual Christian organization in which we belonged. We showed pictures and talked about our experiences and the culture in Jamaica, especially their treatment of Deaf individuals. When we asked for prayers for the children, staff and deaf community, hearts were opening to this mission and without asking, monetary donations were offered and sent to this mission for Deaf in Jamaica.

I returned to my job in Grand Rapids and continued to pursue my goal to open more opportunities and accessibility for the Deaf in my own home town by making contact with several social service agencies. I found the directors of these agencies more than willing to discuss this issue with me. One of the biggest issues reported was finding someone who knew sign language to assist the Deaf who was a qualified interpreter, state certified, and not already working full time in one of the school systems.

When I referred my clients to doctors, social service agencies, or even attorneys, I was often asked to come along with my clients to interpret for them. I refused to do that and reminded them of the law and that I was not an interpreter. I was just a social worker with signing skills. The Deaf deserved to have a certified and qualified interpreter in their private meetings with their doctors or psychiatrist, legal advisers and even employers. When I think back to those days, it still amazes me I was asked, and almost expected, to leave my job to make an appointment to join my client. I am sure those professionals would not leave their jobs to interpret for another professional.

As I continued to contact various agencies about the type of services they provided to the Deaf population, the faster the awareness and interest was growing toward the need and options were being explored to change procedures to comply with the law. My hope and dream to have an interpreter referral service in my home town was becoming a real possibility. It was the right time for changes to occur because of the Deaf Power Movement which stemmed from the 1988 Deaf President Now movement at Gallaudet University. The Deaf students had protested against the board of trustees, almost causing a war because the university hired a hearing president instead of a Deaf president. The Deaf students won and I. King Jordan became the first Deaf president of Gallaudet University. That movement spurred another Deaf movements led by the culturally Deaf, who began advocating for equal rights throughout the United States. The silenced Deaf were now being heard loud and clear.

I decided to contact a certain man, whom I knew had grown up with Deaf parents, and to ask if he would be willing to help me start a center for the Deaf. He was so excited he called a meeting with several other community agency administrators. I was overwhelmed with the turnout that showed up and many thanked me for identifying a need that had not been addressed in our community. Two people stepped up and offered to start applying for grants and asked me to help them by obtaining statistics and the actual number of Deaf in our county.

I couldn't believe how fast this ball was actually rolling! A town meeting was held to ask the Deaf community and those with a hearing loss, if they would be interested in this project and their ideas about other needs to be addressed. Everyone was overjoyed and expressed their support for a center to provide services and referrals for their special needs. My dream was on its way to becoming a huge success!

Everything was moving so rapidly in the direction of fulfilling this goal that I couldn't keep up with working in Grand Rapids and in private practice, taking classes in Lansing and putting more energy into the development of this much needed and worthwhile service. I knew I had to change some things in my life to provide me with the energy to think clear, to stay focused, and to do the research that was needed. Knowing I had to create more time for myself, I wouldn't be able to continue to work two jobs, even if they were each part-time or continue in the Interpreter Training Program while putting the time and effort needed to make this future agency come to fruition. However, I planned to continue to be involved with the advocacy Coalition group which met regularly in Lansing. I had my hands in too many pots and would have to choose which job to let go and back down from some of my social activities and other organizations in which I was an active member.

I chose to keep my private practice in my home town open because it afforded me the time I needed to continue to work diligently educating communities about the needs and legal rights of the Deaf. However, I did regret making a decision to resign from my job in Grand Rapids and to withdraw from my interpreter internship; but I knew this would be best for me and my ultimate goal. During the next year, I spent time between clients, contacting administrators and researching statistics on the number of Deaf not only in my county, but also surrounding counties with the hope to have them join us.

Several counties supported us and helped financially to spread the awareness in their communities as well as starting to provide accessibility for the Deaf in their areas. Soon grant money started coming in. With each grant, there was an understanding that services would also be included for those other counties. As this new agency finally became a reality, letters were sent out in search of a director over the next few months. However, with my experience, contacts and signing skills, I was offered the full-time position of director for the first year.

I took the position and looked forward to fulfill my commitment getting this agency off the ground and to serve and educate the people in our county along with three other supporting counties. It was a very difficult decision for me to make, but I also had to close my private practice. I was reluctant giving up all of this, but I knew it was a necessary choice for the better. I had a huge goal to accomplish at this time and everything else had to take the back seat, at least for a while. As director of this new agency, my first major job was to hire a secretary. I needed someone with knowledge of sign language and computer technical skills. This person needed to be someone the Deaf could trust and who would work with compassion and understanding of those who had a hearing loss and their families.

I reviewed many applications and interviewed several applicants, but I kept returning to the first applicant who was totally Deaf. Her first language was sign language; yet, she could read lips very well. She had graduated from a technical college and came highly recommended. She was patient, compassionate, and understanding of all people with disabilities, as well as those who had no understanding of deafness.

I wanted to hire her immediately after our first interview, but there was friction among our board members who believed a Deaf person would not be a good choice because someone with such a huge disability would have difficulty doing what was needed to be done by a secretary. Some of the board members expressed concerns such as answering incoming phone calls or what she would do if a hearing person stopped in to ask questions, or how she would interact with the administrators of the agencies supporting this new agency.

I was shocked at their responses, especially since this was an agency for the Deaf. I was also aware of several other state agencies that had Deaf staff members and even directors. How could I run an agency for those who were Deaf or had a hearing loss and offer hope for this population for their future, for employment opportunities, and inclusion in society if we denied a job to a Deaf person who had all the skills needed and more than any other applicant?

I reminded them, "A Deaf person can do everything a hearing person can do except hear." This struggle went on for weeks, but I had the final say as the director and I finally hired her against their advice. There was a lot of negative feedback based only on their fears, but she proved herself to be an outstanding, well educated person who could set up and run an office efficiently.

Accommodations did need to be made with a phone router to the computer and with the assistance of TTY relay services. We set up two phone lines in the office; one for me directly and one for her to use with teletype and routers. Through the relay phone system she could take incoming calls from hearing people. Should a hearing person walk in while I was out of the office, she had them write a note for me or she gave them my direct phone number to leave a message. I was very content and happy I had hired her. I admired her skills and she was an excellent worker, whom everyone, including board members, learned to love and accept.

Soon, word got around that an agency for the Deaf was now open. My life became very busy conducting presentations to Rotary Clubs, Lions Clubs, school administrators, mental health providers, hospital staffs, employers, and Senior Resource Agencies. I received phone calls from individuals from all four counties asking about assistive hearing equipment for those who did not use sign language and how to obtain these items.

One of our first success stories was helping a hard of hearing worker keep her job at a hospital. The director of nursing informed us she had just let their best nurse go because the nurse could not hear heartbeats with a stethoscope. We found a digital stethoscope which worked great and the nurse and her supervisor were happy she was able keep her job and return to work.

In another community, I worked closely as a consultant with a case worker who had many Deaf on his case load who needed special equipment to be successful at work or school. Our new agency was proud to successfully help him find solutions.

The interpreter referral service was growing faster than we imagined; but, the difficulty of finding qualified interpreters continued. That sparked another idea. I made an appointment to meet with the directors at two of our local colleges to provide them with supportive statistics on the need for interpreter's, versus the number of Deaf who could benefit from interpreters. I shared with them the high cost of paying interpreters for their traveling expense due to the lack of available interpreters in our community. Although both colleges were interested, Baker College took the lead and in 2004 started the first Interpreter Training Program in West Michigan.

Our new center for those with a hearing loss provided information on the newest assistive devices, programs to educate those with any hearing loss, and made families aware of what is available to them and their legal rights. We also aimed to get job coaches to work with employers and employees to aid those with any degree of a hearing loss understand their job description and to assist with communication between employer and employee. Our local Deaf community soon brought others into our agency for assistance. Eventually they started a club for those who were culturally Deaf and invited others with a hearing loss to attend their meetings and socialize.

Because of my personal deep desire to grow in ASL and provide Deaf with an opportunity to grow in Christ, I decided to start a training program for Christian Interpreters for Deaf. I had attended weekend workshops over the past several years and loved how the interpreters could bring Bible stories to life. I knew three interpreters who did an excellent job with this and decided to contact them about providing training in biblical interpreting, especially for the new interpreters. One very special Christian man, who was an excellent interpreter, said he would be willing to do the trainings. He suggested if we offered CEU'S (Continuing Education Credits) it would help to get more interest from the interpreters because it would help them keep their licenses up to date. I followed through with that request and the turnout for these training sessions was outstanding. The interpreters came from various religious and denominational backgrounds, making interpreting the Bible very interesting as we listened and watched each person's perspective of the meaning of the Bible verses they were to interpret. These sessions lasted all day and were fun and spiritually thrilling for everyone.

I loved working as director of this agency, but also loved my work as a social worker providing therapy to those in need. I had often received calls from various mental health agencies offering me a position to work full-time with their Deaf clients. While I was enjoying my current position, I often thought about returning to private practice someday; but left that idea as a possibility for the future.

One pleasant summer day, a gentleman walked into our office smiling and asked for me. "Hi, I'm Dr. Lamson. I recently read about you in the newspaper and all you are doing to provide services for the Deaf. I just thought I would stop by here and see how things are going for you. I understand you recently went on a mission trip to work with Deaf children. The article also said you were a therapist prior to taking this position. I've wondered if you think you will ever return to that career again."

"That's interesting," I said. "It seems I have thought about that often since taking this job. But for now, I think my hands are full getting this agency off the ground and creating community awareness for the needs of the Deaf and hard of hearing."

"I thought you might say that, but if you ever think of going back to providing therapy, even if only with the Deaf. I offer Christian therapy and have an office a short distance from here. You would be welcomed to use one of the offices one or two days per week. Let me know if you ever decide to consider returning to work as a therapist," he said as he handed me his business card. "I'd love to have someone like you with your background working with me. I do understand your skills are needed in many directions right now, but I do hope you will consider this offer. I pray for God to guide you in your career and in life."

As I stood there watching him walk away, I began to wonder if God had sent him to me to return to work as a therapist. Although, I did seem to have a habit of getting myself into situations where I took on too much responsibility, I knew I could not possibly take on more work. Yet, I wondered if God was leading me to another door I needed to open or was this possibly another one of those times when Satan was playing with my heart and skills?

A few weeks later while driving up the street, I saw a sign with Robert Lamson, Ph.D written on the side of the building. I recognized it as the name of the man who had stopped by my office and offered me space to rent. Out of curiosity, I decided to stop and go inside to check out his office space. I parked my car and walked inside. The waiting room was decorated with very soothing green and pink colors and cozy furniture. I could hear Christian songs playing softly in the back ground.

"Hello," I said to the secretary who had just hung up the phone. "I'm a social worker. Dr. Lamson stopped by my office a few weeks ago and left his card. I was just driving by and thought I would stop in to see what his office is like."

"Would you like to talk with him? I think he is just dictating some notes right now," his secretary asked.

"You don't have to bother him. I just thought I would stop to say hi."

"Let me check with him. I'll let him know you are here."

Dr. Lamson opened the side door to his office and stepped out into the lobby. "I was hoping you would come by someday. Have you given any thought to my offer?"

"I can visualize myself working here, but I really enjoy my job as director of the agency for Deaf," I said as he started to show me around.

"When the time is right for you, call me. You are welcome to stop by anytime, just let me know when you are ready to start."

It seemed he was very persistent, yet patiently waiting, and maybe deep down he knew someday I would return to my career as a therapist.

A few months after that, I received a call from a Deaf parent who had heard I could sign and wanted to bring her child to me for therapy.

I told her I wasn't doing therapy anymore because I had taken a position as a director of this new agency.

"My daughter is thirteen years old and an only child. Her father died a few months ago and she just can't seem to snap back to her old self. Our doctor put her on an antidepressant, but it makes her sleep a lot. Normally, she is very happy and bubbly. Now she just sits and stares. It's like her life is gone."

I felt torn inside. Here was a Deaf child in desperate need for therapy. I knew I could help her work through her grieving. Yet, I hadn't actually spoken to Dr. Lamson about renting space. *Maybe one night after work once a week for 2–3 hours would be something I should consider.*

I made a quick call to Dr. Lamson's office. "Yes, Dr. Lamson is here, but he is with a patient. Can I leave him a message?"

"Yes, tell him Bonnie called. Let him know I may take him up on renting office space a few hours once a week. Please have him call me back as soon as he can."

Dr. Lamson was very happy I had accepted his offer and arranged an office for me to use as often as I liked. I contacted insurance companies and re-enrolled as a practitioner. Then, I called the mother back and we set up a time to meet with her and her daughter for an intake session.

It wasn't long before my practice started growing and I decided to extend my clinical hours to two hours per night, two nights per week and an occasional Saturday.

"Commit to the Lord whatever you do, and your plans will succeed."[55]

Unexpected Visitors
Chapter 34

It was a beautiful spring day and I had just walked in the house from work when the phone rang.

"Hi Bonnie. This is Bobbi calling!" she said sounding very excited and speaking so fast I could barely understand her. "Are you aware the director of the Praise in Sign group is here with some of the kids? They are on a short tour to raise funds for the Mission.

Stunned and not sure I heard her correctly, my mind was flooded with questions. "Here? Where? What do you mean, here? Are they in Grand Rapids or somewhere else in the United States? Where are they?" I was getting excited, too. I thought if there was any way I could arrange my schedule to see them, I would love to show up wherever they are and watch them once again perform Christian songs in ASL.

"Well, I am not sure they are here in Grand Rapids, yet; but I do know the director is somewhere here in Michigan with the kids. He was able to get a special visa to bring the kids to the states for a short concert tour. Remember, Cory, the man who went with us on our mission trip to Jamaica? He and his wife have been arranging their tour schedule. One of the families they were to stay with had to back out at the last minute and the concert where the Praise in Sign group was to perform had to be canceled. Cory is trying to put together an alternative concert tour and find some place for all of them to stay for three days. He and his wife would do it if they could, but they already have other commitments for those three days. Is there any way you and Don can put them up this coming weekend? I know this is sudden. I didn't know anything about this until Cory just called me a little while ago and I thought maybe you might be able to help out."

Without even thinking or asking Don I blurted out, "YES! I'll put them up!" I knew he wouldn't mind and would be happy to help them out, too. "How many of them are kids and how many adults are traveling with them?"

"I think there are only seven or eight of them. I know the director and at least one teacher are traveling with the kids. So there are probably five or six kids."

"I guess we are lucky to have three extra bedrooms and three bathrooms in this new house we just built. We use one of the bedrooms as a den and computer room, but we can rearrange it to put some beds in there. In the back bedroom, we still have the bunk bed Don built for our girls when they were little. It is strong enough for adults, too. We have a double bed in the other bedroom and a sofa sleeper in the basement family room. Plus we also have a blow up twin mattress packed away in a closet. If we need more, I think I can get some cots from DeColores. We do a lot of volunteering for that program and know the board members pretty well. I'll check with them to see if can get a few cots for a weekend.

When Don and I returned from our mission trip to Jamaica, we did a presentation and showed videos of our work and the mission at one of the DeColores meetings. They were all very interested and send a nice donation to the Deaf center in Jamaica. I'm sure they will help us out if needed."

"Oh, by the way," Bobbi continued, "is there any way you might be able to check around and find out if some churches in your area might be able to do a quick concert or even a little special music during church and take a good will donation for them?"

"I'll check with our church to see if they are open to doing anything and ask around to other churches as well. I'll see what I can do."

When Don got home from school, I told him about Bobbi's call and how thrilled I was to be able to provide this hospitality to the kids from Jamaica and their two chaperones. He was glad I had offered to put them up in our home and was excited we would be able to see then again.

"It seems there was a purpose for us to build this house with four bedrooms! I'll help you get things ready for them. We don't have much time to prepare if they are coming this weekend.

The next morning I checked with our church secretary about allowing the Praise in Sign kids to be our special music during church this coming Sunday.

"Oh, I'm sorry, Bonnie, but we already have special music planned for this Sunday's service. However, if you want to put together a quick concert for early Saturday evening, I'm sure we could open the doors for that."

I got busy and called the newspaper. I put a small advertisement in the Thursday and Friday night edition and also our Saturday morning newspaper. I got on the phone and started calling people from church to help me spread the word about these Deaf kids from Jamaica, who would be coming to sign Christian songs in a concert and asked them for donations of cookies and punch to offer refreshments afterward.

Saturday afternoon, my husband and I met up with Cory and his wife who had been transporting the group from church to church for the concerts in the lower southwestern part of Michigan. I rode along with my husband to meet them in Holland. My husband drove Cory's wife back to our house in our car while I rode with Cory in his van to assist in giving directions to our home. It took longer than we thought for us to first find them in Holland and was already getting late in the day. We had to rush back to our house to eat dinner, and then quickly leave in time for them to prepare for their concert at our church. We didn't have enough time after eating to clear the table or unload their luggage and assign their sleeping spaces.

The concert went very well considering how little time we had to advertise and contact people. There was a fairly good turnout for which I was very thankful. For many of those who came, it was the first time they had ever seen any songs signed, especially by deaf people.

After the concert, Don drove both Cory and his wife back to their church in Holland where Cory's wife had left her car. I drove the van back to our house with the praise team so everyone could unload their luggage and start taking showers to get ready for bed. They had plans to be up early the next morning to get to another church for another concert. We had everything organized to occur in a timely fashion.

As everyone climbed out of the van and piled their luggage on my porch and front steps, I began searching for my house key. It was getting to be twilight and I was having difficulty seeing since I had forgotten to leave the front porch light on. All of a sudden I realized that I had never used keys to opened the front door to my house because I always drove my car directly into our garage and entered into the house from there. Don had my car and I didn't have the remote for the garage door! Although his truck, which also had a garage door opener on his visor, was sitting in the driveway, I didn't have any keys to his truck or to access to his remote.

There we were! All eight of us standing outside the house, tired, and exhausted. Seven dark complected Jamaicans in an all-white neighborhood standing there with luggage and loud speakers surrounding them while they lined up along the sidewalk and steps to my house waiting for my husband to come home and let us in. I'm sure there some who passed by our house wondering what was going on. At least they were all quiet!

On Sunday and Monday, I continued to search for more opportunities for them to offer a concert in churches or schools in the area. But, on such a short notice, I wasn't having much luck. Then I thought about my grandsons' parochial school. I called the school secretary, who was confused how deaf kids could present a musical concert for hearing kids. She referred me to the pastor who was very supportive and allowed me to bring the kids in for a short concert. He told the teachers this was an excellent opportunity to create awareness of those who have disabilities and can still serve the Lord. He asked his secretary to send out an email notice immediately to families in the church and to also call the parents of the school children letting them know of this impromptu concert and to invite them to come watch.

After their concert, many parents came up to thank them for sharing such a wonderful gift. Some of them said they never thought about how God could use the deaf to serve Him. For many it was a real eye opener for them to become aware of what deaf people can do.

We returned to my home later that afternoon and helped pack up their belongings as they were to begin their journey north along the shoreline of Lake Michigan after dinner. They would be heading toward the Mackinac Bridge for the kids to see one of Michigan's treasures as they continued to raise funds along the way for their school and mission.

Two years later, a hurricane hit the school again and left tremendous damage. Requests were sent to us asking for donations to help them finance a new roof to the school and repair houses that had been damaged at their center. That request was met with donations from the many churches where lives and hearts had been touched by meeting and interacting with these deaf kids, who had never heard the word or music through their ears but only through their hearts and from the hands of others who cared. These kids were now using their hands to share their praises to the Lord.

"I will praise you, O Lord, with my whole heart; before the "gods" will I sing your praise."[56]

Moving On
Chapter 35

As the months grew closer to the end of my first year as director for the Deaf and hard of hearing center, I was informed by one of the board members that I needed to complete a closing report and start my fiscal planning for the next year. I knew the total income we had received from grants and fund-raisers and had kept track and balanced each month of all the current year expenses. However, I had never worked with social security taxes, FICA, insurance benefits/deductions, workers compensation taxes, and expected percentages for raises. I had been very good at financial planning at home with our family budget, but I never took a course in accounting or how to do fiscal planning for an agency. I had no idea where to begin with these reports.

How on earth would I plan for money coming in and going out without knowing how much money we would be expecting for the next year or exactly from where it would be coming? I thought as I worried about how to do this task. My educational training focused on individual and family relationships, mental health, and substance abuse treatment, not agency fiscal budgets.

I managed to stumble through all of this by asking lots of questions and for help from others who had experience in this area. It took a lot of my time and theirs. I was extremely relieved when it was over. Although, I felt uneasy and wasn't sure I had done everything right. I hoped it would suffice the auditors or for whomever would be reviewing it.

One day just after I completed my first year, I was sent a message to meet with one of the board members. It was also time for my annual evaluation and to review what I had done during the past year as director of this new agency.

"Good afternoon, Bonnie. How are things going for you?" I was asked as I walked into the board member's office.

"Fine, the work is exciting and intense," I said as I proceeded to report on some of the presentations, advocacy, and accomplishments I had completed during my first year as director.

"How is the grant research coming?" he asked.

"I have had very little time to research more grants, but so far have found only one possibility," I responded.

"Well, the board does recognize how hard you have been working to get the word out regarding the needs of the Deaf. You have done a good job making agencies aware of how to make their services more accessible. Everyone understands how much effort you are putting into this agency and how much you really care about providing services to this population."

"That's true. I look at what my life would be like if I was totally deaf and how I'd feel left out if I were completely deaf like a lot of our clients. By helping them, I am also helping me to continue to have opportunities in the future."

"I understand you had quite a struggle with the annual financial planning and needed help to complete that."

"Yes, that is true," I said, feeling my face flush with embarrassment. "I never had any classes on planning finances for a year in advance or how the money would be delegated to certain accounts. I never had any idea how to deal with employee's social security taxes and all the other deductions. It was quite challenging and overwhelming. I think I will need to learn more about how to do that before next year."

"Well, I called you in today because I have something difficult to say knowing how hard you have worked this past year. The board has noticed all the extra efforts you have been put into getting this agency started. However, the board had a meeting to discuss what I have to share with you, now. They all came to an agreement. We need to have someone with more experience as an executive director, especially in the fiduciary department in order to keep this agency going. We need someone who can write grants easily, too. We are also aware of how much you struggled to complete the new fiscal year planning and the amount of help you needed to complete it. We understand you were trained as a social worker and your experience as a therapist did not provide you with all the skills needed for an executive director position."

I felt crushed. Tears flooded my eyes and I felt sick to my stomach.

"Are you firing me?" I asked barely able to get the words out.

"No, we are not firing you. You are a hard worker and have been doing a great job in areas that needed to be done to get this agency started. However, we need to search for someone with more experience running a non-profit business, writing grants, fund-raising and working with the board to keep it going. This is why it is so hard for me to tell you that we want you to stay on until we find the right person. We also discussed suggesting you return to college to get a degree in business management. You lack those skills, but with training and what you have to offer, you could make an excellent executive director."

I felt devastated but I knew he was right. I didn't want to step down. Yet, I didn't want the agency to fall apart either.

"After we find the right person, we hope you will be available to train him or her about what you know regarding the Deaf population, their culture and their accessibility issues. And we hope you will stay around to help out now and then to make sure we are going in the right direction."

What a blow! I felt completely devastated! I also thought about the time Dr. Lamson had come in to my office to meet me and offered me an opportunity to return to work as an outpatient therapist in his office. That incident did not seem like just a coincidence, now. I had not planned to return to my career as a therapist until I got that phone call from a mother who wanted her daughter seen by me in therapy. That's when I felt pulled back into my career as a therapist. Now, as I think back to that time, it seems as if God had planned for and was preparing me for this very event. His plan seemed like a safety net, so to speak, to protect me from loss of income as he led me back to where He wanted me to be. I knew no matter what was happening, God was still leading me in the direction for the purpose He wanted for my life at this time.

"So do not fear, for I am with you; do not be dismayed, for I am your God. I will strengthen you and help you; I will uphold you with my righteous right hand."[57]

Letting Go
Chapter 36

Two months later, shortly after midnight and just three days before Christmas, I was summoned to the hospital by my sister who had been taking care of our dad. When she called she said she brought him to the hospital because he was dehydrated and very weak after a three day bout with the flu. He was just admitted into the hospital when he stood up, collapsed and died. My husband and I rushed to the hospital and stayed there with my sister and her husband until the wee hours of the morning, quietly talking about how quickly he had passed away and how unprepared we all were for this to occur. He had been doing so well. Don and I had taken him out for his 82nd birthday the month before and we were all looking forward to another family Christmas with him.

When we returned home that morning I couldn't get back to sleep. My mind was whirling with a list of things to do before Christmas Eve. In a few hours my sisters and I would have to meet with a funeral director to plan for our dad's funeral, order flowers and due to the weekend and holiday, write his obituary in time for the press to get it into the newspaper. I was also looking forward to having our daughter and son-in-law, who lived out of state, arrive at any time this morning with our four grandchildren. They traveled for hours during the night and would be hungry for breakfast when they arrived. My daughter was looking forward to joining her dad and I this morning to make our annual candy cane yeast breads for our Christmas breakfast. Even though I was tired, I couldn't stay in bed. I needed to get up and to get things ready before I took off to meet my sisters.

The next few days were very difficult for us. In the midst of listening to Christmas songs on the radio and watching the excitement of our young grandchildren, we were grieving. I felt as if I were in a vacuum. Nothing seemed real. I felt numb while going through the holiday rituals of baking and wrapping last minute gifts. I tried to act happy, but I was filled with tears and sadness at the same time. When I finally sat down to relax, I thought about the real meaning of Christmas. Christ came to show God's love for us and give us hope for salvation. This was what Christmas was all about. I should have felt happy because this year my father was celebrating Christmas in heaven with mom and our Lord. Yet, it wasn't the same without him. Our family managed to get through those days with heavy hearts. With the death of my father I felt as if I had reached the last chapter of a good book before being ready to put it down.

The last two months of that year had been very difficult for me. I had lost two meaningful things in my life: my father and my position as the director of the Deaf center. While I had a lot of success creating an awareness of the needs for those with hearing loss, I also felt like I had failed at the same time.

The new year brought many changes. I returned to work knowing I would soon be replaced from the job I loved. I had been thrilled to get the support from so many resources to start this agency. It had meant a lot to me and the Deaf population. Yet, I knew I would be happy to return to working in private practice. I was thankful God had provided this position for me to transition into upon leaving this agency, which I had dreamed of starting and into which I had invested so much of myself.

By the end of January a new director had been hired. I offered to stop by and help him if he needed anything. Although he admitted he knew nothing about the Deaf population or their culture, he was confident everything would be fine. He thanked me for my offer and said he had over twenty years of experience working as a director with non-profits and had worked with many others who had disabilities.

I continued to stop by the center a few times after that, but the new director was not interested in my offers to help out. Finally, I decided it was time to let go and move on. He knew how to reach me, how much I cared about this agency, and my willingness to stay involved. I had hoped he would eventually change his mind, but he never did. Perhaps that was for the better. Although the Deaf community didn't want me to leave nor did they understand why I was leaving, they all stepped in to do what they could to support their new director and this agency.

About four months after my father's death, I discovered he had left a lot of unfinished business and legal matters that needed immediate attention. My sisters were not interested in taking care of these legal matters, so I took over. Not only did I become the executor of his estate, but I eventually took over as my brother's guardian. My brother, who had been diagnosed as a child with what we now know as ADHD and was also slightly cognitively impaired, had suffered from a stroke and needed to be placed in an assisted living center.

With all the repairs needed on my parent's home before we could sell it, my husband (who was now retired) and I decided to purchase the house and utilize my husband's skills to do the repair work. This would cut the cost of hiring a builder or outside help to fix a lot of damage done to the walls and floors by renters. When my husband took out the huge picture window in the living room, we found there was no header to support it. The house lacked insulation and also needed a new roof. The more we began fixing it, the more repairs we found had to be done. There was a lot more work involved than either of us had expected and never imagined how much time and money this would eventually cost us.

While I continued to work as a therapist and re-build my private practice, I also worked part-time at a hospital. After work and on weekends I helped my husband sort through and discard things no longer needed in my parents' home. I spent hours and days on my hands and knees scrubbing and cleaning out the dirt between the cracks of the wooden floors to prepare them for my husband to sand and varnish.

As I worked through each room of the house, tears often came to my eyes as I grieved over memories I had of good times and not so good with my family. When we finally finished the house and put it up for sale, the economy had slowed down and it took months to sell. At one point, I considered selling our own home and moving back into my parents' house, but my husband was against that. Our oldest daughter had designed our new house for her dad to build. I couldn't discount the work they had done and knew it was time to let go of these last concrete memories of my family and past. When my parent's house finally sold, I thought our lives would settle down again.

Things changed again for us. My brother began having physical and medical problems which meant I was often called to the hospital emergency room. Once my brother was stable again, my youngest sister called me with disturbing news.

"Bonnie, I think there is something drastically wrong with me. My legs give out when I walk and I am dropping things all the time. Once I get into the car, I can barely drive. I've seen the doctor, but he doesn't have any answers for me. He can't find anything wrong!"

I encouraged her to make an appointment at Mayo Hospital and have the doctors there evaluate her. She took my advice and returned home devastated with a diagnosis of Lou Gehrig Disease (ALS). She was told she was dying and her body was quickly deteriorating. I wanted to spend as much time as I could with her; but that was limited to a few days per week due to my work and other responsibilities.

On one of the days when I was alone with her, she talked to me about her life and compared it with mine. "Bonnie, you have done a lot of good things in your life. You finished college; something I wish I had done. You have helped a lot of people when they needed you. You helped me tremendously when I went through those trying times earlier in my first marriage. I'll never forget the time Don talked to mom and dad when they found out I was pregnant and you both supported me. I am also so very grateful to Don for what he did. He brought us together again as a family. You have a good life and are very active with so many groups. I envy you and the time you have to do all of that. Now, I am going to say something you may not want to hear, but I'm asking you to just listen to what I am going to say." Then she paused a few minutes and reached for my hand. "While you do all the things you do, I have had the luxury in my life of spending a lot of time with my family and grand kids. I would love to continue to spend more time with them, to be involved with everything they do, and to watch them as they grow up. I won't have that option, but you do. Time with family is so important and I wouldn't have changed those times for anything. You deserve to give yourself and your family that same gift. So, what I am saying is that since you are near retirement age, consider retiring soon. Do it now. Don't wait until it's too late. Take that time now to do things with your kids and grandkids you haven't taken the time to do in the past few years. Let them know they are important, too."

One year later, on a sunny Saturday afternoon, the day before Mother's Day, my sister died peacefully at her home.

I continued to think about what she had said. My kids and grandkids had always been very important to me, but it was true.

I had gotten so busy with work and doing what I "should" do rather than letting go and being more available to those who are the most important to me. I thought about another message I had recently heard from a friend. She said being too busy reminded her of the acronym B.U.S.Y, which stood for Being Under Satan's Yoke.

I hadn't stopped to realize how many things had been going on in my life to distract me from being available to my family. *Perhaps this is time for me to retire,* I thought as I considered what she said and what was going on around me.

About six months after her death there was a slump occurring in our economy and my private practice began to slow down. Many of my clients complained of losing their jobs or their work hours had been cut down to the point they were also losing their insurance benefits and could no longer afford to pay their co-pay for outpatient services. Some of my older clients who were nearing retirement age were being let go by their employers and replaced by younger workers who would willingly work for less money and less hours. There were less opportunities for me to work with the Deaf population because many had either passed away or had moved to other cities where there were more opportunities and the accessibility to local events were easily available to them.

I began to consider retirement as my sister suggested. I had a lot of things I wanted to do in my life. I did want to spend more time with family and grandchildren. Being in that sixty-something age group, I was ready to slow down. I was also gaining awareness of how much my hearing loss was interfering with my ability to hear the soft voices of women and children during therapy sessions. I also considered it was time to have a much needed foot surgery which I had put off for the past few years. Finally, I accepted the fact that it was time for me to retire, slow down, take care of myself, and start spending time enjoying my family.

"Even to your old age and gray hairs, I am He who will sustain you. I have made you and I have carried you; I will sustain you and I will rescue you."[58]

Retirement
Chapter 37

Once I had retired, I started thinking about my friend Bobbi, who had been encouraging me for several years to write a book about the time Martha came to my door and how years later God brought her back into my life. I kept putting this off because didn't know how to write stories. My social work experience had taught me to write reports based on facts. Each time I tried to start writing my story, I thought it would be too boring for someone to read. However, I happened to find a local writers group and attended one of their meetings at the library. I told them about my story and my struggle to write more than just facts. Those in the group, who had published books and articles, told me the best way to get started was to take a creative writing class from Mary, a teacher at our community college. They said she was the best! So I contacted Mary and signed up for her fall class.

Although I felt out of place in a second year college class when I already had a bachelor's and master's degree, I felt even more out of place that first week when I heard younger students in her class read their short stories out loud. They used similes and metaphors, something I hadn't used (or read books using those) in years. I had always written my research papers in APA (American Psychological Association) style. My clinical assessments and reports to doctors were always stated in facts or the client's self-reporting. After listening to some of the students read their work, I felt extremely embarrassed about mine. I was sure I would fail and was ready to withdraw from class. *How could I explain failing a writing class when I carried a better than 3.5 G.P.A. throughout grad school?*

I spoke with Mary about why I thought I should drop her class. She encouraged me to stay in her class and I'm glad I did. Although I do not claim to be a great author, I learned a lot about writing in her class. By the time the semester was over, I felt confident that someday I could write this book, but I still didn't feel I was ready to start.

Just before that semester ended, I met a woman at one of the Chamber of Commerce breakfast meetings. When she asked what I planned to do now that I had retired, I said, "I guess I'll write the book I should have written years ago about my life journey and a deaf girl."

"I know just the person who can help you do that! I'll have to introduce you to Tricia one of these days. She has helped a lot of people around here get their work published. She is a writing coach, editor, and publisher. She can help you with the whole process."

That's nice, I thought, but I didn't really respond to her offer other than to smile. After all, I knew it would take a lot of time and money and I wasn't sure if I really wanted to actually start writing a book.

A few weeks later, I ran into this same woman again at a Business Expo. She noticed me from across the room and rushed over to me smiling and waving. "I've got to introduce you to Tricia. She is right over here in the corner booth."

I walked with her to meet Tricia, but I was doubtful I would want to start this friendship. I had tried to write my book once before and didn't seem to have any interest in starting it now. I really didn't know where or how to start writing my story. It just seemed easier for me to forget it.

Tricia was very pleasant as she handed me her business card. "When do you plan to start writing?"

"I don't know," I replied. "I am just thinking about it."

"What's your book about?" she asked.

I told her about the mysterious deaf girl who had come to my door when I was a child and how later in life God had led me to work with the Deaf population.

"That sounds very interesting! Why don't we set up a time to chat about your book and maybe I can help you get started," she said with sincerity.

"I don't know. I am really busy with the holidays coming."

"Well, here's my card. Call me when you are ready and I'll be happy to help you."

I walked away without any intention of contacting her. I expected I'd never see her again and figured I'd start writing my book when I was ready and when I finished it, I'd contact someone about printing it.

About a month later, at a Christmas party, I ran into Tricia again and once again she asked about my book and if I had considered just taking some time to meet with her to talk about it. We had a pleasant conversation about the holidays and once again I mentioned I was too busy with family events to think about writing.

A few weeks later, I was invited to a presentation for making your own cards. I walked in late and sat down in the only seat left. Once I had settled down and got my computer all set up, I looked up and sitting right next to me was Tricia! *How ironic!* I thought. *This is not just coincidence!* From the way things had been happening in my life, I believed this was another way in which God was not only encouraging me but also providing me an opportunity to start writing this book.

After the card presentation, Tricia and I talked for a while. Once again, she asked me when I was thinking of seriously starting to write.

"Not until after the Christmas holidays," I said. "Maybe sometime in January."

Tricia offered to meet with me the second week in January to give me some idea about what it would take and how she could be of help. "We can just look over the process for when you <u>are</u> ready to write," she said.

I finally agreed to set a date in January to meet with her. When we met, Tricia and I went over the time line of my journey, and events during my life, and how I perceived God had been leading me. Tricia thought a moment and said, "It seems there are two threads in your life: one with the Deaf population and the other your spiritual life. Both are intertwined. I think your journey in life will make a good story."

After hearing about the process, how she could help, and allowing me to work at my own pace, I hired her as my writing coach.

I know God put Tricia in my path to write this book. If I hadn't kept running into her so often in such a short time, I would not be sitting here typing my last pages and as I finish this book.

"There is a time for everything and a season for every activity under heaven."[59]

Summary of Ephphatha
Chapter 38

While I'm coming to the end of writing this book, I know it is not the end of my journey. Life continues to have so much more in store for me and, in fact, for all of us. God isn't done with us until we are called home to Him. I started writing this book because I knew the things which had happened throughout my life, especially when I was younger, was proof God was right there leading me. As I began looking back and reviewing all those events throughout my life, I could see much clearer how God was actually preparing me for a purpose He had in mind. I was also beginning to learn more about myself. Although I knew that everything is in God's hands, I found that at times I failed to put my trust in Him. I also became aware of the pattern I held in my life of becoming overly committed to doing many things to help others while ignoring some of my own needs.

Because of one of the experiences I had after starting to write this book, I decided to add that story to this final chapter as another example of how God continues to communicate with me and leads me to spiritual growth.

I noticed there had been times I seemed to be quite content with my relationship with God and other times in which I was on fire for Him. I also realized if I hadn't reminisced over those past experiences, I would have continued to be unaware of what was occurring in my spiritual life. I gained insight as to how much and how often God actually had made me aware of changes I might need to make to grow closer to Him. Although he didn't verbally speak to me, I became aware of how He had prepared me for events long before I had ever thought such events would become a reality. Each time I faced a challenge or a stressful situation, the Holy Spirit led me to a closer and deeper relationship with the Lord. With each chapter I wrote, I became more acutely aware of this in my journey toward spiritual growth.

About the third month after initially starting to write this book, I woke up at 3:22 am and couldn't fall back to sleep. I had awakened thinking about the chapter I had just written about my Sunday school teacher, Jo, and the love she so willingly shared with everyone. I thought about those things which were so important to me as a child and had become part of my own spiritual growth. I was fortunate to have had the adults in my church bestow feelings of love and joy toward me and the other children in our congregation and making us feel we were important. I felt sad as I realized I hadn't noticed this same kind of support and interactions between generations in churches where we had attended or visited in recent years.

I thought back to those days when our own children were younger. They also had similar experiences in the church where they grew up. In both cases, the adults in those churches took an active part in the lives of the children. But, our children were now grown up and had moved away and we no longer attended that same church.

Feeling restless, I lay there, trying to fall back asleep. Instead, I thought more about the huge inter-generational relationship gap that seemed to be growing between adults and children. I wondered how children who didn't have these kind of experiences at church would feel about growing up and becoming Christians if they never feel valued or experienced the joy of being part of a church family while they were younger.

I recognized my own current feelings of emptiness along with the lack of excitement I used to feel while getting ready to attend church and Sunday school.

A few days later, I told my husband about the night I couldn't sleep and shared with him my thoughts and feelings of apathy and sadness over how things had changed over the years. I asked him if he thought it was just me who might be experiencing these depressive thoughts and feelings.

"No," he said. "I have also noticed how much churches have changed. It seems the interactions we had growing up and experienced in church as a family is much different these days."

Churches had changed quite a bit. People seemed to be in hurry to leave church after the sermon. Everyone, including me, seemed to be very busy. I wondered if this could ever change back to the way things were.

The words stagnant and complacent popped into my mind and I felt stunned. That is one thing Christians should be on guard to resist, but suddenly I realized that was what was exactly happening to me. Even though I was dissatisfied with the changes that kept occurring, I had become accepting and outwardly appeared content.

When churches discontinued Sunday school classes for adults and the children, I was very disappointed. I missed the summer Sunday school picnics at the lake where we played lots of games and held competitions for each individual age group and also played games competing against other age groups. We were not just a church, but a spiritual family inside and outside of church. We knew everyone who attended our church. We were a family, a close knit spiritual church family that expressed love and friendship to everyone.

As I reminisced back to my teen years when I attended our youth group meetings, which also are now almost obsolete in some churches. I thought about the parents who took turns coming to our meetings to help out with lessons, treats, singing, and playing games. They were also involved with lots of other activities with our group such as bowling. During the summer they would occasionally take us to the beach to roast hot dogs or s'mores on a Sunday evening while we all sat around the campfire singing Christian songs. They weren't just someone's parents helping or chaperoning us, they were our mentors and guides.

I loved it when we had combined meetings with other youth from area churches. We had so much fun making new friends and participating with other kids during those teen age years.

In today's world, our lives have become overwhelmed with several after-school activities, sports, and other events. It is not unusual for both parents to be working or holding down two jobs to make ends meet. It's sad, but there is little time available for adding anything more, including church activities, to their already too busy schedules.

One day while driving and reflecting on these changes, my heart felt heavy as I thought about the contrast between then and now. I turned the radio on to our local Christian radio station. I didn't catch the name of the speaker, but he was talking about how people can get caught up doing things out of loyalty. He indicated sometimes even Christians are like this. They go to church out of loyalty to the people they know who will be there, even though they may not get what they need for spiritual or personal growth. That message stuck with me. I could identify with what he was talking about and felt guilty. This seemed to be exactly what was going on in my life. I enjoyed going to church every week and talking with the same people.

A few days after that, but during that same week, and once again while I was driving, I turned on the radio to that same station in time and heard a similar message from a different speaker. This one spoke about how people do things out of habit. He said Christians can become apathetic to what is really important in life by just doing things out of habit or by going through the motions without giving much thought to the meaning. He said we are all creatures of habit and often don't think about what we are actually doing or why. He continued to talk about how Christians can get caught up into going places like to church on a certain day at a certain time out of habit rather than because they are excited to go hear the Word and to be spiritually fed.

Wow, I thought. *It has always been my nature to look for signs from God and if certain things which occurred were God's way of communicating with me. It's certainly amazing I have heard two different speakers this week with similar messages which seem to relate to what my husband and I have been experiencing.*

Both radio speakers emphasized going to church should fill us with joy, love, and hope. They indicated we should leave church feeling inspired and with the purpose of wanting to go out to share with others what we heard. *That is exactly what I had always thought, too! That is what I experienced growing up!*

While my husband and I attended church regularly week after week, we did enjoy the music and liked the people there, but was that really enough? The lack of Sunday school and events which brought us together as a church family felt like a huge gap. I wondered if God was touching my heart to make some changes.

At the next masterminding meeting I attended, we were led in an interesting discussion about success and growth. Our leader asked if we were familiar with the term and meaning of The Hot Poker Principal. He said we are like a poker and talked about how our environment can influence us. Then he said, "If we want to grow in anything, we need to get near the fire where it is hot so we can be useful. Without a fire, a poker becomes cold and is not useful." When I returned home, I shared with Don what we had talked about and my thoughts about exploring some changes we could consider for spiritual growth.

About two months later, we happened to be visiting another church. The pastor started out with the children's sermon and began by taking various items one by one from a bag and asking the children what the purpose was for each item. First, she took out her cell phone and the children responded the purpose was to call or talk to someone. Next she took out a spoon and the children said it was used for eating soup or cereal. Then a pair of scissors and they correctly responded for cutting something. After they identified the purpose of several items, she said, "Did you know everything on earth has a purpose? Even you have a purpose!"

She then turned to the congregation as the children returned to their seats. "Most of us just go through life with our purpose unknown to us. We are clueless of what our future has in store for us or how what we say or do may affect others. We need the Holy Spirit to guide us, to help us see things differently, and to open our eyes. When that happens, we get to see things much differently and how it all fits together. As our life takes on significance, we gain a new view of life and become followers of God's love."

When we left church that day, I understood the extent to which this sermon was what I needed to hear and once again, I believed none of these events were occurring by coincidence.

By writing this book, I have begun to see things differently and how my life has been like a puzzle as the pieces came together to make a clearer picture. I became even more acutely aware of God interacting throughout my life and how led me to do things I never would have dreamed I would do. My eyes were opening as to how everything in my life had fit together in God's plan and recognizing some changes which we needed to start making to continue to grow in our spiritual journey.

I believe we all have more than one purpose. Our lives are like a tree with strong, deep roots. Sometimes a branch may become bent or even broken; but if it is still connected to the strength of the rooted tree, it's source of life, and even though the branch may have fallen or been bent, it is not dead. A new branch can start growing. The old broken branch was only the first part of the branch's life. It can continue to grow and re-start.

Our purpose is very much like that tree branch. Our path changes and grows new again, maybe even becoming quite different. Neither the tree nor its branches are finished just because it had been broken or bent and no longer seen as perfect. The tree continues to have life and a purpose.

Even though my life has changed quite a bit and it seems I am no longer needed in a ministry to the Deaf or to provide therapy, I believe my purpose has changed its course to serve others in ways that aren't always as interesting and exciting as it had been in my past and in my career.

Early in my career, when I felt I was not being used to my full potential, I spoke with a friend who told me a story about a couple who had visited a monastery where one of the monks was translating the Bible in calligraphy. Everyone who saw the monk's work was awed by the artistic beauty of his work. Several years later the couple revisited the monastery and hoped to view the monk's finished work. However, the monk had not finished it. Even more surprising, he was no longer doing calligraphy. Instead, he was cleaning toilets! Being shocked that the monk, who was such a gifted person, was doing this kind of work, the husband asked him how he felt about cleaning toilets and not continuing with the calligraphy. The monk replied, "When you work for the Lord, it doesn't matter what you do."

So it is with our purpose. Whatever we do, when we do it as a servant for God, we are carrying out His will. Although it may not feel like it or it may seem as if what we are doing is not very important, it is all important in God's sight. When God is in our heart leading us, everything we do is for God's purpose. God loves you and is always in your life whether you know it or not. He only asks for us to obey Him and carry out His vision by sharing Him with others. That is our purpose.

We don't know what the future brings for us, but we are all on a journey. What and how things happen along the way are what makes our lives interesting. God provides the doors to be opened. It is up to us to walk through and be open to what lays ahead. For me, my journey started with a deaf girl. I only had to open the door and follow Him.

It is my hope and prayer that you will be also be blessed and have a spiritually fulfilling life. Look at your own life, listen with your heart, and notice where God is leading you. May you open the door of your heart and let the Holy Spirit guide you.

God Bless!

Sincerely,
Bonnie

"Whether you turn to the right or to the left, your ears will hear a voice behind you saying 'this is the way; walk in it.'"[60]

"Thank you for sharing your story! I have always respected my dad's service to his Lord as an ordained minister and his special skill set developed to serve a "niche" of the Lutheran population. But now I have better perspective for the era, its culture and challenges, the sheer enormity of the mission outreach he (and you) faced. An entire population segment, previously ignored--excluded even, was only beginning to be recognized and reached. This was a groundbreaking movement! My heart is now bursting with increased respect and admiration for my dad's humble, faithful servitude to his Master.

--Kim G (Pastor N's daughter)"

Biblography

Bornstein, Harry, Hamilton, Lillian B, Saulnier, Karen Luczak, & Roy, Howard I., editors, The Signed English Dictionary for Preschool and Elementary Levels. Washington D.C: Gallaudet College Press, 1975.

Braddy, Nella, Anne Sullivan Macy, The Story Behind Helen Keller, Garden City NY: Doubleday, Doran & Company, Inc. 1934.

Cousins, Norman, Anatomy of an Illness as Perceived by the Patient; reflection on healing and regeneration, Introduction by Rene Dubos, New York: Norton, 1979 (ISBN: 0-393-01252).

Erikson, Erik, Childhood and Society, New York, NY: W.W. Norton & Co. (ISBN 39331068).

Gannon, Jack R., Deaf Heritage: A Narrative History of Deaf America, Silver Springs, National Association of Deaf, 1981 (ISBN 0-913072-38 9).

Harlan, Lane, A Deaf Artists in Early America: the Worlds of John Brewster JR., Boston: Beacon Press, 2004 (ISBN 0-8070-6616-8).

Maxwell, John C., The 15 Invaluable Laws of Growth: Live them and Reach Your Potential, New York: Center Street Hachette Book Group, 2012, page 90. (ISBN 978-1-59995-366-3).

Woititz, Janet, Adult Children of Alcoholics and Dysfunctional Families, Deerfield Beach Florida: Healthcare Communications, 1987. (ISBN 09-32194-15x).

Young, Veronica L., VHS video, The Pinks and The Blues, New York, NY: Ambrose Video Publishers, 1987.

Songs referred to by chapters in this book:

Chapter 3:
Warner, Anna B (Lyrics). Jesus Loves Me. 1860, Music by Wm. B. Bradbury, 1862.

Chapter 16:
Conty, Sophia and Batya, Naomi, lyrics, 1961. King of Kings and Lord of Lords. Music is an Ancient Hebrew Folk Song. Maranatha,1981. (Words @ 1980, Maranatha! Music (Admin. By The Copyright Company, Nashville, TN).

Chapter 17:
Perronet, Edward 1779, All Hail the Power of Jesus Name. (Public Domain).

Robinson, Robert, 1757, Come Thou Font of Every Blessing (Public Domain).

Chapter 30:
Stevens, Marsha (songwriter), For Those Tears I Died, Balm Publishing, Costa Mesa CA (Arrangements 1995: Produced by Glenna Shepherd "For Those Who Know It Best: Hymns for the Church).

Chapter 32:
Boltz, Ray (songwriter) Thank You, Produced by Steve Millikan & Ray Boltz in album Memories for the Heart, Distributed by Word Entertainment, Inc: Nashville, TN 2001.

Bullock, Geoff (songwriter), The Power of His Love, released by Hillsong Music, 1992.

Father Joncas, Jan Michael (composer based on Psalm 91 and Isaiah 43:31), On Eagles Wings, Douglas Hall Producer, North American Liturgy: recorded 1979.

Gaither, Gloria and William, Because He Lives, 1971.

Zschech, Darlene (lyrics) and Bullock, Geoff (music), I'll Never Be the Same Again. (arranged by Dave Williamson) Australia: released by Hillsong Music, 1993.

Zschech, Darlene (Lyrics) Shout to the Lord, Hillsong Music: Australia, 1993.

End Notes

1. John 15:4 RSV.
2. Proverbs 22:6 KJV.
3. Hebrews 13:2 NIV.
4. Matthew 18:3-4 NIV.
5. Romans 8:31. NIV
6. Psalm 37:4. NIV
7. I John 1:9 NIV.
8. Exodus 20:12 RSV.
9. Romans 8:28 NIV.
10. Psalm 127:3 TLV.
11. John 14:1 NIV.
12. Psalm 32:8 NIV.
13. Psalm 112:7 NIV.
14. Colossians 3:16-17 NIV.
15. Jeremiah 29:11 NIV.
16. Prov. 3:5-6 NIV.
17. Matthew 7:1 NIV.
18. Revelation 3:8 NIV.
19. Psalm 118:24 NIV.
20. Exodus 20:2 NIV.
21. Isaiah 41:10 RSV.
22. Philippians 4:13 NIV.
23. Mark 11:24 NIV.
24. Proverbs 19:21 NIV.
25. Psalm 56:3 NIV.
26. Gannon, pp. 191-192
27. Isaiah 26:3 NIV.

[28] Jeremiah 29:11 NIV.

[29] Matthew 5:14 NIV.

[30] Proverbs 14:30 NIV.

[31] John 14:1 NIV.

[32] Erikson, Childhood and Society.

[33] John 8:7 NIV.

[34] Romans 3:10 NIV.

[35] James 4:11 NIV.

[36] James 2 9-10 NIV.

[37] I Samuel 16:7 NIV.

[38] Romans 5:6 NIV.

[39] John 14:1 NIV.

[40] Mark 12:31 NIV.

[41] Matt 7: 1-6 NIV, author's paraphrase.

[42] John 3:17 NIV.

[43] I Cor. 13:7 RSV.

[44] Psalm 32:8 RSV.

[45] Isaiah 41:10 RSV.

[46] Matt 14:29-31 NIV Author paraphrase.

[47] Psalm 56:3-4 NIV.

[48] Gannon,

[49] Gannon,

[50] Psalms 147:3 NIV.

[51] Public Law 94-142.

[52] Hebrews 13:16 RSV.

[53] John 16:24 NIV.

[54] Proverbs 3:5 NIV.

[55] Proverbs 16:3 NIV.

[56] Psalm 138:1 NIV.

[57] Isaiah 41:10 NIV.

[58] Isaiah 46:4 NIV.

[59] Ecclesiastics 3:1 NIV.

[60] Isaiah 30:21 NIV.

Made in the USA
Lexington, KY
07 June 2017